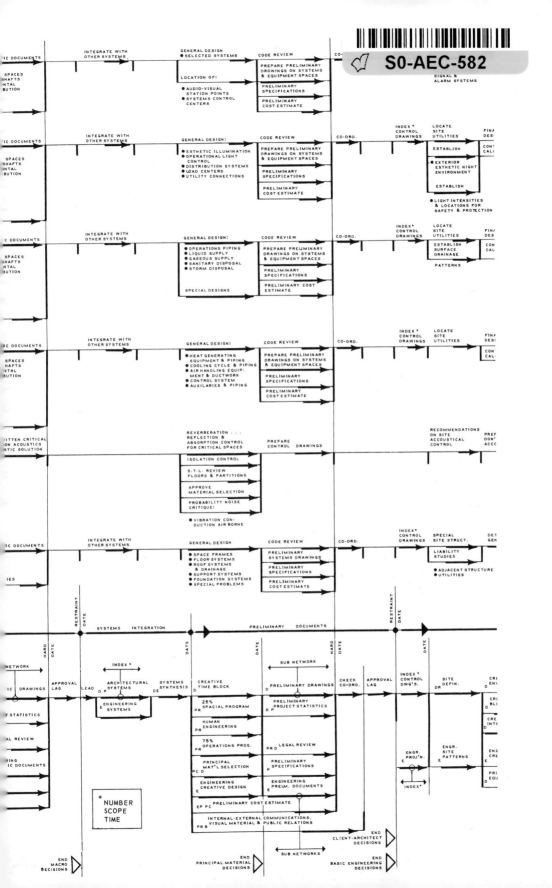

DESIGN COST ANALYSIS

DESIGN
COST
ANALYSIS

FOR ARCHITECTS
AND ENGINEERS

HERBERT SWINBURNE, FAIA

McGRAW-HILL BOOK COMPANY

New York   St. Louis   San Francisco   Auckland   Bogotá
Hamburg   Johannesburg   London   Madrid   Mexico
Montreal   New Delhi   Panama   Paris   São Paulo
Singapore   Sydney   Tokyo   Toronto

Library of Congress Cataloging in Publication Data

Swinburne, Herbert.
  Design cost analysis for architects and engineers.

  Includes index.
  1. Architectural design—Cost control.
2. Building—Cost control. I.' Title.
NA2750.S94   658.1'552   79-13676
ISBN 0-07-062635-9

1234567890   KPKP   89876543210

The editors for this book were Jeremy Robinson and Susan Thomas, the designer was
Scott Chelius, and the production supervisor was Teresa F. Leaden. It was set in Melior by
University Graphics, Inc.

Printed and bound by The Kingsport Press.

TO BERENICE

CONTENTS

CONTENTS

FOREWORD

The problems experienced by Architects and Engineers in controlling the costs of their projects have long been familiar to me. I have spent many years in consulting with the design profession searching for solutions to their most vexing aspect of the design process. Reading the manuscript of this book has convinced me that here at last is the means by which the design professional can understand and control the costs of a project.

This is not a book for estimators; rather, it is for design professionals. Nor is it a "how to" book. It will not transform the architect into an estimator. It contains a mature discussion of the basic theories needed to understand construction costs—how they are generated and how they are applied throughout the design process.

Then, on the premise that to know is to control, the book contains a full primer on the operation of a comprehensive system of estimating—one that is nationally utilized and continually updated. The latter part of the book is organized as a complete teaching aid for use in schools of architecture.

I am confident that the widespread use of the book in teaching would produce a generation of architects to whom construction costs and estimating would be no mystery.

G. Nelson Tower, Jr.
Princeton, New Jersey

PREFACE

WHAT THIS BOOK IS AND IS NOT

First, this is *not* a textbook on how to be a cost estimator. Rather, it is a guide to cost awareness and to where costs are located—a treatise on how to achieve a thorough grasp of the cost control process.

This book also provides guidelines on what questions architects should ask engineers and how to monitor their efforts. Above all, the book is a guide to making crucial design decisions at that stage when cost-saving potential is greatest; it will enable the architect to forecast final construction costs even as the first sketches of a facility are getting under way.

This book presents an array of tools to seek out final construction costs. However, it will unequivocally state that architects and engineers are not always objective about the cost of their respective designs and that a *cost consultant* must be added to the design team. (If none exists in your community, there is one available as close as the telephone.)

This book is divided into three parts: Background, Theory, and Implementation. Some readers may wish to begin with Theory and Implementation and return later to Background. Following is a thumbnail sketch of what is covered in the chapters ahead and in the appendixes.

BACKGROUND

The first five chapters deal with the architect, the owner, and the consulting engineer; then professional services are examined, and the roles and responsibilities of the three major parties together with the contractor are explored. The focus of all these chapters closes in on construction costs and the interaction of the design team during the beginning stages of any project. A look at some recent history, then, will document how complex relationships have evolved over the past century and how these are now changing and shifting at a time of the nation's greatest volume of construction activity. Responsibilities relating to the issues of cost are pinpointed and assigned to owner, to architect, and to engineer. Professional agreements call for *design cost analysis*. Milestone points are established where decisions must be made to realize maximum value. It is pointed out that the architect was never educated or trained in cost estimating, and requires a cost manager who has specialized capabilities in cost targeting during the early conceptual phases of the project. The design team includes the cost manager, who brings objectivity to design decisions.

THEORY

Chapters 6 and 7 are concerned with the theory of cost analysis and involve the owner when defining value and setting scope. The theory is easy. Its application requires diligence, but results are practical and positive. The building program is really a *literary design*, a design composed of words that set a value profile, owner requirements, and user needs. This literary design invokes an architectural design, and the two together generate construction cost; hence the recurrent litany:

$$Program + Design = Cost.$$

IMPLEMENTATION

Chapters 8 and 9 are a complete introduction to the methods of estimating the cost of construction, building system by building system. Besides addressing the cost of building concept complexity and the cost of the exterior wall system, they stress that heavy cost concentrations occur in the *engineering* systems, and constant monitoring is required over their design and component selection to keep total costs in balance.

Chapters 10 and 11 set up a practical program of cost management from the date of receipt of commission until the time of building occupancy. Chapter 10 deals with the program, schematic design, and design development phases of a project; Chapter 11 covers the construction document, bidding, and construction phases.

Hypothetical case studies or experiences drawn from the author's practice will be used in these four chapters to illustrate a systematic approach to complete cost control based on the formula: Program + design = cost.

Some material in the appendixes, together with the front and back endpapers, illustrates the principles of *project control* used by the author over the years. For the most part, however, the appendixes are an extract of many pages from the current edition of *Dodge Construction Systems Costs*, prepared by Wood and Tower, Inc. These data are used to illustrate the principles of *cost control* advanced in this book. Future editions of *Dodge Construction Systems Costs*, available from McGraw-Hill, will assure that these principles can hold firm by permitting the cost data base and locality index to be updated annually.

Herbert Swinburne, FAIA

ACKNOWLEDGMENTS

I wish first to express my appreciation to Oliver D. Filley who persuaded me to write this book and later gave invaluable assistance during the months leading to its completion, then to J. Davidson Stephen for his gentle critique and architectural overview, and finally to Haydn Harris who knows so well how to make the art of cost analysis respond to and blend with the art of conceptual design.

All the buildings illustrated in this book are the work of Nolen-Swinburne and Associates of Philadelphia except for the office buildings, both of which were joint ventures of Nolen-Swinburne and Associates with Marcel Breuer and Herbert Beckhard of New York.

I salute all the photographers who make it possible to experience a building on the two dimensions of a page; their credits appear with each photograph.

Herbert Swinburne, FAIA

DESIGN COST ANALYSIS

INTRODUCTION

Picture this scenario.

The hour of bid opening has arrived. The scene may be an elaborate, ritualized arena of activities for a public bid opening—or it may be a quiet, informal gathering of a few interested people for a private opening. But the time has arrived and the first of eight bids is ready to be opened. A knife slices through the large envelope, papers are pulled out and flattened down, there is a pause until the figures are located on the right line, and then the bid is read out. The architect relaxes and smiles as he notes the figure is just below the construction estimate. The remaining bids may be higher, or even lower, but here is one solid bid; and the contractor is well known for good work.

Now, that's a great scenario, one to be hoped for at *every* bid opening. But here is scenario number two. Papers are pulled out and flattened down, there is a pause until the figures are located on the right line, and then . . . disaster! The figures are 12 percent over the estimate! Questioning looks appear on a face or two; the knife catches noisily on a staple as the second envelope tears open. The person at the head of the table rattles the papers, coughs, and reads flatly: 14 percent over! The knife can hardly slice through the silence in the room, but it moves on to open the remaining bids. One of these is a few thousand lower than the first, but all the others are more than 18 percent over. That cluster of three low bids speaks accusingly. It indicates the architect's estimate was 12 to 14 percent below the "right figure."

That second scenario won't be completed because it has so many variables:

- Negotiate with the low bidder.
- Redesign and rebid as soon as possible.
- Abort the project, as the owner's attorney advises, to recover the losses attributed to the architect.

To avoid that second scenario is the purpose of this book. It will examine the premise that a good building design, knowledgeably based on available technologies and without ambiguities in the drawings and specifications, will produce a bid that is close to a carefully prepared construction cost estimate. A keen sense of market conditions at the time of bidding, to modify that estimate, will produce even greater accuracy. The key phrase in all this is *a carefully prepared estimate*. That means carefully prepared in the early phases of design, building system by building system; and *that* requires monitoring structural, mechanical, and engineering system costs from the beginning of design, with all held in balance until completion of the working drawings. *Design cost analysis* sets up the procedures needed to arrive at a carefully prepared cost estimate.

Not only the architect and his consultants, but building owners, developers, government agencies, and engineering groups are pressed for time to produce a reasonably accurate cost estimate at the inception of a project. When the feasibility of a facility is being determined or when financing has been obtained after months or years of effort, all activities accelerate. All those on the design scene are in a hurry. They are overloaded and overworked. The time for building occupancy has been projected and all are geared to produce results within a compressed time frame. During this period, vital cost information for decision making is not always at hand; a mechanism is needed to help overcome this difficulty. Design cost analysis is such a mechanism.

DESIGN COST ANALYSIS

Design cost analysis has three elements: value, time, and cost—in that order. Value must be analyzed first, since it sets criteria for the completed building. Time is examined next, because the time frame available for design and construction will influence the type of contracts to be used and the financing charges to be expected. Cost is the end result of decisions made about value and time.

Value

The owner expects, even demands, maximum value in his building as a whole. This does not necessarily mean maximum value for each individual building system but rather maximum value in the balance among all building systems. Trade-offs among systems may be made to reach a synergetic whole. The fundamental concept of value analysis may be stated:

Maximum value is achieved when essential function is obtained at minimum cost.

Essential function for the building is defined in a building program. This function goes far beyond a description of spatial requirements and relationships. The concept of value includes the human esthetics of user needs and the social esthetics of environmental and community impacts, as well as the visual esthetics of physical form. Levels of quality must be set for these physical and esthetic requirements and then alternatives of design solution explored to realize lowest cost within defined objectives.

Such a design cost analysis does not necessarily mean designing for the lowest possible cost; it means designing for the lowest cost to achieve stipulated value. For example, a headquarters office building, designed to have stunning visual impact that projects a desired corporate image, may require so high a quality of land, location, of materials, and equipment that very high costs will be incurred. However, even within those programmed requirements, the high costs may be made lower through value analysis. Design, then, is a sensitive and realistic response to the spectrum of values established in the building program. The word *design* includes the sense of *program*. Design and program are inseparable; together they determine the construction cost of any facility. Or, to put it more simply:

Program + Design = Cost

Time

The time required to design and construct a building varies with the conditions imposed by the target date for occupancy. This can be done at a moderate pace using linear procedures of design, bidding, and construction. Or it can be accomplished quickly using one of the many ways of fast tracking, that is, designing and constructing simultaneously with a multitude of bid packages. These will not be discussed here, but the limits of time from start to occupancy, together with the design-and-construct procedures selected, will have a marked influence on construction costs, particularly on large projects. No general rules can be set forth; each project must be analyzed before design and construction procedures can be recommended.

Cost

First of all, a distinction will be made in this book between construction costs and building costs. *Construction costs* will mean the cost of all contracts required to put a building together and complete its site work. These costs include all fixed equipment required for operations and all the change orders agreed to during construction. *Building costs* will mean capital costs, which include land, construction costs, professional fees, loose furnishings, financing charges, and a host of miscellaneous items required to ready the building for occupancy and use.

There are five elements that determine the construction costs of a building: building type, complexity, quality, size, and location. These will all be examined in detail in the chapters ahead, but a brief overview of each element follows.

BUILDING TYPE To specify the kind of building under consideration immediately places it in a cost category that can range from warehouse to medical research facility. The usual classifications of building types are:

Residential	Institutional
Commercial	Religious
Industrial	Recreational
Educational	

These classifications are of no value in arriving at costs per square foot. Later we will be dealing with 41 different building types, each type with an average cost ranging from low to medium to high.

BUILDING COMPLEXITY Complexity is of three kinds.

1. According to its intended purpose, a building may be simple, as is a warehouse, or complex, as is a medical research facility.

2. Architectural design can set complexity or simplicity. Using the same number of square feet in a building plan and using the same quality of material, a designer can add to the cost of a building without even knowing it. The perimeter, form, and shape of a building may be simple or complex, and this can drastically affect mechanical and structural costs.

3. Any one of many building *systems* may be simple or complex within itself without impinging on any other system.

BUILDING QUALITY Quality is of two kinds. One is physical and the other deals with the intangibles of design. Physical quality entails the quality of materials and equipment and the effort applied toward mitigating environmental degradation on and around the site. Intangible quality lies in the sense of building image, amenities for building users, and features compensating for the impact of the building on people in the community that surrounds it. The owner, the architect, and his consultants must all have a solid understanding of these qualities. The intangibles must be set forth in the introduction to the building program, and the physical qualities must be enumerated in the details of that program.

BUILDING SIZE Obviously the size of a building is a major element of its total cost. At the same time, the larger the building, the lower can be its unit cost because of the quantities involved. Size of building is established in the program when *scope* is expressed in terms of the number of net square feet required to satisfy essential function. The ratio of net square feet to the number of gross square feet needed to enclose them is a design decision and has significant cost impact. Building size can spread low and horizontally or high and vertically, each with a different set of site and foundation costs.

BUILDING LOCATION The final element that determines the cost of a building is its location. Exactly the same building constructed in different regions will have differing costs because of dissimilar wage rates, material and shipping costs, and local market conditions. If a national index of the average construction costs in 20 principal cities is set at 100, the location adjustment factor can be as low as 0.66 in Orangeburg, South Carolina, and as high as 1.32 in Anchorage, Alaska, a variance of 100 percent.

CHALLENGING THE ARCHITECT

From time to time, it may seem that the author is unduly hard on architects and consulting engineers when discussing some of their shortcomings in the area of cost control. Possibly so, but these weaknesses are called to attention only to show that improvement is needed—*and* is possible. The profession as a whole is not strong in cost control, and yet methods, procedures, and organizations are available that can assist in achieving better performance; these are all set forth in this book.

Why do so many architects have a mediocre track record in bringing in their buildings on budget and on time? It is true that some architects do have a good record, but the hard fact is inescapable: The public image of architects, and the performance of many of them is not good when it comes to cost control. Over the past several years this image has been made worse by challenges to the profession from new competitors moving onto the scene. These entrepreneurs are aggressive; they claim and even guarantee cost accuracy. They intend to take as much of the action away from architects as they can. Their arguments are always based on better cost control—not better design. They have design professionals on their payrolls, who usually are not at the top level of the decision process in their organizations when program and design directives are set.

The following five sets of statements present a challenge to the architectural profession. When this challenge is understood and resolved, architects will have gone a long way in improving their image.

1. Most architects are very competent in design but not competent in construction cost control. That is a concern to our clients and should be a concern to the profession.

2. Not design alone, but program plus design determines construction cost. Cost is defined as an analyzed balance between initial construction costs and life-cycle costs.

3. Buildings are getting larger and more complex; professional responsibilities and liabilities are expanding. Effective cost control is more difficult, and clients are more demanding.

4. Engineering elements in a building account for 61 percent of construction cost, on the average, while architectural elements account for 39 percent. As prime professional, the architect must know how to manage the distribution of costs in the engineering disciplines.

5. Competitive construction management or design-and-construct orga-

nizations are moving into the architect's territory to fill the void in cost control that the latter has created. Architects must develop authoritative capabilities in design cost analysis.

MEETING THE CHALLENGE

In developing cost-control capabilities, architects must identify cost distribution, by systems, in their buildings during the program and schematic design phases. Here, with planning in a fluid state, they must explore conceptual design alternatives and system trade-offs until they have bracketed their cost targets. During design development of the optimum alternative, architects must achieve balance between funds committed for construction and their designed response to the building program. Here, the building design and cost must be frozen, and both must be held in positive balance through the construction-document phase so that there will be no surprises on the day of bid opening.

It has long been the hope of architects to have the capability of cost analysis available during the program and design phases of a project. One architect puts it succinctly:

> The architect was caught in one of the construction industry's most troublesome traps: By the time costs can be determined, it is often too late to control them. The problem is that presently there is no substantial, comprehensive, and dependable data base behind the systems for cost estimating in the conceptual stages of design. The result is that there are sometimes panic cuts in design features or radical substitutions in materials and methods of construction when the bids are in.[1]

The methods and procedures outlined in this book rest on a very solid, always current data base that will later be described in detail. It is these methods and procedures, linked by computer to a reliable data base under the watchful eye of a cost manager, that make it possible for architects to meet the challenge of cost control.

[1] James Y. Robinson, Jr., "New Data for Cost Estimating at the Conceptual Stage," *AIA Journal*, November 1974, p. 33.

7

PART ONE

BACKGROUND

CHAPTER 1

CONSTRUCTION COSTS AND THE ARCHITECT

For owner or developer, the cost of construction is the most important item in a long list of costs to be considered before a building is completed and occupied. All other costs are dictated by, or are a function of, construction costs. Construction costs are defined as the sum of all dollars paid to contractors to produce a building with all its fixed equipment, together with site development and connections to public utilities.

The average architect knows very little about the cost of construction. Allowing a few percentage points for exceptions, architects as a group are not knowledgeable about current and ever-changing construction costs. At the outset of every building project the owner either tells the architect there are only so many dollars for the work or asks for advice on how much a project will cost. Architects cannot avoid the issue. They must work within defined cost limits, or they must project what the cost of construction will be with reasonable accuracy. The architect's strongest attributes are the ability to design, the ability to organize space functionally and esthetically in ways that meet human and social needs, and the ability to solve problems ranging from micro scale to macro scale. Architects can design handsome buildings and produce drawings and specifications that describe down to the last detail how they are to be constructed. But the Achilles' heel of the profession is its unrealiability in estimating construction costs. That is a difficult statement to understand when it is realized that the building owner was seriously concerned about the cost of his building when he engaged the architect.

Bids for construction on public works frequently come in well above appropriated funds, to the delight of the newspapers, which gleefully follow the cost overruns throughout construction—much to the embarrassment of the architect. These same events, when they occur in the private sector, don't always reach the press, but they do erode professional reputation. Cost underruns, in their own way, are as bad as cost overruns. The owner could have put better quality into the building, built more space, or made some other decision on how to expend those funds, had the surplus been known earlier.

The architectural profession has come to realize that poor performance in cost estimating is not acceptable at all, and it is searching for ways to improve itself. Meanwhile, clients are reacting strongly when building costs are not kept in hand. The number of disputes going into arbitration because of inadequate construction cost control is increasing rapidly, and the alarming rise in rates for professional liability insurance demonstrates that the Achilles' heel must be covered, whatever the cost.

Before we examine how architects can mitigate these difficulties, a review of the background and events leading to the present state of the profession in this regard is needed.

THE NATURE OF THE ARCHITECT

Architects are designers; they are not accountants. Architects are intuitive and paint ideas with a broad brush, rather than deal with costs using a fine pen. They often leap to conclusions without knowing the consequences of their decisions. Scratch almost any architect, and an artist is found underneath. Of course it is true that the typology of architects cannot be couched in general terms that apply to all of them, but on the whole they do comprise a group whose inclination is to think of architecture first as an art form and second as a business. Architects are generalists rather than specialists, and they are sure that creativity is their real business. They prefer to spend more time studying the whole problem to be solved and less on the perfection of its details. Architects, as a rule, don't like to bother too much about construction costs; costs are tedious, time-consuming, and boring.

Still, it is the duty of the architect to be concerned about costs. Indeed, construction costs are an acknowledged professional responsibility and a source of constant worry. But until a final design has been accepted, and materials and quantities determined, how accurate can one be? Architects have always desperately wanted to know what their designs cost while in the conceptual phases, but other than applying some general rules about square-foot cost or material costs and having some conversations with consulting engineers, little can be done to gain full confidence about the accuracy of construction costs prior to final design solution.

Architects, then, by their very nature, spend most of their time on design analysis and little of their time on cost analysis.

THE EDUCATION OF THE ARCHITECT

It is in the nature of the architect to want to go to a school of architecture. A creative, imaginative, artistic personality, seeking ways for personal expression, often finds its outlet in an architectural education. The design faculty are people with similar leanings; students and faculty are comfortable with each other. Great teacher-designers motivate and inspire students who sometimes seek out the teacher rather than the university.

There are approximately 80 schools with accredited programs in architecture. No two programs are alike, and each reflects the personal educational concepts of the dean and faculty of that individual school. All programs must meet standards for a well-integrated and coordinated architectural education as determined by the National Architectural Accrediting Board (NAAB). The curriculum consists of architectural design and of technologies relating to it. It provides a fair understanding of structural, mechanical, and electrical engineering. And it includes work in mathematics and electives in art, history, the humanities, and the social sciences. Many graduate programs are tailored to fit students with a bachelor's degree in disciplines other than architecture. However, there is no room in the curriculum for the study of building economics or construction costs. It is a very rare school that has courses in these subjects, and the purpose here is usually to graduate a student in architectural engineering, rather than architecture.

It takes many years to get a basic architectural education, and still another year for a master's degree. The emphasis in architectural education is on design, and that is as it should be. But to structure a curriculum with no foundation in or sensitivity to construction costs is a serious mistake. Academia is out of touch with the current needs of the profession. Deans of architectural schools well know that competition is fierce among important subjects for a place in the curriculum. Five or six years is little enough time to include all the material needed to graduate a well-rounded architect, but to exclude a basic knowledge of building economics and construction costs is a poor ordering of priorities. To find there is almost unanimity on this exclusion in some 80 schools of architecture is almost unbelievable. Perhaps the real crux of this discussion is that courses in building economics and construction costs are not wanted, and even if they were, the faculty to teach these subjects at a sophisticated level would not be available.

The schools' position on the subject speaks for itself: *design analysis*—yes; *cost analysis*—no.

After graduation, architects are seldom exposed to cost estimating during their period of apprenticeship; they are too busy learning other things. The beginner may be asked to calculate area and volume and to become familiar with the method of estimating costs using a unit price per square foot, however undependable this may be. In addition to gaining office experience, the beginner is preparing for professional examinations and occasionally does study a little about building economics and cost estimating. However, an inspection of all recent professional examinations by the National Council of Architectural Registration Boards shows that almost no questions are asked relating to building economics, and none about cost estimating. The beginner passes the examination, is duly licensed, and becomes a registered architect.

Architectural education, then, has a curious result. Students have studied in the university, studied during the years of apprenticeship, and demonstrated by examination that they are proficient in architecture. They know how to design buildings, improve the environment, and protect the health, safety, and well-being of all the people therein. *But they know almost nothing about construction costs.* When so little value is placed on building economics during the educational process, it is small wonder that architects have difficulties in this area of their professional practice. Over the years, some architects become very efficient in cost estimating because they recognize its importance and emphasize it as they process each project. But too many architects use too much wishful thinking instead of methodical investigating when they estimate the construction costs of their buildings. Why is this so? How can the schools and the profession itself continue this way when the annual volume of all construction is approaching the $200 billion mark? And how did this come to be?

A CENTURY OF CHANGE IN THE ARCHITECTURAL CLIMATE

During the closing decades of the nineteenth century, buildings were relatively simple, erected in stable communities when transportation in the city was based on the horse. Architecture had a human scale, held together by a delightful pedestrian experience. Most people walked from here to there, and buildings were limited in height because the pedestrian experience was vertical as well as horizontal. Architects in those days were few in number and dominated the design of their buildings because little engineering was required. Architects could become master builders because they controlled the entire process of design and construction. Architecture was a gentleman's profession, influenced by the grand Beaux Arts tradition. Clients were people of substance and could well afford the residences and commercial structures they commissioned. Public works were monumental, using styles imported from abroad; they were not designed for efficiency nor for best value. Lesser works and industrial buildings were left for engineers and small houses for carpenters and masons. The constraints of building codes and regulatory agencies belonged to another century.

However, those same nineteenth-century decades contained the seeds of emerging building technologies that would profoundly change architectural practice—slowly at first, but irreversibly—in the following century. Development of the steel frame and the elevator freed buildings from the ground, and structural engineers, as professional specialists, were needed by architects, not only to design the steel cage but also to estimate its construction costs. This new engineering technology then brought forth new architectural forms that challenged the Beaux Arts tradition. The Chicago school led the way as Adler and Sullivan created exciting new skyscrapers. Sullivan was mentor to Frank Lloyd Wright, whose genius contained both architect and engineer and who over the next half century challenged every tradition upheld by architects of the classic school, such as McKim, Mead, and White, or Pope, or Hunt.

Technology planted other seeds in those decades. Gaslight began to give way to Edison's electric light; central heating systems began to replace the fireplace; plumbing moved indoors; the internal combustion engine outran the horse; and the telephone came alive. All these emerging technologies began to change the way buildings were designed and constructed and had great influence on costs. New engineering disciplines arose to bring specialized expertise to the architect. During the twentieth century those technologies gradually became more complex and more esoteric. Building cooling was added to heating; to the steel skeleton was added reinforced concrete, and they both grew into space frames; electricity was extended into electronics, producing control and communication systems; the slide rule was made obsolete by the computer.

The architect was overwhelmed with information needed to design buildings; information supply became information overload. Gradually specialists took over specific building systems which only they could design. Architects began to delegate the design of certain parts of the building to others and thus lost total personal control of the design process. As they did, architects no longer knew the costs of these building elements and depended on others for this information. Today about 61 percent of the construction dollar is expended on building systems which are designed by engineers, not architects. Since the 1950s, engineers and other consultants and technicians have emerged as an integral part of the design team. Architects no longer play a lone role. They share the stage with others, coordinating all activities. But as prime contractor to the building owner, the architect carries complete responsibility for all the players on the team and for the accuracy of cost estimates for all building systems.

During the present century, cities have grown—just as fast as all the technologies—and added hidden social costs to construction costs. As millions of people crowded into ever-tighter spaces, building codes and regulatory agencies were created to maintain physical order, promote safety and health, and prevent environmental degradation. Architecture has developed beyond the concept of a single building on a site; it now must consider not only that building but also its surrounding community and then its relationship to the larger region. Regulations can now say that owners must do more than satisfy the user needs in a building. For instance, the owner must help solve some of the city's transportation problems, and codes stipulate how many cars may be parked in a structure or on the site. Owners must meet certain air pollution requirements, or they must follow regulations on environmental impact. All these social costs must be added to the usual costs of construction and the total adjusted to fit a specific project location, under a variable set of market conditions and at some definite point in time. Architects' abilities to deal with all these matters are not outstanding.

Over the past hundred years, then, architects have been overtaken by a burgeoning technology fostering many engineering disciplines whose practitioners want a piece of the action; in addition, a vast tangle of constraints and regulations has slowly fenced the profession in. It is no wonder that architects have now reached the point where their cost estimating has become less than reliable. They need help. But before we examine how architects can lessen these difficulties, other factors must be considered to show why architects have the public image they do and what moves they must make to improve it.

ESCALATION AND THE BUILDING COST INDEX

As the population of America has grown, so has its physical plant and the infrastructure that serves it. Buildings have not only lost their simplicity but become much larger and much more specialized, generating many building types. Less construction work is done in the field and more in the factory. Shortages in natural resources result in shortages in building materials. Soaring labor and material costs in the construction community have outpaced the rest of the economy and must be added to technological and social costs. As buildings get larger, they take more time to be designed and constructed, and escalation can be a ponderous unknown when building costs several years downstream must be projected. The history of inflation in building costs has produced the curve shown in Figure 1-1.

From 1920 to the end of World War II in 1945, the building cost index was relatively stable, and engineering building systems were relatively simple. Architects could project their building costs tomorrow with some confidence, because they would not be much different from what they were yesterday. After World War II the index leaped higher, and the Korean and Viet Nam encounters added fuel to the fires of inflation, which continued at even greater rates through the 1970s. Today the index is reaching a nearly vertical configuration.

BACKGROUND

Since the unit costs of buildings are now so high, the problem of construction cost control in designing buildings has become critical. Building owners want better value for their construction dollar. Some owners have not been satisfied in this respect by their architects and are seeking services elsewhere.

FIGURE 1-1

BUILDING COST INDEX

(*Reproduced by permission of* Engineering News Record, *New York.*)

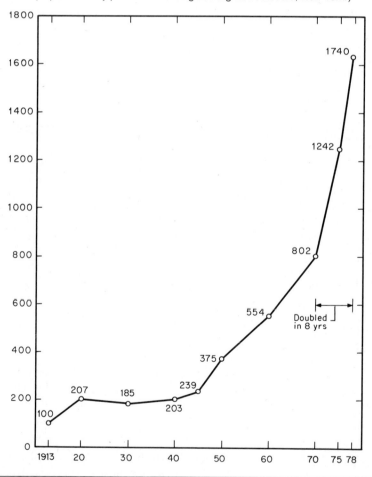

THE ARCHITECT'S PUBLIC IMAGE AND THE NEW COMPETITION

The American Arbitration Association (AAA) is a nationally recognized body that settles disputes within the construction community. It is accepted by professional societies and contractor associations and their members as the authority having jurisdiction when arbitration, rather than action through the courts, is needed about agreements of professional and construction people with the owner and with each other. Accordingly, the volume of arbitration cases involving the architect with the owner, the engineer, and the contractor is a barometer of architectural difficulties. The total yearly number of construction cases brought before the American Arbitration Association has increased over the years; the value of claims and counterclaims is reaching very serious dimensions; and the increase in individual claims in excess of $100,000 is having a severe impact on the professions. Government agencies and private owners who hire architects are aware of these trends. They are also aware of an increase in cases dealing with poor construction cost estimating. None of this is helpful to professionals trying to win public esteem.

Many architectural agreements do not contain an arbitration clause and require other ways of handling disputes. Disputes on public works usually have mechanisms of appeal but leave the "owner" as the court of last resort. Except after arbitration, when decisions are final, anyone can sue anybody in a civil action on a real or imagined grievance. Again, a large number of suits have to do with the architects' inability to match their construction estimates with the actualities of bidding or to negotiate the time and costs of change orders skillfully. Word of these actions seeps out here and there; the public does learn of them, and the lasting impression is not good: Architects are "expensive."

The perception of architects in the world of educational building conjures up words such as *frills, gold plating, monuments,* and others. These unpleasant expressions can be dismissed as the angry reactions of overburdened taxpayers; but, like it or not, this view persists. From elementary schools to college halls, there has been a countrywide history of poor cost estimating followed by frantic rebidding or negotiating to get costs down. When costs are brought down, value is sacrificed. The owner knows this and resents it.

Many will disagree, saying this is not the public image of the architect. Proof to the contrary lies in the fact that a whole new world of competition has been moving in on the architect, while the profession has not been fully aware of its strength. This competition does not say architects cannot design. It is saying that *architects don't know the costs of their designs or that other designs would give equal value at lower cost or better value at the same cost.* Sometimes these charges are true, and sometimes they are simply fabrications intended to exploit the poor image of the architect. The undeniable reality is that architectural services are being offered, in whole or in part, by construction managers, design-build groups, developers, package builders, and specialists in particular building types such as hospitals or branch banks. All these groups have one thing in common. They sell construction costs first and design second. They compete with architects on the basis of cost where they are strong, and not on the basis of design where they are weak. They say to the owner, "Put your project in our hands and we will deliver *on time and on budget.*" That hits architects hard, because as a class, being on time and on budget is hardly what they are noted for.

What can architects do to meet the competition, control construction costs, and improve their public image? They can put a fifth expert on their design team and initiate a new set of procedures that link design to cost analysis.

THE COST MANAGER—A NEW MEMBER ON THE DESIGN TEAM

If architects do not really know construction costs, they have only one possible course: They must put a cost-control expert—a cost manager— on the design team. Note the phrase *on the design team.* That means in the beginning, before irrevocable decisions are made. The cost manager must be a part of the decision process, analyzing the cost consequences of program and design decisions made by the architect and the structural, mechanical, and electrical engineers. Early program and design decisions set the ultimate construction cost of a building and generate this formula, which will later be reviewed in detail:

$$\text{Program} + \text{Design} = \text{Cost}.$$

The first question that arises is: Who will pay the cost manager's fee? There is only one answer: The owner will. If owners demand dependable cost estimating, they will have to pay for it, just as they do for engineering consultation. This is contrary to the standard forms of agreement between owner and architect prepared by the American Institute of Architects. These forms state that complete estimating services are not included in the basic fee and will be an extra. This subject will be discussed further in Chapter 3.

The second question that arises is: Where will we find a cost manager? Ideally this manager would be located near the architect or in the vicinity of the project, where local construction practices and market conditions are known firsthand. However, if this service is not available locally, there are cost-management organizations, which are well staffed and are able to operate on a national level and to work with professional firms at any location. Specific construction cost information is stored in their computers for all parts of the country. Communication at first is by telephone, then by mail, and later in person.

Later chapters will set forth procedures for working with the cost manager. These require time, effort, and self-discipline, but they will put the architect into the decision process leading to cost control.

Design analysis and cost analysis become simultaneous operations, leading directly to *design cost analysis.*

CONSTRUCTION COST CONTROL BY THE ARCHITECT

Architects have a wealth of cost information at their fingertips. The cost data used to illustrate the principles set forth in this book are taken from the 1979 edition of *Dodge Construction Systems Costs*[2] This cost information is updated each year so that the examples and concepts presented here will always be current when used with each new annual edition. Cost information is gathered from 485 cities in the 50 states, Canada, and Puerto Rico. Construction costs are based on an average national index, and location adjustment factors make it possible to estimate costs in any part of the country, keyed to the zip-code address where a project is located.

Table 1-1 shows the national average 1979 construction costs per square foot for 43 different building types, beginning with the least expensive and ranging up to the most costly. Within each building type, costs are separated into three average levels of quality, from low to high.

[2] Dodge Building Cost Services (McGraw-Hill Information Systems Company) with Wood & Tower Inc., *1979 Dodge Construction Systems Costs,* McGraw-Hill, New York, 1978.

TABLE 1-1

AVERAGE CONSTRUCTION COSTS
(dollars/square foot)

	Building type	Low avg.	Average	High avg.
1.	Shopping centers	$20.14	$23.54	$28.06
2.	Apartments, low rise	18.67	25.18	27.95
3.	Service stations	24.02	25.70	28.05
4.	Warehouses	20.06	26.82	31.38
5.	Apartments, high rise	24.51	27.16	30.76
6.	Light manufacturing	22.44	27.50	38.72
7.	Multistory housing	23.59	27.78	34.70
8.	Auto dealers	28.64	30.78	32.46
9.	Educational service center	29.78	32.51	38.28
10.	Stores and shops	25.23	33.22	41.96
11.	Supermarkets	25.48	34.00	36.75
12.	Chemical process plants	25.64	34.14	39.20
13.	Warehouses, refrigerated	28.09	34.80	42.28
14.	Community centers	34.24	36.70	40.99
15.	Racketball and health clubs	35.02	38.76	41.00
16.	Heavy manufacturing	25.26	38.64	52.03
17.	Nursing homes	30.44	38.78	49.02
18.	Food processing plants	25.96	38.90	58.21
19.	Hotels	31.82	39.04	41.52
20.	Office buildings	37.38	39.98	48.20
21.	Department stores	33.71	40.10	42.50
22.	Homes for the aged	35.40	40.24	45.43
23.	Dormitories	38.58	40.86	45.61
24.	Elementary schools	35.61	41.42	46.16
25.	Fire stations	40.42	43.24	48.57
26.	Vocational schools	36.28	44.52	55.30
27.	Secondary and high schools	41.94	44.98	47.58
28.	Computer centers	43.05	47.56	50.20
29.	Corporate headquarters office buildings	45.10	48.00	55.51
30.	Health centers	43.28	49.84	52.92
31.	Theaters and playhouses	47.20	50.46	55.96
32.	Prisons	43.40	50.48	55.10
33.	Museums	42.15	51.74	54.72
34.	Restaurants	42.15	54.48	59.64
35.	Churches	38.42	50.68	76.92
36.	University classrooms	54.82	59.78	67.55
37.	Public libraries	56.82	60.38	68.05
38.	Branch banks	48.15	60.60	70.14
39.	College libraries	60.00	63.88	71.77
40.	Laboratory buildings	43.39	63.90	67.64
41.	Courthouses	59.00	66.08	72.63
42.	Main banks	63.99	70.08	82.36
43.	General hospitals	69.00	79.82	85.63

It is interesting to note how the cost of one particular type relates to its neighbors above and below and how it is positioned in the full spectrum of all building types. These data can be of considerable value to architects when setting cost range possibilities during the programming and schematic design phases. The costs shown here should only be used as guidelines, as they reflect national averages. To illustrate just how far these national averages can vary, refer to the location adjustment factors in Table A-1 in Appendix A. Orangeburg, South Carolina, is found to be lowest at 66 percent, and Anchorage, Alaska, tops all cities at 132 percent. These comparative figures demonstrate how dangerous it is simply to compare the cost of one building with that of another of the same type.

Since so much of the construction dollar goes into engineering systems, architects need advance information on the *probable distribution of engineering costs* during the early phases of schematic design. The cost manager has these data; they are hard data, not intuitive. This will be examined in detail later, but Table 1-2 illustrates a cost breakdown for a

TABLE 1-2

LABORATORY BUILDING

Building system	Low average $/sq ft	Low average % tot	Average $/sq ft	Average % tot	High average $/sq ft	High average % tot
Foundations	$ 2.26	5.2%	$ 2.42	3.8%	$ 2.50	3.7%
Floors on grade	0.84	1.9	0.90	1.4	0.92	1.4
Superstructure	6.20	14.3	10.94	17.1	11.16	16.5
Roofing	0.96	2.2	1.02	1.6	1.06	1.6
Exterior walls	4.36	10.0	6.80	10.6	7.28	10.8
Partitions	3.06	7.1	3.28	5.1	3.52	5.2
Wall finishes	1.80	4.1	1.94	3.0	2.06	3.0
Floor finishes	1.28	2.9	1.36	2.1	1.46	2.2
Ceiling finishes	1.24	2.9	1.34	2.1	1.44	2.1
Conveying systems	0.86	2.0	0.92	1.4	0.98	1.4
Specialties	1.88	4.3	2.02	3.2	2.16	3.2
Fixed equipment	3.57	8.2	5.10	8.0	5.46	8.1
HVAC	6.06	14.0	10.76	16.8	11.50	17.0
Plumbing	3.92	9.0	6.34	9.9	6.78	10.0
Electrical	5.10	11.8	8.76	13.7	9.36	13.8
Construction cost	$43.39	100%	$63.90	100%	$67.64	100%

Source: Dodge Building Cost Services (McGraw-Hill Information Systems Company) with Wood & Tower Inc., *1979 Dodge Construction Systems Costs*, McGraw-Hill, New York. 1978.

laboratory building. The cost per square foot is shown for fifteen building systems, over three levels of quality. General conditions, overhead, and profit are spread throughout the fifteen systems. Also note that gross construction cost does not include site work; this item can vary over such a wide range that it would distort the actual cost of construction allocated to each system. Site work must be estimated separately and added to construction cost.

It has been noted that depending solely on the square-foot costs of a building is dangerous because of differences in location and quality. Architects are prone to compare their building costs with those of others, and if they don't, their clients do. For example, the cost of a laboratory in Orangeburg @ 66% of the national average could run from $28.64 to as high as $44.64. In Anchorage @ 132% it could run from $57.27 to $89.28. This atypical (but true) comparison projects costs ranging from $28.64 to $89.28. It does bring home a point. When location and quality factors are closer together it is very easy to be mistaken about square-foot costs. The only way to be confident in cost control is to have the cost manager on the design team.

Table 1-2 also illustrates another point that is a surprise to many architects. The average cost column itemizes six engineering systems. These total $40.12 or 63% of the construction dollar! The only places the architect can affect costs are in exterior walls and interior partitions. The architect certainly needs a cost manager here—someone to keep a tight leash on engineering costs. If a particular engineering system design goes above these average costs, how will the difference be made up? It can't come out of an architectural system; it *must* come out of some other engineering system.

The argument is now complete. A cost manager is to be placed on the architect's design team if the latter is to control construction costs. The cost manager will link design decisions to cost consequences and analyze both together, beginning at the inception of every project.

It is now necessary to examine architectural services over the second half of this century and see how much change there has been relating to value, time, and cost. The same forces that have put a cost manager into the design picture are those forces that have induced change in architectural services.

CHAPTER 2
ARCHITECTURAL SERVICES AND CHANGE

The last chapter pointed out the substantial changes that have taken place in the past century in building technology, in population growth, and in escalating construction costs. Since the nineteen-fifties all these changes have accelerated exponentially, and this in turn has induced many changes within the architectural profession and in the way services are provided to individuals and institutions. Social, economic, and now environmental forces lean ever more heavily on the design professions, and further changes are to be expected.

CHANGES IN GROWTH INDICATORS RELEVANT TO CONSTRUCTION

As one family in five changes homes each year, as industry moves from north-eastern and north-central America into the Sunbelt, as all the population squeezes ever closer together, as environmental and regulatory constraints have multiplied, and as inflation impedes true growth in the economy, a trail of statistics has been left as shown in Table 2-1.

The data in this table reflect the recent history of growth in size, complexity, and costs, not only for the nation but also for the construction community and the design professionals who create the built environ-

TABLE 2-1

GROWTH INDICATORS RELEVANT TO CONSTRUCTION

(in millions)

Indicator	Source	1950	1960	1970	1975	1980
Population	1	151	180	204	213*	
Existing housing units	1	45	58	68	79	
Gross national product, $	2	284,769	503,734	977,080	1,516,338	
Value of construction put in place, $	3	33,575	54,738	94,855	132,043	
Federal budget outlays, $	4	42,600	92,200	196,600	326,100	
Business expenditures for plant and equipment, $	2	17,832	36,750	79,710	112,780	
Personal consumption expenditures, $	5	191,000	325,000	617,000	979,000	
U.S. fuel consumption in barrels per day of oil, equivalent	6	16	21	32		48*

*Estimate
Sources: 1. U.S. Bureau of the Census
2. U.S. Bureau of Economic Analysis
3. U.S. Department of Commerce
4. Office of Management and Budget
5. U.S. Office of Business Economics
6. Joint Congressional Committee on Atomic Energy Report, 1973

ment the nation needs. Over this same period of time the character of architectural services has changed, or has been added to, to meet the growth trends. Three patterns of architectural services are capable of definition, and a fourth is in sight. Some architects have not favored these new patterns and have resisted change, tending to continue old ways of doing business. Peter Drucker has this to say about such tendencies:

What exists is getting old. To say that most executives spend most of their time tackling the problems of today is euphemism. They spend most of their time on the problems of yesterday. Executives spend more of their time trying to unmake the past than on anything else.

This to a large extent is inevitable. What exists today is of necessity the product of yesterday. . . . Indeed, every business regards what happened in the past as normal, with a strong inclination to reject as abnormal whatever does not fit the pattern.

No matter how wise, forward looking, or courageous the decisions and actions were when first made, they will have been overtaken by events by the time they become normal behavior and the routine of a business. . . .

It is always futile to restore normality; "normality" is only the reality of yesterday. The job is not to impose yesterday's normal on a changed today; but to change the business, its behavior, its attitudes, its expectations—as well as its products, its markets, and its distributive channels—to fit the new realities.[1]

The past realities of the architectural business will now be examined as well as the realities of today. Figure 2-1 shows in graphic form, but not to scale, four patterns of architectural services—three existing over the past decades and one sure to appear over the next ten years. The diagram shows the sequential activities of service and the lengths of time needed to perform those services from one decade to another. The key here is the vertical line showing the time when zoning and other public approvals are received. How much professional service is required to gain public approval, and after approval, how much service is required to design and build the project? Service varies from building to building, of course, but some general premises can be made as each decade is surveyed.

TRADITIONAL SERVICES IN THE 1950s

Services in this decade carried on the traditions of the past. They were a sequential, linear flow of preliminary design, construction documents, and supervision of construction. Codes and zoning laws were not too complex for the most part, and the time for zoning and other public approvals of a project was usually predictable, routine, and short. Except for the Korean war, which critically curtailed the supply of some building materials, the business of construction had few surprises. By the end of the decade, construction projects were blooming countrywide, and industry was getting set for the soaring sixties. Relations between architect and

[1] Peter F. Drucker, *Managing for Results*, Harper and Row, New York, 1964, p. 8.

PATTERNS OF ARCHITECTURAL SERVICE

FIGURE 2-1

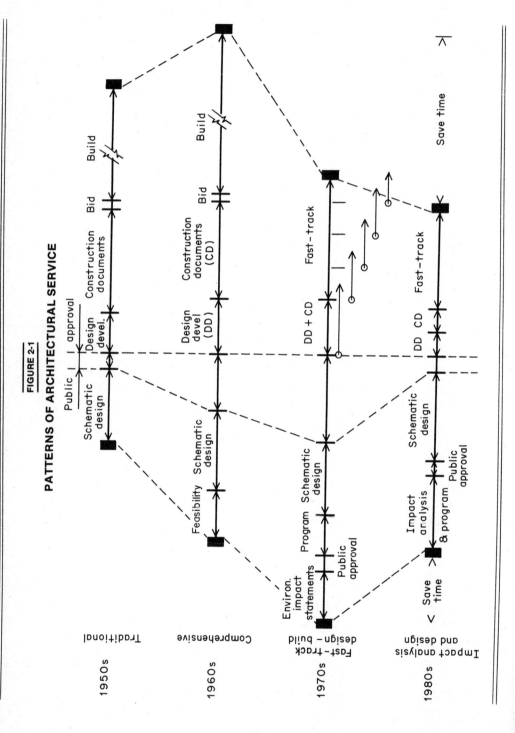

client and architect and contractor were stable and cordial, and the idea of errors-and-omissions insurance had not yet been born. Construction costs could be reasonably projected using the cost-per-square-foot method. Cost consultants were few and far between. As the pace of construction quickened and the volume and complexity of buildings grew, the old traditional ways of service didn't fit the needs of the times. Traditional services did not vanish, but it was clear that other ways of doing things were at hand.

COMPREHENSIVE SERVICES OF THE 1960s

These years saw the architects blocking out a much larger role for their services. No longer satisfied to wait until a client with land and money called and asked for a building to be designed, architects became aggressive. They did as Drucker advised; they changed their attitudes and their business and looked for new markets. They wanted to be involved "up front" when projects were born so they could take part in the basic decisions that influenced building design. In a statement on comprehensive services, the American Institute of Architects pointed out that architects must continue their traditional role, but modify it as required to respond to the needs of the times. Services should be expanded to perform or coordinate all the diverse activities required by building projects, including environmental design. These also included feasibility studies, financial analysis, location and site analysis, operational programming, building programming, and promotional services. (All this is summed up in Figure 2-1 for the 1960s with the one word *feasibility*.)

That was indeed an expansion of services. However, many architects maintained they were in business to practice architecture, and having little aptitude for comprehensive services, continued to practice just architecture. Many still feel the same way.

During this decade the regulatory process became much more complicated and stringent. Zoning laws were often tested in the courts. Public hearings challenged the construction of housing and buildings; hearings could stretch out for weeks and months. Billions of dollars of work were financed in whole or in part with federal funds, and every government agency had its own book of rules the architect had to follow. With additional services to perform and with public approvals more difficult to obtain, the average time for architectural services from inception of a proj-

29

ect to receipt of public approval was much longer in the sixties than in the fifties.

With additional services came additional responsibilities. Many firms, particularly the larger ones, staffed up to meet the new levels of competence required for comprehensive services. These were the years when many architectural-engineering (A-E) firms were organized to meet the new challenges of the times, and, with other disciplines added, offered full in-house professional services including cost-management capabilities. Many more cost-consultant firms were available to architects in those years, but most architects continued to estimate construction costs by the traditional square-foot method, or a variation of that method. The computer began to find its way into a few offices but was very slow in gaining acceptance. Very few computer programs could be used for architectural purposes; most were better suited to the engineering disciplines, which took to them readily.

Construction projects became larger; large projects became multibuilding projects. New towns were designed and built; city planning grew into regional planning. More engineering systems made buildings more complex and difficult to supervise during construction. The standard form of architectural agreements was changed; architects *observed* construction, they no longer supervised it. Lawsuits proliferated over grievances involving design and construction. Errors-and-omissions insurance was invented, and with this protection came exposure, and the number of suits expanded again. Relations between architects and contractors were not as cordial as they had been during the fifties. With the growth that came in this decade and with larger projects, the average time it took to construct a building after receipt of public approvals was longer in the sixties than in the fifties.

It was also in the sixties that the architect began to be thought of as expensive, because a disproportionate number of architects could no longer control construction costs. The times themselves had much to do with this. For example, this decade saw rapid expansion of the use of air conditioning, of elaborate control systems in all building types, of television and audiovisual systems in education, and of sophisticated equipment in hospitals. It was the buildings themselves that became expensive, not the architects. However, as architects added more services to the traditional ones, as buildings became more complex, and as engineers did more of the work, it was true that architects did not control the cost of buildings as well as they had in the nineteen-fifties.

FAST-TRACK AND DESIGN-BUILD SERVICES IN THE 1970s

This decade saw the development of two more types of architectural service, each having adherents and opponents and each requiring a high level of architectural, engineering, and management skills, as well as a full command of construction methods. The fast-track method is organized to reduce the time needed for construction, making possible earlier occupancy and reducing financing costs. During the sixties large projects took years to build, and something had to be done to speed up the work. Who can properly estimate labor and material costs three and five years downstream? In fast-track, as soon as the schematic design is accepted and public approvals are received, the construction manager (who sometimes is the architect) breaks the project down into a series of phased bid packages. Work in the field can be started immediately, and materials and equipment requiring long lead times are ordered. As final design and documentation for separate building systems are finished, they in turn are bid in separate bid packages, until the building is complete. Tight scheduling and coordination is a must.

During this decade a swarm of package builders and others invaded the design professional's field and offered owners a design-build package. Architects and engineers countered by getting into the development business themselves. They organized joint ventures and consortiums in any number of ways that might be attractive to clients. Design-build uses the fast-track method of construction, but it does so at a fixed price and with a single responsibility. Architects supply services to the point of single responsibility and not to the owner, and great care is needed to avoid conflicts of interest.

The seventies added to the public approval difficulties by introducing federal and state regulations with respect to environmental impact and by passing the Occupational Safety and Health Act (OSHA). Now environmental impact statements had to be filed for approval even before projects were designed. In some urban centers the logjam of projects awaiting approval backed up for endless months. Another ill-defined layer of safety in building construction had been added to those already in effect. An inescapable fact emerges clearly: This decade realized a reduction of construction time by fast tracking, but it concurrently added up-front regulations that lengthened the time for design and approvals.

These years saw the computer gain substantial holds on the architectural profession, not only in drafting but also in design itself. The advent of energy conservation and new regulations setting energy budgets for buildings make it clear that building envelope, form, siting, and region could no longer be left to intuitive design. Architectural design will need computer analysis just as does mechanical design. Construction cost analysis by computer is now commonplace. The cost manager's data system is now accessible to the architect through office terminals connected to the managers' programs and data base by telephone. This surely fits the new realities of today.

IMPACT ANALYSIS AND DESIGN SERVICES IN THE 1980s

The eighties will continue to use all patterns of service. The traditional, linear form will continue in use for smaller projects. The trend is clear, however. New methods must be found to shorten the delivery time for the design and approval process, just as new methods shortened construction time in the seventies. The construction problem was really a management problem. It needed no new theories or technology. Design and approval must contend with social, economic, and environmental factors, all having impact on the design solution. Government regulations and public demands of communities affected by a new building project place severe constraints on design. Ways must be developed to balance public needs with the design objective, which is to deliver best value to the building owner. Figure 2-1, for the eighties, labels this process *impact analysis and design*. Before describing this, it is necessary to examine some methods and tools that will be available in the eighties to help implement this concept.

THE DESIGN DECISION PROCESS

A final design solution is the combined result of thousands of decisions. These decisions are made independently by many people, and some independent decisions can ricochet among other previously made decisions with devastating effect. It is necessary to formalize the decision process in design and to examine its parts, so that once the process is understood, design can flow naturally and easily without requiring any thought.

WHO MAKES DECISIONS?

The decision process begins by coming to an agreement on *who* it is that shall make decisions. In building design, architects make both basic decisions and minor decisions, sometimes with and sometimes without the advice and counsel of their engineering consultants. Architects stand ready to accept their own work; it is a personal expression. J. K. Galbraith recognized that the individual is appreciated more than the group when he says:

> The individual has far more standing in our culture than the group. An individual has a presumption of accomplishment; a committee has a presumption of inaction. . . . To have, in pursuit of truth, to assert the superiority of the organization over the individual for important social tasks is a taxing prospect.
>
> Yet it is a necessary task. It is not to individuals but to organizations that power in the business enterprise and power in the society has passed. And modern economic society can only be understood as an effort, wholly successful, to synthesize by organization a group personality far superior for its purposes to a natural person and with the added advantage of immortality.
>
> The need for such a personality begins with the circumstance that in modern industry a large number of decisions, and all that are important, draw on information possessed by more than one man. Typically they draw on the specialized scientific and technical knowledge, the accumulated information or experience and the artistic or intuitive sense of many persons. And this is guided by further information which is assembled, analyzed, and interpreted by professionals using highly technical equipment. The final decision will be informed only as it draws systematically on all those whose information is relevant.[2]

Design decisions in the 1980s will be made by a design team composed of the architect, the structural and mechanical engineers, and the cost manager, known as ASMEC and described in Chapter 4. It is this group that will make design decisions.

[2] John Kenneth Galbraith, *The New Industrial State*, Houghton Mifflin, Boston, 1967, pp. 60–61.

HOW ARE DESIGN DECISIONS MADE?

Creative design concepts (synthesis) are generated by the architect subjectively and intuitively. Engineers contribute to and support the concept subjectively and analytically. Cost managers examine architectural *and* engineering designs analytically and objectively. Martin Starr has this to say about decisions and design:

> Because decision problems are complex, it is impossible for any study to evaluate with precision all the relevant factors. The gap is filled by judgment, intuition, and the application of whatever we mean by common sense. As long as the gap exists, unique . . . viewpoints will continue to exist.
>
> Great stress has always been placed on analysis in the production management field. But synthesis has not been similarly favored. The explanation is that synthesis has been relegated to the intuition and judgment of executives. It shall continue to be, but not exclusively. There is a basis for objective synthesis. The desire for synthesis is not academic. Pre-designed systems . . . must be synthesized in an external and objective fashion. There is no other way.[3]

And that is *how* the design team, ASMEC, makes decisions. Design decisions should not be made until ASMEC has considered the design carefully and contributed to that design intuitively, subjectively, analytically, and objectively.

WHEN SHOULD DESIGN DECISIONS BE MADE?

As early as possible. Early decisions are basic decisions that establish design and cost. Right, objective decisions produce maximum benefit. Without full consideration by ASMEC, wrong decisions can produce maximum penalty. A wrong decision about community reaction to a proposed building, made during the impact-analysis phase could result in the project's never being built for lack of public approval. It is important to make the right decision in selecting a schematic design concept from among a group of alternatives. That basic decision is the first in a chain of

---

[3] Martin Kenneth Starr, *Production Management: Systems and Synthesis*, Prentice-Hall, Englewood Cliffs, N.J., 1964, pp. 48 and 54.

decisions, all of which must be made within the limiting parameters of that concept. Design and cost flexibility are available cnly through building system selection. Then the decision chain follows: once a building system is selected, design and cost flexibility is limited to subsystem and component selection within the boundaries of that system.

Figure 2-2 illustrates the cost of wrong and right decisions and shows

FIGURE 2-2

THE COST OF DESIGN DECISIONS

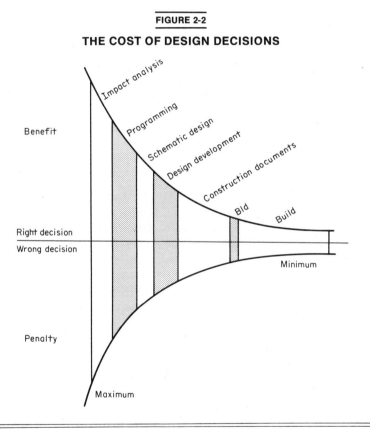

that maximum penalties and benefits accrue from the early stages of a project and that after the design phase there is little that can be done to change its cost. It also points out how unrewarding it is to try to lower costs after bids have been received. Implied in the whole diagram is the necessary presence of the cost manager every step along the way.

COST ESTIMATING BY COMPUTER

It has been said that for some jobs people are ideally suited, and for others the computer has definite advantages. There is no doubt that the computer will be doing cost estimating in the 1980s, using the concepts and programs developed by people; it will see widespread use. The architects' resistance to use of the computer will disappear, and this decade will produce large networks of terminals connected to the cost manager's system.

COMPUTER-AIDED DESIGN

More architects will be using computers in the late eighties to help solve design problems, as well as for automated computer drafting. Applied Research of Cambridge, Limited (ARC), an architectural and research firm, describes its computer-aided design program, developed in the nineteen-seventies, this way:

> It is an integrated, interactive computer-aided design system. It accepts information from the design team, by building systems, and gradually assembles a fully detailed three dimensional model of the building in the memory of the computer. Using this model it carries out a large set of evaluation procedures to assist the design team toward better building by predicting the cost and performance of alternative solutions. It uses the inherent logic of the building method to check the validity and consistency of design decisions and, whenever possible it automates the detail design process. The model is used to generate interim documentation on the progress of the design. When the model is complete, it is used as the automatic source of the drawings and schedules required for bidding and construction.[4]

Other research efforts are underway leading to computer-aided design. Toward the end of the eighties computer-aided design will be computer-linked to cost. Finally the architect and engineers will be able to address themselves to the job of design, and the cost manager to design cost analysis, leaving the chores of drawing and calculation to the computer.

Figure 2-3, prepared by ARC, shows how, with computer-aided design,

[4] C. W. Haskins, *Integrated Computer-Aided Building and the OXSYS Project*, Applied Research of Cambridge, Limited, Cambridge, Mass., June 1964, p. 1.

the greatest amount of time and resources is put into design effort and relatively little into preparation of construction documents. Note how the curve of the right decision of Figure 2-3 compares with ARC's traditional method and how, with computer-aided design, the ability to make right decisions over a longer period of time is enhanced because of the level of effort put out during the schematic design phase.

FIGURE 2-3

DECISION IMPACTS AS SEEN BY ARC

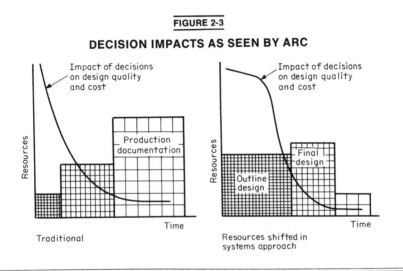

Traditional

Resources shifted in systems approach

This design-decision process then, together with computer-aided design and cost-setting, is one of the main tools expected to assist design professionals in the eighties.

THE CONCEPT OF IMPACT ANALYSIS AND DESIGN

When a building is placed on a site, it not only has physical and biological impact on the environment, but it also has economic and social impact on the community if the project is of any magnitude. Zoning and other regulatory approvals will be in two stages: one for environmental, social, and economic impacts, and one for the building itself. Public approvals are delayed or denied not because the appearance of a building is not acceptable, but rather because the building is not wanted at all. It will degrade the environment. Or it will disturb a sense of community values, overload a local traffic network or school system, upset a tax base, or do any of a host of things laden with high emotional content. Principles taken from planning can be used to analyze the impact of a building on its surrounding community while the building itself is being programmed. Social, economic, and environmental analyses can be made and a rationale prepared that will objectively balance the needs of the community with the needs of the building owner. Enough experience has been gained in the seventies to demonstrate that this will be commonplace in the eighties when environmental, demographic, and economic data can be conveniently stored in computer memory.

Building design will be computer aided and stored in memory according to systems, subsystems, and components. Design cost analysis will be done by the same computer, directly linked to the cost manager's programs and data base. Most of the design professional's time will be spent on just that—design, exploring alternative systems, and seeking best value. Architectural service in the 1980s has exciting possibilities.

CHAPTER 3

BUILDING COSTS AND THE BUILDING OWNER

The building owner—the architect's client—is concerned not only with construction costs but also with all the many other costs that go to make up the total cost of a building. These building costs are substantial and relate directly or indirectly to the cost of construction. As clients, building owners expect their architects to be knowledgeable about, and sensitive to, all the costs that constitute building costs.

When clients select their architect for a commission, they are concerned about building costs and about building design. Clients are more involved in design than they are given credit for. Pier Luigi Nervi, the noted Italian engineer and builder, had this to say about clients:

> The overall quality of the architecture of a nation is more influenced by the tendencies and cultural level of the clients than by the knowledge and esthetic sensibility of its architects.
>
> The client influences the architectural solution directly. Consciously or unconsciously, by defining the general outline of the structure, by choosing the designer, and by accepting or rejecting the designer's project, he

becomes a decisive element of the architectural solution. The private client will obviously ask the collaboration of a designer whose works he appreciates, and will direct the chosen designer towards his own ideal during discussions of the project . . . [1]

Clients, then, select their architects with design as well as costs in mind. It is good to know their thinking and what they expect from their design professionals.

THE CLIENT PROFILE

Clients can be separated into two broad categories: those in the private sector of the economy and those in the public sector. Each sector has projects that range from the very small to the very large. Public projects are funded initially by direct appropriations or bond issues; their operating and maintenance costs are supported by taxes. Private projects are funded from existing financial reserves or through borrowing from many diverse sources. But, public or private, all clients are extremely careful, or required by law, to manage the expenditure of funds wisely.

Most government clients, and most private clients with large building programs, require conformance with their own particular rules, regulations, and procedures. Those clients without experience who build only once, or a few times, depend on their architects to lead them through the maze of design and construction. The architect's freedom from constraints varies from client to client.

The communication link between client and architect is vital. It can take one of three forms, depending on how the client wishes to be represented. First is the client as an individual person. This is a one-to-one relationship and is ideal because the client is the owner, understands any problems under consideration, and has the authority to make immediate and final decisions. Next is the client—such as a school, country club, or church—represented by a building committee. Small building committees, numbering three, are preferable; larger committees of five or seven have wide divergences of opinion and are difficult to deal with. The decisions of building committees can be vetoed by a president or a board, but

---

[1] Pier Luigi Nervi, *Structures*, F. W. Dodge Corporation, McGraw-Hill Information Systems Company, Inc., New York, 1967, p. 3.

this is the most common form of client representation in the private sector. Finally there is the client represented by staff, where the client, public or private, has a constant volume of buildings to design and construct. This can be an informal process or a highly departmentalized series of reviews and approvals where architects and engineers follow the book. At best, with a staff as client, procedures can be enlightened and helpful. At worst, working with a staff as client is stultifying and cumbersome.

Clients may be large or small, informal or disciplined, public or private, but with few exceptions they have four common demands:

- That the architect complete their project within budget.
- That the architect complete their project on time.
- That the project function to their satisfaction.
- That the quality of design meet their criteria.

Clients, whoever they may be, will hold the architect personally and financially accountable if professional performance falls short of these demands. Clients can be very exacting people.

VALUE IN A BUILDING

Maximum value, as the client sees it, is achieved when essential function is obtained at minimum cost. But value in a building is of three kinds: quality value, use value, and esthetic value. These values are all established in the building program.

Quality Value

Buildings can be said to have three broad levels of quality in materials and equipment: low, average, and high. It is the owner's prerogative to set the level of quality wanted in a building and to insist on having that level at the lowest possible cost. A Mogul can call for marble in the Taj Mahal, and a magnate can call for concrete block in a national chain of cut-rate drug stores. Quality of materials, however, has nothing to do with quality of design. Outstanding design can be achieved with concrete block, and poor design can be immortalized in marble.

Use Value

Buildings are programmed around user needs as well as owner requirements. All buildings are constructed to house certain specific operations. These operations are performed by people or machines or both. Machine operation requirements are always satisfied, or the machine will not work. Human operational needs are not so well understood, or they are neglected or denied. In general, human values are well served when people are physically comfortable in a building, when the interior environment has good thermal, luminous, and acoustical characteristics, and when people are psychologically secure (without feelings of vertigo or claustrophobia) and are not subjected to building sway or vibration. Human user needs are denied when, for instance, an industrial process generates extreme heat that debilitates the operator or in a completely windowless building.

Esthetic Value

Visual and artistic qualities add esthetic value to a building. Buildings designed to fit well into the landscape and harmonize with surrounding buildings add esthetic value to the community. As Nervi said, when clients know good design and seek out those architects whose work they admire, good esthetic value is assured. It can be added that clients not interested in good design or esthetic values will not seek those qualities in their architects; such clients believe esthetic expression is too expensive. This, of course, is not necessarily so.

COST OF A BUILDING

The cost of a building to an owner can be visualized in three parts. The first part is the cost of construction; this is basic because the owner's needs establish what the functions and size a building should be, and the resulting design sets construction costs. All other costs are related to, or are a function of, construction costs. The second part of the cost of a building includes all those expenses that an owner must incur, other than construction, before a building can be occupied. The third part of the cost of a building takes in all the expenses incurred by the owner during its useful life. These latter are life-cycle costs, and the cost of operations and maintenance depends in large part on the initial cost and on the quality of the architectural and engineering building systems. Low initial building costs achieved by the sacrifice of quality can result in high life-cycle costs.

Figure 3-1 illustrates these three parts of the cost of a building. The first column shows that, on the average, architectural building systems account for about 39 percent of the construction costs, structural engi-

FIGURE 3-1

THE COST OF A BUILDING

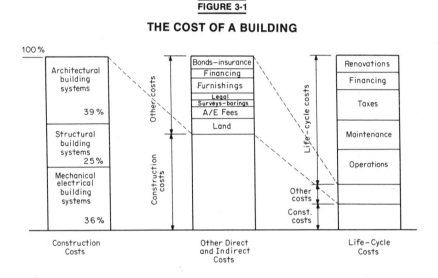

neering systems 25 percent, and mechanical engineering systems 36 percent. The second column illustrates other costs before occupancy; land is a large variable and can be significantly high in downtown urban locations. The third column shows that total building costs over many years dwarf the initial cost of construction.

Figure 3-1 gives only a broad picture of the owner's building costs. Some owners have all the expertise needed to determine their costs; they establish the number of dollars available for construction, negotiate a fee with their architect, pin down all other costs, and determine their entire fiscal future. Other owners depend on architects and their engineers and cost managers for a good deal of this information, and these design professionals must speak the language of dollars as spoken by the building owner. Table 3-1 shows in detail a Project Cost Checklist that combines the first two columns in Figure 3-1; these represent all owner costs until occupancy. Table 3-2 is an Operating Expenses Checklist, itemizing

TABLE 3-1

PROJECT COST PROJECTION CHECKLIST

	Submitted	Stabilized
Taxes (ad valorem)		
Insurance		
Payroll		
Payroll taxes and fringe benefits		
Utilities		
Water		
Gas		
Electricity		
Contract maintenance		
Scavenger		
Elevator		
Pest control		
HVAC		
Landscaping		
Painting and decorating		
Advertising		
Legal		
Accounting		
Supplies		
Repairs and replacements		
Equipment		
Furniture		
Building		
Reserves for replacement (or actual cost of replacement)		
Carpets		
Drapes		
Equipment		
Appliances		
Etc.		
Management		
Parking		
Licenses, permits, fees, and business taxes		
Contributions		
Subscriptions and dues		
Contingencies		
Transportation and travel		
Communications		
Entertainment		
Total		

Source: C. W. Griffin, *Development Building: The Team Approach,* American Institute of Architects, Washington, D.C., 1972, p. 49.

TABLE 3-2

OPERATING EXPENSES CHECKLIST

Projection of Direct and Indirect Costs

A. Land
  1. Survey _____
  2. Soil test _____
  3. Abstract or title policy _____
  4. Legal _____
  5. Appraisal _____
  6. Real estate fees _____
  7. Interest (holding costs) _____
  8. Demolition costs _____
  9. Feasibility studies _____
  10. Taxes (holding costs) _____
      Total land _____
B. Site preparation _____
C. Architectural and engineering _____
D. Contractor's cost estimate
  1. Buildings _____
  2. Paving and site work _____
E. Mortgage loan fee _____
F. Interim loan fee _____
G. Interim interest _____
H. Insurance during construction _____
I. Taxes during construction _____
J. Appraisal fee _____
K. Legal fees _____
L. Accounting _____
M. Project overhead _____
N. Title costs _____
O. Survey _____
P. Landscaping _____
Q. Furniture, furnishings, fixtures, and supplies _____
R. Professional fees (decorators, mg't. studies) _____
S. Advertising and public relations _____
T. Permits, licenses, and fees _____
U. Performance bond _____
      Total direct and indirect costs _____

Source: C. W. Griffin, *Development Building: The Team Approach,* American Institute of Architects, Washington, D.C., 1972, p. 50.

expenses during occupancy. These two checklists summarize all the minutiae with which a private building owner must be concerned, and,
except for interest and taxes, apply to a public building owner as well.

PROFESSIONAL FEES

An architect delivers services to a client *for a fee,* and sometimes clients
look at professional fee arrangements with a jaundiced eye.

There is no single right way to calculate a fee for services. Many
arrangements are possible, but there are four methods that are used most
frequently. These have been developed over the years to satisfy the various conditions under which buildings must be designed. The four methods are:

1. Percentage of construction costs
2. Professional fee plus expenses
3. Multiple of direct personnel expense
4. Fixed fee (lump sum)

In recent years, many clients have questioned some of these methods
and are calling for other ways to arrive at professional fees.

Percentage of Construction Cost

This method is required by law in many governmental jurisdictions. Others require a fixed fee. The public image of the architect's fee is a standard
6 percent, most of which is profit. It is true that, depending on building
size and complexity, fees normally range between 4 and 8 percent; cus-
tom residential work is seen at 10 percent, and difficult remodeling work
is not uncommon at 12 or 14 percent. Some clients are asking: "Who picks
the numbers? Are services directly related to construction cost and size?"
Clients are unhappy when extras occur during construction, and when
the architect's fee automatically increases with each extra, their unhap-
piness knows no bounds. Contractors bid a job based on the architect's
plans for a fixed sum. Why can't the architect do likewise?

Professional Fee plus Fixed Expenses

This method of fee computation is usually used when the expertise of a
certain firm of solid reputation is needed but when the scope of work to
be done is not known or detailed research and costly explorations are

necessary. This is not a common form of fee arrangement. Any architect would agree to it at any time, as there is no way to lose; profit is measurable and realized in advance.

Multiple of Direct Personnel Expense

This method is not uncommon and may be very useful when a firm is on retainer with a repeating client who is frequently in need of services and whose confidence in the firm has been built up over the years. It is also an excellent method for open-ended services where scope of work is not known, such as the development and continuous updating of master plans for large universities. The selection of the multiplication factor is negotiable and ranges from a difficult 2.0 to a satisfactory high of 3.0. Some clients complain about the high salaries of competent professionals, but that is what it takes to produce competent service. Clients sometimes wonder if the time is being spent wisely or efficiently; but again, the client must have confidence in the architect, or another kind of fee arrangement should be made.

Fixed Fee (Lump Sum)

This method appeals to many clients, and some will contract for services in no other way. The client likes it because it yields an exact figure that can be put into a budget and recommended to a board or agency with confidence that it won't change over time. Architects do not feel too comfortable with this method because they must accurately diagnose the scope of architectural and engineering work to be done, provide for all the contingencies that creative work entails, and still come up with a hard bottom-line figure.

Since the Supreme Court has ruled that codes of ethics can no longer prohibit competitive bidding by professionals on the basis of fee, this method is bound to increase in popularity. However, it contains some dangerous possibilities. Clients can compare one fixed fee with another, but they cannot compare the quality and reliability of service that those fees will deliver. When comparing one fee with another, clients will have to ask competing architects such questions as these to establish the scope and timing of services.

- Who, specifically, will form the project design team? What are their biographies?

- What are the numbers and kinds of consultants to be used, and who are they?
- How many work-hours of effort are budgeted for the project at what hourly rate, and what is the management plan for implementation?
- What construction cost controls will be employed, and who will perform them?

In the future, more and more clients can be expected to move away from the first three indeterminate methods of fee computation. They will move toward the fixed-fee method because it is reasonable and objective. Architects should be prepared to meet this new client demand.

The American Institute of Architects has published an excellent document covering ways of computing professional fees for specific kinds of designated services.[2] It describes in great detail how to arrive at a fixed fee. A sample work sheet is shown in Figure B-4 in Appendix B.

[2] *Compensation Guidelines for Architectural and Engineering Services,* American Institute of Architects, Washington, D.C., 1978.

CHAPTER 4

CONSTRUCTION COSTS, CONSULTING ENGINEERS, AND THE DESIGN TEAM

We have examined how buildings have become much more complex in the twentieth century and now require a host of engineering services that were never needed in the historic styles of architecture. We have also seen how architectural services have changed to meet the new conditions.

Structural engineering, with the capabilities of structrual steel and reinforced concrete, made it possible for architects to articulate form through structural expression, and this in turn led the way to the development of so-called modern or contemporary architecture. The architect and the structural engineer understood each other. Some architects like Frank Lloyd Wright had an uncanny feel for structural engineering; some structural engineers like Pier Luigi Nervi had an equally uncanny feel for architecture.

Architects, however, do not have the same rapport with mechanical and electrical engineers. Piping, ductwork, and conduits are (with outstanding exceptions) buried in interstitial space, hidden from the eye. Mechanical spaces, risers, and distance from finish ceiling to floor above are made small by the architect to conserve square footage and volume.

The engineer wants these same spaces larger to accommodate equipment and piping and to provide for servicing after installation. If there is a conflict between building systems, then piping and ductwork have a lower priority than columns and beams; structural integrity must be preserved. In general, mechanical and electrical engineers must cut, patch, and fit around architectural form and its structure.

Suddenly during the late 1970s this picture changed. With energy resources dwindling and with the unit cost of energy skyrocketing, federal and state governments established a series of mandatory energy regulations that completely changed the ground rules about how to design a building. The energy budget became as important as the construction budget. Life-cycle costing took on new meaning, because the energy consumed over the lifetime of a building became a dominant feature of mechanical and electrical design. Heat generated by either system must be trapped and recycled; both systems are interactive and must be designed together, not separately.

The architectural concept of the building itself, of its form, shape, fenestration, mass, and exposure, must now be as sensitive to mechanical and electrical principles as it has been to structural principles. Architects can no longer design beautiful buildings and ignore their cost to build or their cost to operate. Architects now depend on their engineering consultants more than ever before. These relationships between architects and engineers must now be studied in detail, particularly the heavy professional and legal responsibilities they share. And, finally, since construction costs of the building they design together are basic to those relationships, a fifth chair is pulled up to the conference table for the new member on the design team—the construction cost manager.

ENGINEERS' SHARE OF THE CONSTRUCTION DOLLAR

Engineers carry a larger part of the construction dollar in their designs than most architects realize. Well over half the cost of construction is found in engineering building systems, and the distribution of costs among those systems varies widely depending on the building type. Cost control begins with a knowledge of the costs of engineering systems, by building type, during the programming and design phases of a project. It is during these same stages, however, that cost information is difficult to get from engineers. Structural engineers usually are easier to deal with than mechanical or electrical engineers. After a structural system has been identified, its cost can be projected with reasonable accuracy; and after core borings have been analyzed the cost of foundation design can be projected with some confidence. Also, since the form and mass of a building generate structural components, the architect and structural engineer have a natural tendency to work together at the outset of design.

Mechanical and electrical engineers are reluctant to be as specific about costs as the structural engineers. They reason that design has not been set in its final form, and it would be a waste of time and money to pursue various alternative plans until the design has crystalized. Architects are notorious, they say, for changing their minds; wait until the schematic design is set, and then serious engineering solutions will be explored during the design development phase of the work.

It is also true that many architects don't want to be involved too early with engineers, arguing that engineering is a secondary consideration during the creative process, and the costs of engineering systems can't possibly be rationalized in early stages. These architects work out their solutions first and *then* ask their engineers to "fit in" their systems somehow. This of course, is not design cost analysis. Engineering and architectural costs must be approximated in the beginning stages of architectural and engineering design, and trade-offs must be made among all systems to remain within budget. This means architects and engineers must start the building design process together and stay together until completion.

All through this book, the building systems listed below will be used to analyze the cost of construction.

- Foundations
- Floors on grade
- Superstructure
- Roofing
- Exterior walls
- Partitions
- Wall finishes
- Floor finishes
- Ceiling finishes
- Conveying systems
- Specialties
- Fixed equipment
- HVAC
- Plumbing
- Electrical

Site work is also a building system, but will not be included in the schematic design phase except as an indefinite additional cost. Site work costs fluctuate widely from zero to 20 percent of construction cost and distort the cost ratios of other building systems when included in the first stages of building design.

These systems will be examined in detail in Chapter 8. They will now be regrouped to show how they are distributed to architects or engineers or are shared by both disciplines, as follows:

Architectural Systems	Shared Systems	Engineering Systems
Roofing	Conveying systems	Foundations
Exterior walls		Floors on grade
Partitions		Superstructure
Wall finishes		HVAC
Floor finishes		Plumbing
Ceiling finishes		Electrical
Specialties		
Fixed equipment		

Eight architectural systems and six engineering systems designed by different engineering specialtists: this is the way building systems are distributed among the disciplines. Architects and engineers both contribute to the design of conveying systems, so it is placed in the shared category.

Table A-3 in Appendix A shows the cost breakdown, by building systems, for college and university libraries. If the data from the center column of average cost per square foot and percentage of total are regrouped as in Figure 4-1, then the distribution of costs by disciplines becomes apparent.

It is startling to note that after equal assignment of shared costs, engineers are responsible for 59 percent of the construction dollar, and the architect 41 percent. An analysis of the percentage column shows that all the large-cost numbers are with the engineers, and except for exterior walls, the architect has little maneuvering room. If a project comes in above the budget, the figures show how quickly value can be lost when the architect negotiates to get the figure down. The building superstructure is not negotiable; HVAC and electric are close to nonnegotiable. That leaves only building systems, and they account for few construction dollars. One thing is obvious: The big dollars are in engineering. Therefore the architect must monitor all engineering decisions closely and be aware of the cost consequences of engineering design.

Conclusions cannot be reached by sifting the data of one particular building type. The distribution of the costs of engineering and architectural systems varies markedly by building types, and yet there are some

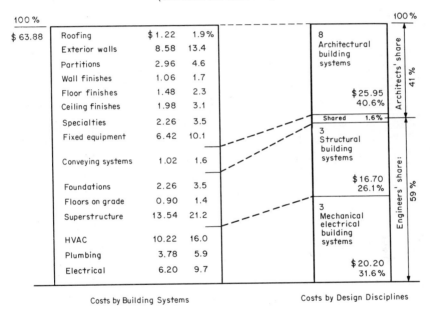

FIGURE 4-1

THE ENGINEERS' SHARE OF AVERAGE CONSTRUCTION COSTS FOR A COLLEGE LIBRARY

(Site costs are excluded.)

surprising similarities. To illustrate this, other building types will be compared with the library; each is quite different from the others, and their unit cost per square foot ranges from $23.54 to $79.82, site work excluded. Detailed cost breakdowns for these buildings are found in Table A-3 in Appendix A. Again, using average costs from the middle column and rearranging them according to engineering, architectural, and shared systems, the distribution of costs emerges as shown in Table 4-1.

The tabulations, as a percentage of building costs, show in the first three numbered columns the distribution among architectural and *all* engineering systems; the last three columns show a breakdown of all

TABLE 4-1

DISTRIBUTION OF AVERAGE COSTS AMONG ARCHITECTURAL AND ENGINEERING SYSTEMS

Average cost/sq ft*	Building type	1 % Arch. systems	2 % All Eng. systems	3 % Shared System	4 Struct. eng.	5 Mechan. eng.	6 Elect. eng.
$23.54	Shopping center	34.7	65.3	0	28.9	21.8	14.6
36.70	Community center	45.7	54.3	0	30.1	14.8	9.4
48.00	Headquarters office building	41.4	57.4	1.5	26.5	23.0	7.9
59.78	University class-room building	38.4	60.1	1.5	22.3	25.2	12.6
63.90	Laboratory building	35.9	62.7	1.4	22.3	26.7	13.7
79.82	General hospital	34.6	62.6	2.8	16.5	30.1	16.0
	Average percentage all types	38.4	60.4	1.2	24.4	23.6	12.4

*Cost of site work not included.

engineering systems into the specialized components of structural, mechanical, and electrical systems.

An examination of these data shows the following:

- After shared costs are divided equally, the average cost percentage of architectural systems for the six building types if 39 percent and for engineering systems 61 percent, as shown in the first three numbered columns. This is just one percentage point away from the college library.

- This average distribution of 39 to 61 percent is fairly constant for all building types, irrespective of their unit cost per square foot. An examination of 43 building types shows that the architect's share of construction costs seldom reaches the mid 40 percent range and even more rarely exceeds 50 percent.

- A complex, expensive general hospital has a percentage distribution almost the same as a simple shopping center.
- Although the cost percentages of all the engineering systems in column two show a reasonable consistency, the variations among the engineering *specialties* have a wide swing, at times as much as 100 percent.
- One conclusion is inescapable: The cost of engineering systems exceeds those of architectural systems by a broad margin.

Although the architect's share of the construction dollar is low, it is the architectural design—shape, form, and selection of materials for the building itself—that sets the configurations of all engineering systems. Architects must not make unilateral decisions about design that might throw engineering costs out of line. Architects have the responsibility to know the broad distribution of the construction dollar among all design activities. From the earliest stages of design, all designers must contribute to the solution and, with the cost manager on the design team, apply the principles of *design cost analysis*. Average costs and their distribution only indicate a general set of conditions. The cost manager is needed to bring the right figures and the right percentages to a particular building in a specific location at a definite time. Averages, though, do point up one fact: If there are overruns in engineering costs, there will not be enough slack in architectural systems to absorb them.

If the engineers' share of the work is so great and its cost is so important, it follows that the professional and legal relationships and responsibilities among all parties on the design team must be spelled out very carefully.

THE ARCHITECT AS PRIME CONTRACTOR

In large A-E firms, where engineering services are performed in house, the firm as a whole is responsible to the owner for all services. However, the architectural firm that engages engineering consultants assumes sole responsibility for all services—*both architectural and engineering*. Agreements between architects and all consultants thus take on a new dimension.

The manner in which each engineering firm is linked to the architect, but not to the others, can impose conditions of stress at times. Communications among the professions is not what it should be. The form of agreement between architect and engineer has been set by professional societies, but good as they are, they are not specific enough in certain respects.

The architect's agreements with the owner can be drawn up in many ways. In government work, the government agency itself usually develops its own form. Here, architectural services are carefully specified and maximum work costs spelled out in detail. Very explicit paragraphs are inserted regarding the architect's responsibility for professional performance and technical accuracy. For example, the government's review of, acceptance of, and payment for professional services does not relieve the architect of liability for negligent performance under the contract, and the government can assert its right of recovery in such a case *either during or after* performance of the contract. This is strong language, and the architect must hold all consultants to the same conditions.

In private work, agreements are as many and as varied as there are owners and architects to write them. A widely used standard form of agreement between architect and owner has been prepared by the American Institute of Architects.[1] This is an excellent document in all respects, save one. It straddles the fence on "probable construction cost," saying in essence that despite any previous budgets or estimates, the architect does not warrant that bids or negotiated prices will not vary from them. It also requires that if a fixed limit for construction costs is to be a condition of the agreement, then additional contingent conditions for design, bidding, and escalation shall be agreed upon in writing.

Although the usual government form of agreement sets forth with great specificity the cost of construction, the AIA form of agreement carefully avoids any specificity. One form demands great accuracy, and the other says it is not possible. Owners are now applying strong pressure on architects to be more specific; these demands must be passed on to consulting engineers. *Design cost analysis* plus a *cost manager* can lead to greater reliability in budgeting and cost estimating.

Whether construction costs are enumerated in the agreement or not, they become specific at a later date in correspondence, estimates, reports, and even conversations. The project acquires a cost frame that the archi-

---

[1] AIA Document B141, *Standard Form of Agreement between Owner and Architect,* American Institute of Architects, Washington, D.C., 1977.

tect will be held to, and that, together with services, sets the stage: construction costs and professional services. *Services*, remember, are engineering as well as architectural. But only the architect's signature is on the agreement with the owner. *It is the architect who contracts to deliver all services.*

Architects are prime contractors, and engineers are subcontractors. It's that simple. If difficulties arise in engineering services or engineering estimates, the owner holds the architect responsible, not the engineers. If litigation or arbitration ensues, it is the architect who is the target, not the engineer. Of course, architects or their insurance companies can seek redress from the engineers later, but by this time things have reached that point of no return which only lawyers enjoy. It is essential, then, that the agreement between architect and engineer receive close study. There must be a clear meeting of the minds on how they will be working with each other.

THE REALITIES ON AN ARCHITECT-ENGINEER AGREEMENT

Chapter 3 has reviewed in detail how the owners of today's buildings demand completion on time and within budget; yet the Standard Form of Agreement between Architect and Engineer, as prepared by the American Institute of Architects, uses the following three paragraphs to describe the engineer's responsibilities to the architect in preparing cost estimates:

> The Engineer shall cooperate with the Architect in determining the proper share of the construction budget which shall be allocated to This Part of the Project.
>
> Statements of Probable Construction Cost and Detailed Cost Estimates prepared by the Engineer represent his best judgment as a design professional familiar with the construction industry. It is recognized, however, that neither the Engineer nor the Architect has any control over the cost of labor, materials or equipment, over the contractor's methods of determining bid prices, or over competitive bidding or market conditions. Accordingly, the Engineer cannot and does not guarantee that bids will not vary from any Statement of Probable Construction Cost or other cost estimate prepared by him.

When a fixed limit of Construction Cost is established as a condition of the Prime Agreement, the Architect and the Engineer shall establish, if practicable, a fixed limit of Construction Cost for This Part of the Project which shall include a bidding contingency of ten percent unless another amount is agreed upon in writing. When such a fixed limit is established, the Engineer, after consultation with the Architect, shall be permitted to determine what materials, equipment, component systems and types of construction are to be included in the Contract Documents with respect to This Part of the Project, and to make reasonable adjustments in the scope of This Part of the Project to bring it within the fixed limit. If required, the Engineer shall assist the Architect in including in the Contract Documents alternate bids to adjust the Construction Cost to the fixed limit.[2]

That language says one thing clearly: If the owner has a fixed limit on construction costs, the engineer must have 10 percent, or some other number, as a bidding contingency; and further, the engineer has full authority to determine the design of the system. That is not cost control, but an admission that the project is in trouble already. This is not the best way to start a working relationship between architect and engineer. Certainly an agreement between an architect and engineering consultants could not be left in this form if the architect had signed an agreement with a governmental agency calling for a fixed limit on construction cost.

This AIA agreement is comprehensive in the fine legal points that should be covered in a contract, such as: termination of agreement, ownership of documents, and arbitration. The document, however, is vague or silent on such things as time, insurance, job safety, and errors and omissions. Finally, one document is used for all engineers and not tailored to the specifics of different kinds of engineering services.

Following is a letter the author has used when engaging engineering consultants, and it refers to a form of agreement between our firm and the engineer. A portion of this form of agreement is found in Appendix B, Figure B-1. This one is specifically tailored for mechanical and electrical engineering services; a different form was used for structural engineers. Some consultants considered the terms too exacting and would not sign, but since our responsibilities to the owner, as we saw them, were no less exacting, we required the same understanding with consulting engineers. The document is included here to call attention to the serious mutual responsibilities shared by architects and engineers.

---

[2] AIA Document C141, *Standard Form of Agreement between Architect and Engineer,* American Institute of Architects, Washington, D.C., 1974, pp. 5 and 8.

NOLEN-SWINBURNE AND ASSOCIATES

Gentlemen:

On an average project in our office, the value of construction costs on systems designed by consulting engineers amounts to 60 percent of the total. Today, at our present workload level, this runs into a significant number of dollars, and since the professional responsibilities are so heavy, Nolen-Swinburne and Associates have decided they must enter into agreements with their Consultants, having a clear-cut understanding of our mutual obligations.

It is widely recognized that legal and financial obligations are interpreted strictly by the courts today. Today the number of suits instigated throughout the Profession by the Owner and by parties other than the Owner, make it necessary that we carefully establish boundaries of responsibility. Since the courts are holding the Architect responsible for all his work, we are forced to insist that the Consultants who work with us share those same responsibilities to the extent of their participation in the work. Accordingly, we are enclosing a letter form of agreement.

It is long, we know, but we didn't know how to make it shorter and still cover all the points that needed consideration. We think it is fair. We think, for the most part, any top professional accepts these responsibilities. Where we narrow down in insurance or some fine points, we can only say: As Architects we know we are accountable and when we are involved on projects of this magnitude, those who work with us as consultants must accept the risks involved and insure themselves accordingly.

We hope you agree.

Yours very truly,
HERBERT H. SWINBURNE

THE DESIGN TEAM AND DESIGN COST ANALYSIS

Design, in the sense used here, is not architectural design; it is *building design*. Building design includes elements of design other than architecture, and a true design team includes members from each of the engineering disciplines. The design team also includes a cost manager who deals creatively with building costs. This design team: architect, structural engineer, mechanical engineer, electrical engineer and cost manager, has five players whose titles generate the acronym ASMEC. There are other design specialists who, from time to time, will be involved, such as an acoustical engineer or civil engineer, but these five principal players will be the design team. Each member of the team contributes to the design solution and carries weight in advancing ideas, but the architect, as the prime contractor, is first among equals. The architect is also first among equals, because it is this generalist who creates the building concept or series of concepts, and consulting engineers and the cost manager must react to those concepts. ASMEC's objective is to reach a final design solution that has a harmony among its physical parts as well as a harmony in its economic structure.

The nature of the design team is to be *value seeking*. Best value is the considered balance among functional, esthetic, and economic requirements established in the building program that now must be satisfied in the building design. ASMEC, in seeking best value, will have to adjust individual building systems as they interface with each other, and this will mean much give-and-take among the five players. ASMEC's decision process is structured to eliminate wrong decisions; no functional or esthetic commitments are made until their costs have been analyzed. Chapters 9 and 10 will scrutinize all cost-related activities, step by step, as an aid to decision making.

ASMEC, then, is a dynamic entity as it puts the parts and the costs of a building together. This interaction, under the overall guidance of the architect, is complex and interlocking. Informal communication among the players on the team is essential for day-to-day activities, and formal written communication is required at milestone events. Information, scheduling, monitoring, coordinating—all are needed to generate and maintain positive project control. A format for such control is to be found on the endpapers of this book. Program, design, and production activities are shown from the time of receipt of commission until the project is ready for bidding. Activities are also shown in separate, but concurrent, networks of all the disciplines; cost control is not shown as a separate network as it must be involved in all of them. Datelines for scheduling are established which recognize that allowance must be made for unprogrammed lag time. This project schedule is a broad one and not all the activities shown will always be required, but it can be modified to fit the specifics of any project. It is a good checklist and will help keep all members of ASMEC in phase. If each stated activity is carefully acted upon and if the cost of each activity is analyzed, the final building design will be in balance with its initial cost and life-cycle cost.

CHAPTER 5
ARCHITECT-OWNER-CONTRACTOR RELATIONSHIPS AND RESPONSIBILITIES

So far we have looked at architects, owners, and consulting engineers, but we have not looked at contractors or at the structure of relationships formed when all these parties are assembled for the purpose of designing and constructing a facility. Nor have we examined the roles and responsibilities architects assume (or share with others) once this assemblage has been put together. It is the building owner, the client, who decides what kind of organization is needed to provide design services and what kind of organization should construct the facility. The architect-owner-contractor combination can take many forms. These various combinations will now be analyzed, because the responsibility for determining construction costs during design, and maintaining them during construction, changes with each combination.

Picture, if you will, several chains of legal agreements: first between owner and architect and then between architect and engineers, cost manager, and special consultants; next between owner and general contractor and then between contractor and many subcontractors and material and equipment suppliers; and eventually between subcontractors and sub-

subcontractors. These chains of agreements can be further complicated if the owner requires several separate prime contractors other than the general contractor. Or there may be no prime contractors at all—only a *construction manager* with a completely different set of legal relationships. This skein becomes more tangled when the architect is a joint venture or consortium whose internal agreements assign responsibilities to the several parties. In setting up the groups to design and build the facility, the chains of agreements must be pulled together to form a closed loop, encircling the common purpose. There must be no loose ends and no weak links.

Owners have three broad options to choose from when bringing together the organizations needed to design and build a facility. They can:

1. Select one organization to design the facility and another organization to build it.
2. Select one organization that will both design and build the facility.
3. Set up their own organization to design, build, and operate the facility for their account.

Each of these three options will now be examined in detail. The first two can have many variations. All contractors and construction managers deal with subcontractors and suppliers of material and equipment, but consultants to architects range much further than ASMEC. The following list covers the more important consultants; it is not intended to be all inclusive.

Engineers	*Others*
Structural	Cost manager
Mechanical	Legal
Electrical	Financial
Civil	Planning
Geological	Landscape
Acoustical	Interior design
Illuminating	Food service
Traffic and parking	Building-type specialist
	Economist
	Sociologist

ONE ORGANIZATION TO DESIGN, ANOTHER TO BUILD

Under this option the owner has the choice of four sets of owner-architect relationships in contracting for design services (as shown in Figure 5-1), and four sets of owner-contractor relationships when ready to build (Figure 5-2). Owners who are new to the building process usually select the simpler relationships. Owners wise in the ways of building, with large projects, often seek more sophisticated ones. Public agencies have no choice; relationships are mandated by law or regulations.

Owner-Architect Relationships

Depending on project size, project complexity, and time schedule, the owner may select an arrangement where (1) the architect or (2) the architect-engineer has sole responsibility to design the project and represent the owner with the contractor during construction. Or the owner may choose to form (3) a joint venture, where those responsibilites are shared, or (4) a consortium, where responsibilities can be tangential or nonexistent. The four structural forms for these combinations are shown in Figure 5-1, and the chain of the agreements that set up relationships between parties is represented by a line with a solid dot in the middle. The dashed line between architect and contractor, although there is no contractual link between the two, represents the fact that the architect is acting as agent for the owner.

ARCHITECT AS PRIME PROFESSIONAL. The first diagram in Figure 5-1 shows the architect as prime professional in a triangular relationship with owner and contractor. For a designated fee the architect provides all professional services and is completely responsible to the owner for them. The architect assembles a team, designs the facility, and then as agent for the owner sees that it is built by the contractor in accordance with the construction drawings and specifications.

The architect in turn concludes agreements with the other members of the ASMEC team and with any other special consultants whose expertise is needed but who are not on the architect's staff. These agreements describe the responsibilities among the respective parties, but in doing so, they do not relieve the architect of any obligations to the owner. The architect is responsible for all acts of commission and omission and for

FIGURE 5-1

OWNER-ARCHITECT RELATIONSHIPS

(a) Architect as prime professional; (b) architect-engineer as prime professional; (c) architect in a joint venture; (d) architect in a consortium.

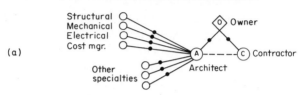

(a)

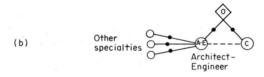

(b)

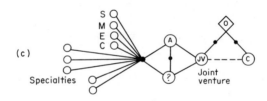

(c)

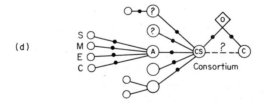

(d)

FIGURE 5-2

OWNER-CONTRACTOR RELATIONSHIPS

(*a*) Single contract; (*b*) single contract, fast-track; (*c*) multiple prime contracts; (*d*) construction manager.

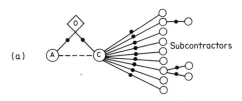

(a)

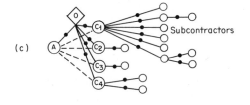

(b)

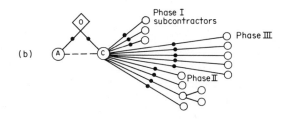

(c)

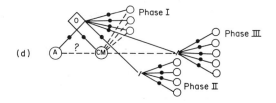

(d)

every error of any member of ASMEC or other consultants. Owners hold architects accountable first; architects can then hold consultants accountable to them.

ARCHITECT-ENGINEER AS PRIME PROFESSIONAL. The second diagram in Figure 5-1 is similar in all respects to the first, except that the engineering disciplines are in house and all services managed as a single entity. Special consultants are engaged only when their expertise is not within the firm's capabilities. Responsibilities to the owner are identical to those described above in the first example.

ARCHITECT IN A JOINT VENTURE. The third diagram illustrates an aggregation of two or more professional firms who formally agree among themselves to produce design services for an owner, usually for very large contracts. The joint venture may be formed by several architectural firms or by any combination of architectural and engineering firms. Services are rendered for a fee, and profits from that fee may be distributed among the joint venturers in any agreed-upon proportion, but professional responsibilities are borne by each to the full extent of that firm's resources. The agreement with the owner is signed by all joint venturers, and all are jointly accountable to, and act as agent for, the owner. Agreements with consultants are signed by all joint venturers, or authority may be delegated to one individual to sign on behalf of all. In essence, this is the same arrangement as when the architect is prime professional, except that duties and responsibilities are shared by all, rather than borne by one.

ARCHITECT IN A CONSORTIUM. The fourth diagram shows one possible structure for a consortium; there are so many variations from this format that it can be said that seldom are any two alike. It is an aggregation of many nonprofessional and professional companies to design projects and cope with unusual problems of very large magnitude and of national and international scale. The contract with an owner is signed by the lead member of the consortium who has the authority to act as its *single point of responsibility*. The architect may be one of the companies in the consortium with authority to set up a full ASMEC team, or the architect may be engaged for architectural services only, working with, but contractually independent from, other engineering consultants hired by the consortium. Some disciplines may be represented not by consultants but by in-house employees of some member of the consortium. (This condition is represented by a line connecting two parties without a solid dot in the middle.)

A consortium is ad hoc in nature and can have a high risk factor. The architect must know precisely all the relationships and responsibilities involved and have them set forth clearly in writing.

OWNER-CONTRACTOR RELATIONSHIPS   Once more, depending on the size and complexity of the project and on the time schedule, and usually with advice from an architect, the owner has four sets of options to choose from, each establishing a different pattern of relationships with contractors and subcontractors: (1) single general contract, (2) single general contract, fast-track, (3) multiple prime contracts, and (4) construction manager. These combinations are all shown in Figure 5-2.

When these four owner-contractor options are paired with the four owner-architect options, it is seen that the owner has sixteen sets of possible relationships if the facility is to be designed by one organization and built by another. On first consideration this may seem complex, but it is not. Rather, it gives the owner great flexibility in tailoring design and construction services to the specific needs of a project from the small and simple to the large and complicated and from a leisurely pace to an accelerated schedule.

SINGLE GENERAL CONTRACT   The first diagram in Figure 5-2 shows the simplest of owner-contractor relationships. The agreement calls for a facility to be completed within a certain time for a stipulated price. The price may be arrived at through a formal bidding process or, in private work, by informal negotiations with a preselected contractor. It is the contractor's option how much of the work of construction will be subcontracted and what will be done using the contractor's forces. Agreements are signed with selected subcontractors and material suppliers; subcontractors in turn may have agreements with others to help carry out their work. The contractor closes out the selection of subcontractors as soon as possible and submits their names to the architect for approval. The total cost of all subcontract work plus the cost of the general contractor's work are itemized and sent to the architect for examination. This cost summary is known as a *schedule of values*, and when approved, is the basis for the contractor to prepare monthly requests for payment as the work progresses. The contractor also prepares a time schedule showing when each subcontractor is expected to begin and complete that portion of the work.

The contractor's superintendent on the site coordinates the work of all subcontractors, expedites where necessary, and together with the contractor's office staff delivers the completed facility in accordance with the time schedule. Bad weather, strikes, and other delays can play havoc with any time schedule, but a good contractor accustomed to these adversities can deliver on time.

SINGLE GENERAL CONTRACT, FAST-TRACK The second diagram in Figure 5-2 shows that the only difference here from the first method just described is that subcontracts, instead of being closed out early on the basis of a completed set of plans and specifications, are let out in phased packages. For example, subcontracts can be let for clearing, grading, excavation, and foundations before the architect has completed the drawings and specifications for subsequent stages of work. Also equipment requiring long lead times, such as electrical switch gear, can be ordered long before the subcontractor concerned has been signed on. Other bid packages are let from time to time as the contractor, working with the architect, decides which ones become necessary to maintain the time schedule.

MULTIPLE PRIME CONTRACTS Many public agencies require that prime contracts be given not only to the general contractor but to heating and ventilating, plumbing, electrical, and other designated contractors. This awkward and difficult arrangement is illustrated in the third diagram. Each prime contractor signs an agreement with the owner which stipulates that each contractor is responsible only to the owner but that they should all work together harmoniously. The general contractor is assigned the task of scheduling and coordinating. This authority to schedule and coordinate is not always effective, since all contractors are paid directly by the owner and not through the general contractor. A slow contractor can hold up the work of other contractors. The general contractor has no real power or authority and can only complain about holdups and call on the architect for help. But, in spite of their disadvantages, multiple prime contracts are preferred by some owners and required by law in some places.

CONSTRUCTION MANAGER The *construction manager* (CM) has a relationship with the owner altogether different from that of the contractor, as shown in the fourth diagram. This diagram indicates a fast-track method for construction, but the CM can also employ conventional methods of bidding and construction. The CM performs services for a fee, and all subcontractors have agreements with the owner. The CM, not the architect, is responsible for cost control, his work beginning with the architect during the design stages and finishing with the last set of sub-contract awards. The CM is responsible for scheduling and supervising the work of all subcontractors and suppliers and is reimbursed at cost for items of the "general conditions" not supplied by subcontractors. The form of owner–construction-manager agreement has many variations, and the CM's responsibilities are different for each. Some agreements call for a guaranteed maximum cost, and some do not.

The exclusive role of owner's agent, formerly played by the architect has changed. As we have said, in all matters of cost the CM and not the architect, is responsible to the owner. This includes project budgeting, estimating, assembling and awarding bid packages, and negotiating the cost of change orders. The CM calls for bids and negotiates their award with the owner. The CM has taken over some of the responsibilities cus-tomarily handled by the architect, and it is necessary that the architect's new position be clearly established in the agreement with the owner.

ONE ORGANIZATION TO DESIGN AND BUILD

Some owners prefer to deal with an organization that provides single-point responsibility for both designing and building a facility. This is known as a *design-build* operation. A variation on design-build is known as a *turnkey* operation, where, under a predetermined buy-back agree-ment, the design-build organization constructs a facility that satisfies the owner's building program while retaining title to the land and improve-ments. When the facility is completed and accepted, the owner makes payment in full and receives title.

Owner-Design-Build Relationships

The design-build organization (Figure 5-3) can range from a small con-tractor who designs and sells custom-built houses a few at a time to large organizations with far-flung operations. These firms have complete in-house capabilities that can design and then build anywhere in the coun-try, or in some cases anywhere in the world. The only thing they do not supply is subcontractors whom they engage in the vicinity of the project. Some design-build firms may lack certain disciplines or specialties on their staff and go outside to get them. Rarely do they engage an architect for complete services.

Design-Build, Architect in Charge

Recently architects themsleves have begun to enter the construction business. This opens up a whole new world of architect-owner relationships where the architect can add to the usual professional capabilities the role of designer-builder as shown in Figure 5-3. Now, instead of being engaged but rarely for full professional services, the architect can take charge of an entire operation.

FIGURE 5-3

OWNER–DESIGN-BUILD RELATIONSHIPS

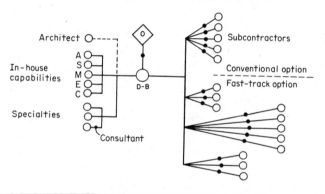

No one knows how the courts will interpret the new responsibilities and liabilities assumed by architects as builders, and no one knows how surety companies will react to this new group requiring construction bonds and insurance, as they seek still to retain professional liability insurance. The 1980s will be an interesting decade as architects move into the field of construction.

THE OWNER DESIGNS, BUILDS, AND OPERATES

When building owners decide to build for their own use or for investment purposes, the ultimate organization emerges as in Figure 5-4. In the interest of best value it should be noted that the ultimate organization does not necessarily produce an ultimate architecture.

Owner builders or investment builders have in-house design capabilities, or they contract for design services to meet their programmed needs. These builders have complete construction and management capabilities of their own and engage subcontractors, using conventional or fast-track methods of construction. After the facility is completed, owners manage all operations or contract for others to do so under their direct control. The decision process is simple: All agreements are made with the owner, who manages the results called for in the agreements.

FIGURE 5-4

OWN–DESIGN-BUILD–OPERATE RELATIONSHIPS

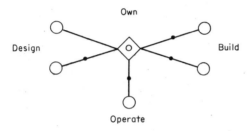

ROLES AND RESPONSIBILITIES

Responsibility is always concentrated at a single point under all design-build conditions. But when design is done under the terms of an owner-architect agreement and the building is constructed by a contractor according to an owner-contractor agreement, it is possible for serious differences to arise between architect and contractor as they both interpret their respective obligations to the owner.

The *general conditions* of the contract, prepared by the architect and incorporated into the agreement signed by owner and contractor, spell out those rules and responsibilities. Some of the more important ones—those that affect cost and quality of construction—will now be examined in detail. This dichotomy of responsibility must be made clear. When procedures go awry during construction, except when there are strikes or acts of God, it is because one party or the other has not performed as stipulated. Large sums of money may be at stake. Responsibility ends with accountability.

Approval of Subcontractors

Contractors do not build buildings; subcontractors do. Care and attention, including prequalification procedures, are just as important in selecting subcontractors as they are in selecting a general contractor. Good subcontractors supply—on schedule—materials, equipment, and workmanship of quality; poor subcontractors do not. Most of the cost of construction is eventually paid to subcontractors. Therefore it is essential to the owner's best interest that the right ones be chosen. On public work, subcontractor approvals follow standard agency procedures, not those recommended here. On projects where a construction manager is in charge of cost control and subcontractor selection, the architect may or may not have a voice in subcontractor approval.

A very common scenario for bidding and start-up of construction goes like this: Within the very short time allowed for bidding, the general contractor has called for prices from dozens of subcontractors. The latter hurriedly examine the plans and specifications, put together their quotations, and, so that their figures will not be exposed to competitors, wait until the contractor's deadline before turning them in. Then the contractor, now under great pressure, winnows all the numbers, wondering how reliable this one is, knowing he can do better than that one, constantly adjusting here and there until a final set of figures is made. To this is added the contractor's costs, overhead, and profit. The total number is typed up on an architect's or agency's form and rushed over at the last minute to bid-opening. If successful, after award of contract the contractor plays one subcontractor against another to pull down the price. These savings accrue to the contractor, not the owner. This is not exactly the best way to find subcontractors of the highest quality, but the agreement between contractor and subcontractor usually does require the latter to build or install in strict accordance with the architect's drawings and specifications. The architect must be satisfied.

Soon after the award of contract, the architect receives a letter from the contractor containing a long list of subcontractors and requesting approval of them. (Or two or three letters are received from time to time, asking approval of groups of "subs.") The architect then considers the list, talks with the owner about his satisfactions and doubts, negotiates with the contractor by telephone if necessary, and finally writes a letter approving his choices. The final list of approved subcontractors sets the background and general climate of construction operations. End of scenario.

It was the author's conviction that the subcontractor-approval process required much more precise handling. First, a subcontractor rating system was set up on simple, three by five filing cards. After the completion of a project, every sub that worked on that job was rated: *Excellent, good, fair,* or *not acceptable.* Over the years a valuable record was compiled as each subcontractor, working on many different jobs, developed a pattern of performance. It is painful to reject a subcontractor, but if the record indicates poor performance, it is an obligation to the owner that the request for approval be turned down.

Furthermore, the practice of approving subcontractors as a group was discontinued in all private work. They were to be approved one at a time, and then only under carefully specified conditions. A form letter of approval was drafted to call the attention of each subcontractor to those conditions of approval in precise terms. It also stressed once again that the general contractor was personally responsible to the owner for the quality and scheduling of that particular subcontractor's work. That form is found in Figure B-2 in Appendix B.

Approval of Shop Drawings

The work that subcontractors perform for, or supply to, the general contractor is shown in detail on the *shop drawings.* Architects involve themselves too much in reviewing and approving shop drawings, and contractors and superintendents are delighted to have them do so. By allowing the line of responsibility from subcontractor through superintendent and contractor to become blurred, the architect may, by implication, assume liability for costly change orders in the field due to improperly processed shop drawings. From the day the first batterboards go up on a job site, the superintendent is responsible for building layout and dimensions, as it is the superintendent who supervises and coordinates the work of all subcontractors. Shop drawings submitted to the architect before the contractor has examined them and stamped them approved should not be reviewed but returned. For an authoritative statement on the subject of shop drawings, see Figure B-8 in Appendix B.

Supervision and Observation

It is the role of contractors to be responsible for supervising the construction of buildings. That is why their representatives on the site are called superintendent: they supervise. That is their job. It is the role of architects to see whether or not the superintendents are carrying out their assignments in accordance with the plans and specifications. They observe, and that is *their* job. Architects have no dealings of any kind with subcontractors on the site. They deal only with the superintendent, who in turn supervises the subcontractors in accordance with the shop drawings which have been approved by the contractor.

Safety

Safety on a project is of two kinds. First consideration is for the people working on the site and the people in close proximity to it. The second is for the owner's improvements on the site and all the materials stored there. Responsibility for safety is shared by contractor and architect, each however in a different way. It is the contractor's responsibility to develop and maintain safe conditions for all building workers at all times. It is the responsibility of the architect to see that safe conditions do in fact exist, and if not, to notify the contractor, who must immediately correct the reported unsafe condition.

Unsafe conditions can lead to structural failure of parts of a building and to loss of life as well. This in turn can result in substantial, even catastrophic, extras in construction costs and expensive, long-drawn-out litigation. It is the author's practice, shortly after construction is underway, to issue a letter to the contractor (with a copy to the owner) on the subject of safety. It puts the contractor and the owner on notice that we are seriously interested in the business of safety. Our field representatives are well indoctrinated in continuous follow-up. Safety is on the agenda at every job meeting. The letter on safety can be found in Figure B-3 in Appendix B.

RECORD KEEPING

Architects, owners, and contractors have defined roles and responsibilities, and they also have responsibilities that are only implied and not well defined. There is no substitute for a written record that demonstrates how seriously these responsibilities were considered and carried out.

Every meeting between architect and owner and every office and job meeting between architect and contractor must be recorded in detail, as well as meetings between architects and consultants. Every drawing approved by an owner or public agency must be on record. Project correspondence must be complete and readily accessible. Project diaries, personal diaries, and telephone logs must be filled out each day. Shop drawings and material samples that have had final approvals must be available. Important primary records must be preserved for many years—some indefinitely. One never knows when they may be needed.

There is no substitute for a written record, not even a competent witness with a good memory.

The author has served as arbitrator on many difficult cases of disagreement between architect and owner and between architect and contractor. It is his conviction that many of those cases would never have reached the stage of arbitration if the architects had only kept a written record of events during design and during construction. Personal recollections, verbalizations, and expert witnesses' testimony are awkward, or suspicious, or unreliable, or dulled by passing time. There is no substitute for a written record.

For a full discussion about preserving the record, see Figure B-7 in Appendix B.

TIME FOR REFLECTION

It very often pays for a partner or principal in an architectural firm to sit back and consider in broad perspective the relationships and responsibilities shared by architect, owner, and contractor—on all the projects in the office. Each project is different, certainly, but in overview they are very much alike. A sensitive professional knows when relationships are harmonious or beginning to go askew. It is essential that these relationships be constantly examined, reinforced, and kept on track. Formal and informal communication among all three parties is essential. Problems must be met head-on when they arise and settled as soon as possible: they must not be deferred. If problems cannot be resolved, a written record of the facts must be at hand to establish a solid, professional position.

But if unhurried time is set aside to reflect on these relationships, any obstacles that lie ahead can be anticipated, and steps can be taken to prevent the hardening of attitudes that causes difficult confrontations.

PART TWO

THEORY

CHAPTER 6

A SYSTEMATIC APPROACH TO DESIGN COST ANALYSIS

Architects, when dealing with conceptual design, diligently seek the right solution, and no effort is spared. When the concept has crystallized it is refined and honed to a state of excellence. Then an attempt is made to determine its cost, and sometimes that cost is found to be too high. But, conceptual design has fixed the final cost of construction, and, short of scrapping that design and starting over again, little can be done to influence its certain destiny. Design sets cost.

However, it is possible that elements of the building program, not design, might be responsible for excessive costs. The scope of the project and its functional areas may be excessive or the quality of building systems too high, setting up conditions that are not commensurate with available funds.

A systematic approach to design cost analysis begins with three requisites: (1) a reconsideration of just what is meant by the word *design*, (2) detailed knowledge of relevant construction costs made available to the designer, and (3) a creative process that integrates design decisions with a cost analysis of those decisions—a design train of thought that says:

"Color, light, cost, texture, form . . . "

where the word *cost* is blended with other words used to characterize architectural design.

DESIGN

When a properly detailed program is prepared to meet the needs of a building owner, without anyone's actually realizing it, the program itself is a design in words for that building—a *literary design*. This literary design is a directive to architects and engineers. It tells them what elements the building must contain, what the functional relationships must be, what quality level of materials must be used, what owner requirements and user needs must be satisfied, and the approximate construction and project costs the owner anticipates. (These will be examined in detail in Chapter 7.)

The literary design also establishes the number of square feet net that the building must contain and here, too, contributes to setting the cost of the building. The literary design is known in the professions as the *building program*. No attempt is being made here to change the language, only to extend its meaning. The building program is truly a design directive.

The word *design*, as used in the professions, is a verb that means to put a drawing instrument actively to paper and freely manipulate lines in a three-dimensional way that visually captures ideas and intuitions of the mind. Here we will call it *graphic design* to separate this process from literary design. Graphic design is a three-dimensional interpretation of literary design. When graphic design is complete, it establishes measurable form, contents, quality, and cost for the building as a whole and for building systems in particular. The word *design*, then, as shown in Figure 6-1, includes both literary design and graphic design; the two are inseparably linked, and together they set the cost of a building. With this understanding, we will continue to use the professional expressions *building program* and *design*, leading (once more) to the axiom:

Program + Design = Cost.

KNOWLEDGE OF CONSTRUCTION COSTS

In today's professional world, all architects and engineers must speak the language of cost and have the advice of expert cost consultants at their elbows as they make design decisions. Edward Heller agrees when he says, "Knowledge of cost . . . is probably the most powerful single tool ever devised to achieve cost reduction. It convinces us in most cases that cost is too high, pinpoints the areas where costs are most out of line, and enables us to attack the most lucrative areas."[1] Designers have two

FIGURE 6-1

DESIGN COST ANALYSIS

Program + design = cost. (Diagram not to scale.)

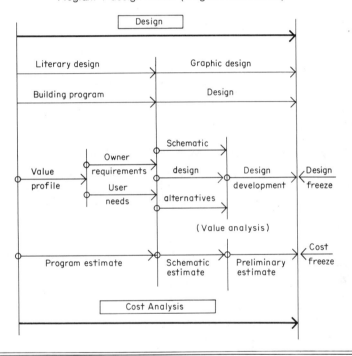

sources to provide them with detailed, positive knowledge of construction costs. First, there are several publications, such as *Dodge Construction Systems Costs*,[2] that update construction costs annually and provide location adjustments so that they are applicable in all parts of the country.

---

[1] Edward D. Heller, *Value Management*, Addison-Wesley, Reading, Mass., 1971, p. 34.

[2] Dodge Building Cost Services (McGraw-Hill Information Systems Company) with Wood & Tower, Inc., *1979 Dodge Construction Systems Costs*, McGraw-Hill, New York, 1978.

They can be extremely useful to the designer as will be demonstrated in Chapter 8. The second source, of course, is the cost manager. To undertake any substantial construction project without the assistance of a cost manager is asking for trouble. It can be compared to attempting the design of an elaborate air-conditioning system without the help of a mechanical engineer. When expertise is needed it must be hired. A design team is not complete without a cost manager.

DESIGN COST ANALYSIS

If program plus design is equal to cost, then it follows that the building the owner desires (program plus design) must be kept in balance with the funds committed for its completion (cost). This balancing mechanism is *cost control*. Cost control examines the cost of all the pieces in a building design, looks ahead to the time when the building will be completed, forecasts shifting cost probabilities, and advises the design team of the consequences of their design decisions. The process of cost control begins by establishing a realistic budget for construction based on the building program to assure that the program itself does not call for more than the available funds can deliver. After the budget is set, cost control becomes a seesaw that first seeks its balance in the wide swings of alternative solutions in the schematic design phase, then approaches balance during the narrowing swings of building systems selection in the design development phase, and finally achieves full balance of all costs in the construction document phase after subsystem and component design is complete.

Cost control demands a constant state of awareness. This means awareness of shifts in size, function, complexity, and quality as well as awareness of any cost oscillations caused by design decisions. Thus, continuously, cost control shows how to correct imbalances between the building desired and its final cost when completed. This is shown in Figure 6-2.

Design cost analysis, in seeking maximum value at least cost during the schematic and design development phases, is constantly making a value analysis of the building as a whole as well as its individual systems. Six specific areas of analysis are covered. Value analysis, as used here, always operates within a defined level of quality and deals only with cost as measured in dollars. Value is also measured in terms of esthetics, certainly, and as a design expression, esthetics may be either simple or very complex. The costs of esthetics, in terms of spatial amenities above functional norms and in terms of complexity of detail, will be made known to the design team. Best value, as determined by the use or image of a building, may require these costs, but they must be analyzed to see if they cause any economic imbalance that will have to be compensated for in other ways.

FIGURE 6-2

COST CONTROL

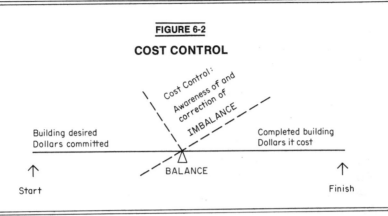

1. An analysis is made of the areas assigned to the various building functions and calls attention to any excessive space allocations.

2. An analysis is made of the ratio of square feet net to square feet gross. This ratio is compared with ratios typical for that particular building type as shown in Table A-2 in Appendix A, and if it is found excessive, further design studies are called for.

3. An analysis is made of the ratio of the area of perimeter walls to the gross floor area of the building. If this ratio is found excessive, again, further design studies are suggested.

4. An analysis is made of the complexity of architectural details, both exterior and interior. Complexities leading to higher costs are identified.

5. A careful analysis of the quality and useful life of all building systems is made, and possibilities are examined to see what trade-offs can be made among systems to retain value but reduce costs.

6. Finally, an analysis is made to verify that all steps have been taken to accomplish the owner's long-range plans with minimum future costs, all as set forth in the building program.

DESIGN COST COORDINATION

On the endpapers of this book is a *Project Control Schedule* that the author has used in his practice for many years. It is shown as a lineal, sequential form of architectural service, but it can be rearranged for fast tracking. It lists all possible activities that architects and engineers must consider on a project from the time of receipt of commission until the start of construction. Concurrent activities are listed on separate networks, or systems, and hard, milestone dates are located for each major phase of the work.

Design cost analysis, as just described, is constantly on track with the activities of architects and engineers, beginning with building economics in the program phase. Note that study and integration of all building systems is required after approval of the schematic design.

Each specific activity listed on the schedule requires many decisions, and it is here where coordination is essential. Cost control is locked into project control, realistically and 100 percent of the time. Study of this Project Control Schedule is recommended. It is a good roadmap and helps to keep program, design, and cost on track and in balance.

DESIGN COST FREEZE

A management consultant, specializing in architectural and architect-engineer firms, made a startling observation after many years of practice and over 150 clients. He said it was his experience that no two firms had ever been alike. They were different in many ways, but one thing they all had in common: After approval of the design development drawings, they kept on changing the design of the building.

When a design is changed, the cost of a building changes. Solid cost control requires a design cost freeze. If a final building design is not satisfactory to the architect, it should not be submitted to the owner for approval.

ACCURACY OF CONSTRUCTION-COST ESTIMATES

Accuracy and control are tightly joined. The percentage of cost-estimate accuracy is directly proportional to the percentage of cost control; 100 percent cost control means it must be working 100 percent of the time.

The percentage of accuracy is also directly proportional to the progress of the design. At the end of the program phase, the percentage of accuracy is plus or minus 12 to 13 percent, thus bracketing the cost target by some 25 percent. At the end of the schematic design stage an allowance of seven or eight percent is made for design contingencies. At the end of the design development phase the contingency factor is down to 5 percent. And when the construction document is drawn up, a detailed construction estimate that takes into account the market conditions at the time of bidding should be within one or two points of the low bid or negotiated contract. A reserve of 3 percent of the contract price must be set aside for project contingencies during construction. Unforeseeable costs such as sub-surface problems, strikes, or bad weather must be expected. For reconstruction and renovation work, accuracy factors and contingencies are higher than the above figures to reflect the unknown conditions behind all visible surfaces.

But let it be repeated: Without serious, constant cost control, accuracy in the construction cost estimate is beyond reach.

MARKET CONDITIONS

Cost control can achieve 80 to 90 percent accuracy when dealing with measurable quantities described in the drawings and specifications, but market conditions exist in the economy over which there can be no control, only informed forecasting. These market conditions are:

Inflation / escalation

Time of year

Bidding load on other projects in area

Labor supply / strikes / impending negotiations

Union shop / open shop

Material shortages

Industrial capacity / backlog on critical items

Weather conditions

Cost of construction money

Hunger factor / profit and overload

Building escalation costs can be projected ahead to an estimated mid-point of construction and, at a predetermined rate, the estimate can be adjusted to reflect these costs. All other market conditions must be studied carefully, and, using judgment and common sense, the cost estimate is adjusted to compensate for these conditions. Such a procedure should bring the accuracy factor to within a point or two of the low bid or negotiated contract.

THE BUILDING PROGRAM

Since designing with words—*literary design*—has such an impact on setting construction costs, it will be examined more fully in the following chapter.

CHAPTER 7

LITERARY DESIGN— THE BUILDING PROGRAM

The architect does not hand a contractor a rough sketch of a building that is to be constructed. Rather, the contractor is given a precise set of instructions in the form of drawings and specifications. Similarly the owner should not give the architect a rough idea about a needed building. Rather, a detailed document must be developed that precisely defines how a building must function and perform in order to achieve desired objectives.

This chapter will show how construction cost control begins with programming. A building program is a cost document. The program states the size of a proposed building, sets forth the quality of building systems, and describes the building's human environment. These program features generate a design solution in gross square feet where construction costs are finalized. No attempt at cost control is complete without a full knowledge of the cost-generating elements in a well-thought-out building program.

A good building program depends on who writes it. Since the literary design will be interpreted by the architect through graphic design, and since the architect is expected to know the cost consequences generated by the program, it is the architect who should write the program. It should not be written by a specialist or a technician with no experience in architecture or engineering. A good building program is more than a list of needed spaces, giving their names and required sizes. A good building program begins with general concepts for the building and then moves through several levels of increasing detail, ending with the specific requirements for each individual space. These requirements are not limited to physical needs; they must also address human needs—the way people move about in a space and use it. While a program separates spaces and functions, one from another, it is simultaneously arranging people into groups of different sizes and configurations, and the resulting group dynamics have important effects on how well a building performs.

A good building program is as simple or as complicated as the building itself. Some programs can be carried in the designer's head, while others must itemize and describe in great detail. In any event, the program should be sufficient to give the owner and the architect a clear understanding of the size of the building and what rooms it will contain, and also what human factors must be considered so that the building will perform properly. The criteria for judging and evaluating a building that is completed and in use must be the same criteria established in the building program. If a physical element or human amenity is inadequate or missing in a completed facility, it is the building program that will have been at fault.

A good program is a communication link between owner and architect; it creates mutual understanding. Remember, we have pointed out that clients are very exacting people, whether public or private, and they hold their architects personally and financially accountable to:

1. Complete *their* project within budget.
2. Complete *their* project on time.
3. Assure that the project functions to *their* satisfaction.
4. Assure that the quality of design meets *their* criteria.

The purpose of a good literary design, then, is to define clearly the required scope and expected performance of a building in such a way that, when completed in accordance with that program, owners will not be disappointed, however exacting they may be.

THE STRUCTURE OF A BUILDING PROGRAM

As shown in Figure 6-1 a building program has three elements. First there is a *value profile* that sets the approach and tone that will be used to limit the boundaries of the other two elements, *owner requirements* and *user needs.* These three elements interact with each other and must be examined in detail, for it is here in literary design where the cost of a building is born. We will now examine the full range of complexities that a building program might contain, with the understanding that they may or may not be needed in any specific program. However, and this must be stressed, it is very easy to under-program a building, and this can lead to serious difficulties in the design phases. The architect and ASMEC must have full knowledge of the owner's expectations and incorporate all of them in the program.(See Figure 7-1.)

VALUE PROFILE

The value profile establishes: (1) the desired levels of quality for the building and all its systems; (2) the quality of visual esthetics; and (3) the quality of human esthetics. In general terms it sets the climate for the

FIG. 7-1 VALUE PROFILE The owner requirements for this chapel at a boy's high school stipulated that it should be remote from the school and attached to the faculty residence. It should fit naturally into the landscape without disturbing it. Materials should be durable and of high quality but the design should be quiet and unpretentious. *(La Salle High School. Photo by the author.)*

FIG. 7-2 VISUAL ESTHETICS   Visual esthetics can be interpreted in many ways. Here is a hospital specializing in cancers of the skin. A limited budget mandated that construction dollars be concentrated in the mechanical systems and built-in equipment. The resulting architectural design was unadorned and austere in every respect except for one contrasting statement: the sculptural form of a welcoming protecting entrance for all those who had to come here. *(Temple University Skin and Cancer Hospital. Photo by Lawrence S. Williams, Inc.)*

designer's approach to solving the problems of owner requirements and user needs. Very often the building owner is also the building user, making it easier to describe desired levels of quality. The investment owner, who intends to retain ownership over a long period of years and lease out to various users, looks at levels of quality quite differently. The developer or speculator, who builds to sell to others as soon as possible, is more interested in the level of his profit; but even here it has been demonstrated that a building of highest quality, with outstanding visual and human esthetics, can produce the greatest profit.

The quality of a building and its systems, as described verbally, can range from the very austere to the luxurious. A building can be rich and enduring, or it can be described as lavish and ostentatious. Rather than austere, a building can be cheap and short-lived. Or inexpensive, temporary buildings can last a lifetime where properly maintained. The desired image that a building should project has economic, artistic, and emotional implications. These should be carefully discussed by owner and architect and set forth at the beginning of the building program.

Owners are not designers, but designers, through the building program, should make clear to owners how they intend to approach the visual esthetics of the job. If owners had an advance picture in words about their building—something about materials, color, scale, and other design attributes—they might not be surprised or disappointed when they first saw the schematic design. Visual esthetics is an artistic expression and contributes greatly to value in a building. It does not, of itself, cost money; rather, it requires sensitivity. It requires sensitivity in the owner, who should seek it, and sensitivity in the architect, whose talent bestows it (to the degree that the architect is blessed with talent).(See Figure 7-2.)

However, someone once said that in judging and evaluating a completed building, one should first be sure that it performs and functions as intended; if it does, then, and only then, should one consider the qualities of visual esthetics. If a building is beautiful but operates poorly, it is a failure. If a building is more a work of fine architectural sculpture than a work of fine performance, then its visual esthetics has no value.

Human esthetics is even more difficult to describe verbally than visual esthetics; but much emphasis will be placed on it here, because this quality relates to user needs and building performance. Programming is not only concerned with the organization and relationships of spaces. It must also analyze the activities of people: how they move around, form into groups, and converse. Programming must also deal with the subtle ambience of the interior and exterior environments where these activities take place. This is the architecture of group dynamics, rather than the architecture of space. The whole idea of designing around the activities of people is what makes a building work, whether the activities are as strenuous as operating a hydraulic press or as reposeful as exchanging ideas in a seminar room. Each building user has a chain of activities that must be performed from the moment of approaching and entering a building until that person leaves. This is a pedestrian experience mixed with stop and go. Human esthetics contributes substantially to value, and agreement must be reached on how much importance is to be attached to this factor, as it has significant impact on the cost of a building.(See Figure 7-3, 7-4.)

The value profile is not an easy document to put together, but its importance cannot be overestimated. It sets the framework and posture for all subsequent programming of owner requirements and user needs. The value profile is a joint venture of owner and architect, and the architect

FIG. 7-3 HUMAN ESTHETICS—INTERIOR The individual person and his or her activities within a building must be carefully programmed. Each person walks around in a small bubble of space and reacts, sometimes unconsciously, to the designed environment, which may or may not have provided essential user needs. *(La Salle College Science Building. Photo by La Salle College News Bureau.)*

FIG. 7-4 HUMAN ESTHETICS—EXTERIOR Considerations for the human factor must be programmed into the spaces between buildings. Some people are always in a hurry but many are not, and people-pockets can be designed for those who want to enjoy the outdoors. Human esthetics does not permit paved parking lots right up to the building line to the exclusion of any people space. *(Temple University Campus. Photo by the author.)*

must have the skill and sensitivity to convey the qualities of building, people, activities, and beauty. Every decision made about the several kinds of quality affects the cost of construction.

OWNER REQUIREMENTS

Owner requirements, as set forth in the building program, include definite commitments by the owner, limits on the architect, and specific avenues of exploration on which recommendations will be submitted to the owner for approval. These following owner requirements set the stage for all subsequent program and design decisions:

- Scope
- Time
- Cost
- Impacts
- Useful life

Some requirements are adjustable; others are not. Those that are adjustable can vary from project to project. When the value profile has been properly set and the owner requirements have been reduced to writing, there is a clear understanding between owner and architect of the design problem to be solved.

Scope

The scope of a project has two parts: immediate and long-range needs. Immediate needs require a building on a specific site and of a certain size. (Size becomes certain after completion of the *user needs* program.) Long-range needs, if any, will estimate allowances for: *expansibility,* either horizontally or vertically; *flexibility* needed to achieve new spatial arrangements; and *convertibility* allowing change in the functions of a space or a building to satisfy new needs. Expansibility, flexibility and convertibility all add to the initial cost of a building without adding to initial value, but they do add to future value. Each must be considered carefully. Correct decisions made here about the scope of a project positively affect the cost of construction.

Time

Careful estimates must be made of the time necessary to program, design, construct, and occupy a facility. These schedules must be balanced against other time constraints, for example: A high school should be on line, ready to use, at the opening of a fall semester; or a new building must be ready to occupy on a date certain, because the lease on present space will not be renewed. There are any number of reasons why a project may have to be accelerated, and this will affect the way it will have to be designed and constructed. In any event, time may be crucial, or it may not be; a clear understanding is necessary. Each decision made here about the time allocated to complete a project affects the cost of construction.

Cost

Owners' attitudes about costs have been reviewed in Chapter 3. Costs are of three kinds: construction costs, project costs, and life-cycle costs. How cost data are collected and analyzed differs from one project to the next, but the owner usually presents one of three alternatives to the architect: (1) the owner is ready to commit a fixed sum for construction; (2) the owner is ready to commit a fixed sum for all project costs including construction; or (3) the owner will wait until the building program is complete and a program budget established. This will determine construction and other project costs, and whether or not it is then feasible to proceed.

Impacts

Laws and regulations covering environmental impact will have to be followed, and these can be strict in some localities and minimal in others. Some owners are very sensitive to physical and biological degradation and are willing to spend appreciable sums over and above legal requirements in order to mitigate impact; others are not. Community impacts of certain projects can be substantial and very expensive to resolve. Traffic and parking, air and water pollution, population density, school enrollment, and the local tax base are only a few of the social and political concerns that must be addressed. The building program, at the very beginning, must establish the owner's limits of cooperation with reference to environmental and community impacts. The owner's decisions can have great influence on architectural design as it seeks a solution having the least impact, which in turn can drive up costs and make the project economically unfeasible.

Useful Life

The building program should call attention to the estimated life expectancy of the project itself and to its separate building systems. This will influence the degree of flexibility that may be needed in the building as well as the selection of components and subsystems when life-cycle costs are estimated. The U.S. Army Construction Engineering Research Laboratory has this to say about estimating the life expectancy of new and existing facilities:

Several criteria may be used to define the life expectancy of facilities.

Physical Life   This is the time period after which a facility can no longer perform its function because increasing physical deterioration has rendered it useless. If there are no cost constraints, maintenance and repair activities can indefinitely extend the physical life of a facility.

Functional Life   This is the length of time until the need for the facility no longer exists or until the facility cannot effectively fulfill its original function. The physical life of a facility often exceeds its functional life by many years.

Economic Life   Economic life is exhausted when a financial evaluation indicates that replacement is more economical than retention. With most facilities physical life exceeds economic life.

Since the physical life of a facility normally exceeds both functional and economic life, the actual life-span of the building is normally limited by functional and economic considerations.[1]

Some building types have a short functional life; for example, a hospital has a very short functional life in certain departments because of the rapid obsolescence of equipment and medical procedures. An example of economic life can be found in selecting a boiler for a building's heating system. If, in order to reduce initial cost, a boiler of low quality is selected, it will be less costly to replace it in 20 years than to keep it running, thus adding to life-cycle costs.

The building program should address, in general terms, the expected balance among the functional, economic, and physical lives of its several building systems. Each decision made here will affect the cost of construction.

THE LEVELS OF A BUILDING PROGRAM

Whether the program be simple or complex, it must never be oversimplified. An oversimplified program leads to omissions or misinterpretation

---

[1]Jeffry G. Kirby et al., *Estimating Life Expectancy of Facilities*, Army Construction Engineering Research Laboratory, Champagne, Ill., April 1974, p. 7.

FIG. 7-5 PROGRAM LEVEL 1: THE SITE On a site of over 200 acres, this community college of several thousands was dispersed informally along a curving main street and anchored at one end to the old estate house where the college was born. Except for visitors' parking and service areas, automobiles were distributed among the trees, unseen from the main campus. All buildings were grouped to reinforce the importance of the individual student and of small group interactions. The principles of social organization and pedestrian experience were carefully programmed before any spatial solutions were attempted. Later, when making design decisions, if there was any conflict between student and faculty interests, the decision favored the student. *(Bucks County Community College. Photo of model by the author.)*

of the owner's expectations by the designer. This in turn leads to a poor cost estimate or to change orders and extra costs during construction.

Before dealing with user needs, an architect must know how to express those needs from perspectives of many levels, from the site and overall building concept down to the smallest unit of space, the individual room. Following are six levels of programming for the complex project. For simpler projects some levels may be combined or even eliminated.

The Site

The real physical, natural, geological, and climatic conditions of the site on which the building is located is the first level of programming. How the site relates to the larger community about it and how the site itself is used are of paramount consideration. (See Figure 7-5.) Broad principles of site use and landscaping must be outlined in the building program.

The Building

The second level of programming deals with the overall concept of the building(s). Is it to be a megastructure or a dispersed plan? High rise or low rise? Is the building to make a bold and challenging statement, or is it to be an organic expression growing out of the site? Some of these questions may be answered only by the investigation of alternatives during the schematic design phase. However, the owner will have some positive convictions, or at least some strong leanings in one direction or another. Programming at this level generates a better understanding between owner and architect, and it helps to eliminate owner surprise or disappointment at the first showing of architectural design. (See Figures 7-6 and 7-7.)

The Cluster

This third level examines how the principle assemblages of building functions are to be arranged with respect to each other and how they are to be disposed about the site. It is concerned with pedestrian lines of traffic internally and with pedestrian and automobile traffic, parking, and building services, externally. Literary design here translates owner requirements into design terms. (See Figure 7-8.)

The Group

Clusters are subdivided into groups where related sets of prescribed functions and activities take place. This fourth level of programming deals with the very essence of building performance as it sets matrices of proximity and internal communications. It is here where architectural group dynamics begin. A well-thought-out program for all of these departments produces a building that functions properly. (See Figure 7-9.)

The Unit Space

This fifth level is the final unit of space, the individual room. It can be as small as a janitor's closet or as large as an enclosed football field with room for thousands of spectators. The program describes in detail each typical unit of space, including the specific activities intended there and built-in equipment needed by those activities. The interior environment is described in terms of the physical requirements of thermal, visual, and

FIGS. 7-6 & 7-7 PROGRAM LEVEL 2: THE BUILDING Simple program, large open uncluttered spaces, simple building. This building proclaims its unity without disturbing the sweep of a magnificent site. It floats above the ground and is entered at that level from a principal pedestrian walkway. *(Gwynedd Mercy Student Center. Photo by Lawrence S. Williams, Inc.)*

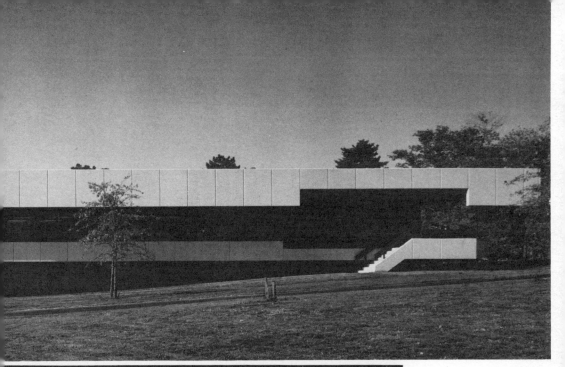

FIG. 7-8 PROGRAM LEVEL 3: THE CLUSTER The master plan for this community college shows six groups of buildings all gathered into one enormous cluster arranged around a central mall. Although the program called for groups to be separated at the ground level, they were all united at the second floor with a continuous looping all-weather pedestrian concourse. *(Mercer County Community College. Photo by Lawrence S. Williams, Inc.)*

FIG. 7-9 PROGRAM LEVEL 4: THE GROUP The Building program here called for pitched roofs only, and a market survey revealed that bearing masonry wall construction would be less expensive than steel or concrete frame. These highly articulated groups reflect early program and design decisions about roofs and masonry. *(Bucks County Community College. Photo by Walter J. Kaufman.)*

FIG. 7-10 PROGRAM LEVEL 5: THE UNIT SPACE The single room is the final test of design. Does architectural form fit the programmed needs of the user? *(Swinburne Residence. Photo by the author.)*

FIG. 7-12 PROGRAM LEVEL 6: SPACE FURNISHINGS—INFORMAL Clustered furniture groups can be designed to favor the lone individual, the few, or the many. People can have many choices about where they would like to sit depending on their mood at any moment. Group sizes and locations cannot be haphazard or incidental at the whim of the designer; they must be studiously programmed. *(Gwynedd Mercy Student Center. Photo by Lawrence S. Williams, Inc.)*

FIG. 7-11 PROGRAM LEVEL 6: SPACE FURNISHINGS—FORMAL When the group size is large, the building program can still require that the space be inviting, even intimate, and caution against the hard unimaginative. *(Gwynedd Mercy Academic Center. Photo by Cortlandt Hubbard.)*

acoustical criteria as well as such human criteria as privacy, degree of control or freedom, and group size. The description of each unit of space can be stated in a very few words or as thoroughly as shown in Figure 10-2.

The Space Furnishings

This sixth and final level completes the concept of architectural group dynamics. Activity patterns are reinforced or hampered by the arrangement of furniture. Group size and location can also be set by furniture distribution. (See Figures 7-11 and 7-12.)

USER NEEDS

At every level, when programming a building, it is necessary to keep in mind that the purpose of having a building at all is to house people in such a way that they can perform certain operations in particular places under comfortable conditions. To do this, four subprograms are necessary to describe required performance for the building as diagrammed in Figure 7-13. A *human program* is combined with an *operations program*,

FIG. 7-13 PROGRAMMING FOR USER NEEDS AT ANY LEVEL

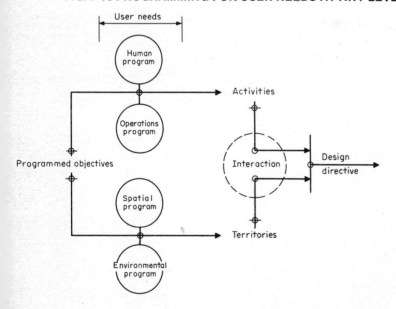

FIG. 7-14 USER NEEDS The interaction of people performing certain operations with equipment all within a flexible space using sophisticated environmental controls were meticulously programmed in this building. *(Temple University Communications Center. Photo by Lawrence S. Williams, Inc.)*

and together these define activities at any level. Next, a *spatial program* is combined with an *environmental program*, and together these define the territories where activities take place. Or, as illustrated in Figure 7-14, human activities take place in defined territories, producing a desired reaction or performance. This description is a part of literary design—a directive that architects and engineers must respond to during the graphic design phases.

The Human Program

This program deals with people: how to arrange them formally or informally, in any required active or passive situation and with due regard to their needs, health, and safety. It sets the degree of control over their movements, privacy, and initiatives.

The Operations Program

This program describes the physical arrangement of machinery, equipment, and furnishings and such supply and energy sources as may be required to accomplish tasks such as selling, teaching, sleeping, manufacturing, or playing.

The Spatial Program

This program deals with areas and volumes. It is concerned with the three dimensions of length, breadth, and height; with clearances, relationships, and proximities; and with flexibility, expansibility, and convertibility. This program sets forth the human engineering between people and machines or equipment, and also the distances between one person and another.

The Environmental Program

The environmental program, whether exterior or interior, is divided into two parts: the physical environment and the behavioral environment.

The physical program sets the thermal, luminary, and acoustical conditions required by *human beings* performing certain *operations* in a specific *space*. It is concerned with the meteorological conditions of sun, wind, rain, and snow as they relate to the building's orientation and exposure. It recognizes the variation of the four seasons as the building is used, and it acknowledges that a building has a nighttime character far different from its daytime character.

The behavioral program recognizes that the ambience in which people find themselves can have a subtle influence on their behavior or attitudes. Material, shape, color, texture, and light can be organized in ways that make activities productive and pleasant, or in ways that frustrate and offend. The behavior program does not call for a pallet of certain materials and then describe a design; rather, in general terms, it calls for the atmosphere—the mood, feeling, or character—desired within a given space.

PROJECT CONTROL

On the endpapers of this book, the preceding four user programs are to be found in the Project Control Schedule, first during the program phase. The schedule also shows some programming during the preliminary design phase, indicating that not all programming can be completed until then, particularly in the mechanical and electrical engineering aspects of design.

THE PEDESTRIAN EXPERIENCE

The user programs all relate to the building, the people in and around it, and the activities they perform. However, implicitly included in those programs at every level, although not specifically mentioned, are the dynamics associated with a person or group moving through the building(s) for varying periods of time. The special character of this *pedestrian experience* is that it is related to not one but many spaces. The pattern of motion can have great influence on design. The kinesthetic experience of walking along paths, walkways and corridors and through large and small spaces is closely allied with user satisfaction and building performance. In large structures without recognizable nodes to focus on, it is easy to lose a sense of direction and location. Figure 7-15 takes one student through a dispersed community college campus of many separate buildings, such as that shown in Figure 7-5. As students must flow through the area from early morning until late afternoon, the pedestrian experience was made an important part of this design. Now that all public buildings are required to accommodate the disabled, designing for the pedestrian experience is more exacting than ever.

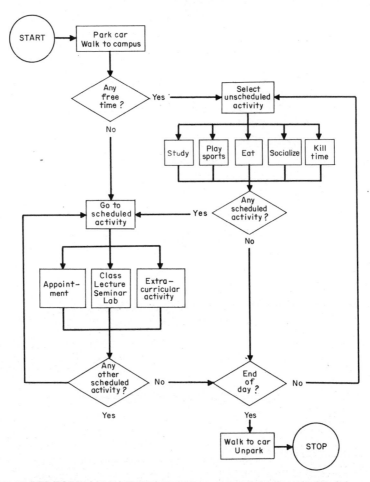

FIG 7-15 PEDESTRIAN PATTERNS FOR A COMMUNITY COLLEGE

HOW TO WRITE A BUILDING PROGRAM

There are no rules for writing a program. Each project, each owner, and each set of conditions is different. The purpose of this chapter has been to call attention to all those elements of program that may be considered for any particular building. Once again the admonition is given: the program is important because it sets the size and quality of a building and shares the responsibility in determining its cost. Remember:

Program + Design = Cost.

FIG. 7-16 THE PEDESTRIAN EXPERIENCE Patterns of people flow, rather than a predetermined visual esthetics, should set pedestrian relationships among groups and clusters. *(Gwynedd Mercy Academic Center. Photo by the author.)*

PART THREE

IMPLEMENTATION

CHAPTER 8

BUILDING SYSTEMS— THE KEY TO COST CONTROL

Program + design = cost. Program and design define a building's size and essential functions; program and design set architectural form and decide broad questions of material selection and engineering requirements. Cost control must be initiated during the conceptual stages; the cost target must be bracketed, and then refined with greater and greater precision.

Architects and cost consultants have tried, with varying degrees of success, to develop reliable methods for projecting costs during the design stages. Methods have ranged from very simple to very complex, but only two will be examined here before looking at design cost analysis based on building systems. The first is the *square-foot method*, which is fraught with many dangers, and the second is the *quantity survey method*, which is inflexible and has other shortcomings.

THE DANGERS IN ESTIMATING BY THE SQUARE FOOT

It makes sense to measure the square- or cubic-foot cost of a completed building; it is a factual record of a specific project. It does not make sense to estimate by unit area or volume the future cost of a building yet to be constructed or to compare the cost of one completed building with another completed building, using such raw data. Cost comparisons by the square-foot method are not only misleading, but dangerous when relied upon to forecast a low bid. There are many reasons for this:

1. The quality of two buildings of the same building type can vary significantly. (See Table 1-1.)
2. The locality of buildings being compared can have widely different construction cost indices. (See Locality Adjustments in Table A-1 in Appendix A.)
3. The methods of calculating building area and volume may be different, or, as is more often the case, calculations are rough and the arithmetic bad. In the early design stages two independent people, using the same set of plans, will arrive at two sets of figures that can be as much as 10 percent apart. The AIA Document D101, shown in Figure B-5 in Appendix B, gives an excellent method for computing area and volume.
4. Published cost data vary from publication to publication. Separate contracts for fixed equipment may or may not be included in the unit price. Professionals who publish their cost data never place themselves in an unfavorable light.

The square-foot method of cost estimating has many variations, such as using different unit costs for different functional areas of the building. This increases precision, but in general, the method is still not dependable. Exception can be made for the firm specializing in one building type, doing work in a particular region, and using a consistent method of computation. This much can be said for the square-foot method: it is far more dependable in establishing a rough budget for a building than using such unit costs as cost per hospital bed or cost per stadium seat.

THE SHORTCOMINGS IN ESTIMATING BY USING A QUANTITY SURVEY

A detailed material quantity takeoff should be undertaken somewhere within the time when construction documents are 50 to 95 percent complete. When carefully done this is accurate and dependable, subject only to local market conditions at the time of bidding. A detailed cost estimate is necessary information when bidding or negotiating a construction agreement. It also serves as a check against the contractor's schedule of values, and in verifying monthly requests for payments or change orders; but it is cumbersome and awkward when used during design and has no value at all in the program phase.

The form of a detailed cost estimate is based on the Uniform Construction Index (UCI) format for cost analysis. This in turn is derived from the specifications format developed by the Construction Specifications Institute (CSI). The UCI cost analysis follows the 16 subdivisions tabulated below. Cost elements are broken down into labor and materials for items of work that the contractor or construction manager may place with subcontractors or execute themselves.

1. General requirements
2. Site work
3. Concrete
4. Masonry
5. Metals
6. Wood and plastics
7. Thermal and moisture protection
8. Doors and windows
9. Finishes
10. Specialties
11. Equipment
12. Furnishings
13. Special construction
14. Conveying systems
15. Mechanical
16. Electrical

This format is useful to contractors and subcontractors, but not to architects and engineers. It is cumbersome and inflexible, and the quantities of materials needed are not known during the design phase. The UCI analysis is associated with the construction process, not the design process. It does not become effective until the project is well into the construction document phase, and accuracy at this time comes too late. The quantity survey is not the answer to cost control during the design phase.

DESIGN COST ANALYSIS BY BUILDING SYSTEMS

Design cost analysis by building systems is a method of estimating construction costs in the program and design phases, or as one architect puts it, "translates . . . the language of construction into the language of conceptual design."[1]

Design cost analysis produces a cost sketch synchronized with each design sketch. Cost estimating procedures should naturally, and concur-

[1]James Y. Robinson, Jr., *Current Techniques in Architectural Practice*, McGraw-Hill, New York, 1976, p. 136.

rently, follow design procedures. The responsibility of the design team is to produce this synchronous, interactive cost control during design, and that is done using a building system format, not a building trade format.

What Is Conceptual Design?

The architect, in creating the basic concept for a building, first organizes units of space into functional relationships that meet programmed needs. Next, all spaces are connected with mechanical and electrical assemblages and with pedestrian and vehicular systems for people and services. Then the architect creates a series of spatial configurations that give the building its form, and this in turn is adjusted to fit into the site and the larger community with the best possible harmony of urban or suburban expression. Appropriate materials, equipment and furnishings are selected to make the building operational, useful, and a delight to live, work, or play in.

Oversimplified, this is conceptual design.

Architects, as they design, are thinking about the overall concept of a building—its functions and proximity relationships. They are thinking of those large elements that will make their building come alive and operate. They are thinking in terms of *building systems*. They are not thinking about the tons of steel or the thousands of bricks or all the work-hours of labor needed to put the building together. Architects think in terms of *building systems*, because in design these are the true, basic constituents. Architects create space and architectural form by manipulating building systems. Engineers devise the systems that support the architectural concept. With the cost manager estimating the costs of all systems, the entire design team, ASMEC, is concurrently engaged in design as it focuses on all building systems and simultaneously weighs design and cost. Trade-offs among alternative systems are examined and adjustments made as ASMEC seeks better value for the building as a whole. As the solution shapes up and the alternatives narrow down, the building systems slowly become better defined. The construction cost range during the design phases is held within a predetermined design contingency. Later, in the construction document phase, the building systems become definite, measurable, and cost-quantifiable, and the design contingency is no longer needed.

To make clear this method of design cost analysis, we must now examine building systems in detail and learn how their costs are computed. This is an exercise in awareness and understanding for both the architect and the engineer.

114

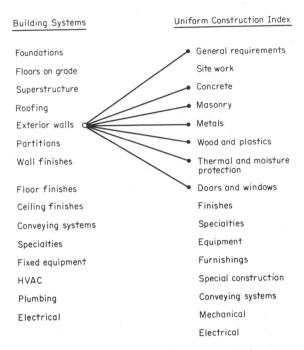

Building Systems	Uniform Construction Index
Foundations	General requirements
Floors on grade	Site work
Superstructure	Concrete
Roofing	Masonry
Exterior walls	Metals
Partitions	Wood and plastics
Wall finishes	Thermal and moisture protection
Floor finishes	Doors and windows
Ceiling finishes	Finishes
Conveying systems	Specialties
Specialties	Equipment
Fixed equipment	Furnishings
HVAC	Special construction
Plumbing	Conveying systems
Electrical	Mechanical
	Electrical

FIG. 8-1 COMPARISON OF BUILDING SYSTEMS FORMAT WITH THAT OF UNIFORM CONSTRUCTION INDEX

BUILDING SYSTEMS, SUBSYSTEMS AND COMPONENTS

Several years ago, a collaboration of the American Institute of Architects and the General Services Administration introduced a method of cost control using building systems, known as Mastercost. This is still in the development stage, awaiting the organization of a rational cost data base. Other organizations have pursued similar methods, and there is now no doubt that serious efforts are under way to increase the use of this principle in cost control among the design professions. It is a powerful tool.

The procedures for design cost analysis set forth in this book are based on fifteen building systems. They are repeated in Figure 8-1 so that they may be compared with the UCI format of sixteen divisions.

Figure 8-1 demonstrates how one building system, exterior walls, might be composed of materials that come from seven divisions of the UCI format. The cost of this system, although drawn from many sources, will be expressed as a system cost. This gives great simplicity and flexibility when manipulating design by systems.

Later in this chapter building systems will be examined in detail, but first, in order to understand what a building system is, it is necessary to define systems in general. Martin Kenneth Starr puts it this way:

> A system is a group of activities, functions, or components that can be bounded. The rule for bounding these activities, functions and components is: *all relevant interdependencies, interactions and relationships must be enclosed within the* boundaries of the system.[2]

All building systems treated in this book meet that definition, for example: The *exterior walls system* shown in Figure 8-7 indicates the various *components* that might be used to build that wall; they are all necessary before the system is independent and stands alone. Another example: An *electrical building system* consists of these *subsystems:*

Power generation	Special systems
Power transmission	Communications
Service and distribution	Heating and cooling
Lighting	Controls and instrumentation

One particular building may not require all the enumerated subsystems, but the electrical design of that building requires the selection of relevant subsystems that satisfy essential function; design sets the boundary of the system.

A building system, then, is to be thought of as an independent entity made up of those components and subsystems required to fulfill essential function. The cost of a building system can be computed independently without impacting on the cost of other systems, *unless a conscious design decision is made that it should do so.* This permits component and subsystem design, and their costs, to be changed as needed to maintain best value. The key to cost control, then, lies within each building system.

CONSTRUCTION COST DATA BASE

Our method of estimating by building systems must be supported by detailed knowledge of construction costs (labor and materials) for all possible combinations of components and subsystems that can be assembled into the fifteen building systems. This data base is available in *Dodge Construction Systems Costs* and is utilized in the procedures for design

[2]Martin Kenneth Starr, *Production Management: Systems and Synthesis*, Prentice-Hall, Englewood Cliffs, N.J., 1964, p. 34.

cost analysis presented in this book. Methods for collecting these data are uniform, the data are always current, and they are immediately accessible for computer manipulation.

Table 8-1 is a data sample showing locality adjustment indices for 22 building trades in four selected cities. The first column lists the national index, which is the average of 20 principal cities in the United States. The specific adjustments for the four individual cities show wide variations. Fresno, California, shows more than twice as much for labor as does

TABLE 8-1

LOCALITY ADJUSTMENT INDICES FOR LABOR AND MATERIALS FOR 22 TRADE CATEGORIES SHOWING 20-CITY AVERAGE WITH VARIATIONS FOR FOUR SELECTED CITIES

Trade Rates	20-C	Fresno, California 93744		Greenville, S. Carolina 29602		Gulfport, Mississippi 39501		Harrisburg, Pennsylvania 17105	
		Local	Adj.	Local	Adj.	Local	Adj.	Local	Adj.
Asbestos worker	16.15	19.50	1.21	8.45	0.52	11.70	0.72	12.13	0.75
Bricklayer	13.88	14.68	1.06	7.60	0.55	10.30	0.74	12.55	0.90
Carpenter	13.81	17.61	1.28	7.08	0.51	5.24	0.38	12.09	0.88
Cement mason	13.45	16.53	1.23	6.73	0.50	9.40	0.70	12.09	0.90
Electrician	16.56	18.89	1.14	8.45	0.51	12.51	0.76	13.68	0.83
Glazier	13.31	13.50	1.01	7.08	0.53	8.19	0.61	10.71	0.80
Laborer	10.83	14.04	1.30	4.15	0.38	5.87	0.54	8.60	0.79
Lather	13.40	15.01	1.12	6.14	0.46	9.94	0.74	11.22	0.84
Oiler	12.09	16.38	1.36	5.26	0.44	8.77	0.73	11.03	0.91
Oper eng, hoisting	13.74	18.35	1.34	6.96	0.51	9.59	0.70	14.40	1.05
Oper eng, excavation	13.74	18.15	1.32	6.96	0.51	9.59	0.70	15.75	1.15
Painter	12.69	15.02	1.18	5.85	0.46	10.04	0.79	9.70	0.76
Pipefitter	16.85	19.59	1.16	9.10	0.54	13.36	0.79	14.00	0.83
Plasterer	13.22	14.67	1.11	7.08	0.54	10.00	0.76	10.83	0.82
Plumber	16.95	22.22	1.31	8.45	0.50	13.48	0.80	14.00	0.83
Reinforcing ironworker	14.77	17.71	1.20	7.60	0.52	10.53	0.71	14.64	0.99
Roofer	13.14	16.56	1.26	5.85	0.45	8.75	0.67	11.54	0.88
Sheet metal worker	16.33	19.42	1.19	8.45	0.52	11.05	0.68	14.87	0.91
Structural irownworker	14.75	17.71	1.20	7.60	0.52	10.53	0.71	14.64	0.99
Teamster	11.02	15.32	1.39	5.03	0.46	8.19	0.74	9.18	0.83
Title setter	13.00	13.63	1.05	6.14	0.47	10.00	0.77	11.93	0.92
Waterproofer	13.16	16.56	1.26	7.02	0.53	8.75	0.66	11.54	0.88
Average labor adjustment			1.21		0.50		0.70		0.88
Average material adjustment			1.03		0.94		1.02		0.89

Source: Dodge Building Cost Services (McGraw-Hill Information Systems Company) with Wood & Tower Inc. *1979 Dodge Construction Systems Costs,* McGraw-Hill, New York, 1978.

Greenville, South Carolina, although both cities pay about the same for building materials.

The cost of building materials is also gathered to pinpoint their regional variations. Table 8-2 lists the materials most commonly used in construction and form the base of the survey.

TABLE 8-2

MATERIAL COST TO CONTRACTORS AND SUPPLIERS

Material	Unit	Basic quantity
1. Concrete, 3000# ready mix	cu yd	100
2. Concrete block, 8″	each	each
3. Plywood, 4′ × 8′ × ½″, sheathing grade	sq ft	2,000
4. Lumber, 2″ × 4″, construction grade	bd ft	2,000
5. Gypsum board, ½″	sq ft	2,000
6. Asphalt shingle, 235#	square	15
7. Reinforcing bars, no. 4	pounds	per lb
8. Structural steel, no erection	tons	per ton
9. Galvanized electric conduit, ¾″	lin ft	100
10. Copper pipe, type L, 2″	lin ft	100

These data on labor and material rates are updated regularly. Locality adjustments are computed for each city, and the adjustments for 115 selected cities are published annually as shown in Table A-1 in Appendix A.

Cost figures are based on national averages of the 20 cities, which are then modified by computer for a specific project location, identified by its zip code address.

The data base described here is used for the detailed quantity survey, previously described. It is the language of construction that must now be translated into the language of systems. The data base is stored in a computer following the 16-division UCI format. There is then a large history of completed buildings stored under each building type, and the computer has been programmed to translate these costs to 15-system costs for use during the design phases. This is done automatically by selecting the costs of all components and subsystems that are bounded by a system and adding them up to arrive at a system cost. Design cost analysis using building systems is the key to cost control, and it becomes really effective through the accuracy achieved by using a reliable construction cost data base.

PROCEDURES FOR COST CONTROL OF BUILDING SYSTEMS

The cost manager will advise the architect on the cost of early design concepts and alternatives, but the architect must have an innate feel for building systems and how to select components and subsystems, not on the basis of their absolute prices but rather on the basis of their cost relative to each other. As systems are manipulated to create a desired design concept their costs are manipulated simultaneously, and design decisions are not made until esthetics and design have been balanced with construction economics. The designer should be generally familiar with the current average costs of the architectural systems shown in Table A-4 in Appendix A. The costs organized on the vertical axis range from the least expensive to the most expensive materials, and on the horizontal axis from buildings of low quality to those of high. Material components, as a design decision, should be selected to achieve best value at least cost; keeping in mind that esthetic quality is an ingredient of value.

A few systems will now be examined in detail. In Chapter 9 procedures will be examined to illustrate how a cost manager pulls the costs of all systems together to arrive at a total construction cost. The first system to be studied will be one of the superstructure subsystems.

The Superstructure System

The superstructure has been chosen for investigation because it is an inherent part of architectural form, and it is usually the architect, rather than the structural engineer, who selects the type of structural system and sets the bay sizes. Some architects belong to the design school that believes only a concrete structure can produce exciting architecture; others believe that structural steel is far more sophisticated. Each school has its leaders and followers. This discussion will show no preference for either. The economics of the structure should play an important part in the selection of either system, and this should be weighed against the designer's personal preference.

The superstructure system consists of three subsystems:

1. Vertical support assemblies
2. Primary and secondary framing assemblies
3. Deck assemblies

FIG. 8-2 STRUCTURAL SUPER-SYSTEM The supersystem may be routine or imaginative, with complicated cost implications. *(Headquarters Office Building for Health, Education, and Welfare. Photo by Lautman Photography.)*

The following alternative design examples are limited to primary and secondary framing assemblies, as these best illustrate early basic conceptual design. Investigations will be made by using examples that illustrate how to select (1) materials for a framing assembly, (2) appropriate bay size and live loads, and (3) building form and perimeter. Calculations are based on 1979 costs for framing assemblies tabulated in Table A-5 and modified by locality adjustment factors shown in Table A-1, both in Appendix A.

STRUCTURAL STEEL OR PRECAST CONCRETE? A hotel in Miami, Florida, proposes to add a 52′ 0″ × 102′ 0″ one-story extension to its main building, requiring bays 25′ 0″ × 25′ 0″, as shown in Figure 8-3. The roof deck is to be concrete with a 200# live load, supporting a heavily landscaped terrace. The first floor is open and will be used as a sheltered recreation area. Which framing assembly is less costly, structural steel or precast concrete?

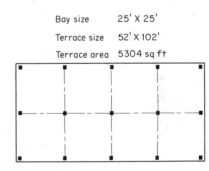

Bay size	25′ X 25′
Terrace size	52′ X 102′
Terrace area	5304 sq ft

FIG. 8-3 A STRUCTURAL FRAMING SYSTEM FOR STEEL OR PRECAST CONCRETE

Alternative 1: Steel

Primary framing @ $1.29/sq ft
 Span factor—0.8
 Load factor—1.7 $1.29 \times 0.8 \times 1.7 = \$1.75/\text{sq ft}$
Secondary framing @ $2.03 sq ft
 Span factor—0.8
 Load factor—1.7 $$\$2.03 \times 0.8 \times 1.7 \quad \frac{= \$2.76}{\$4.51/\text{sq ft}}$$

Locality adjustment
  (0.84–Miami, Fla.) $\$4.51 \times 0.84 = \$3.79/sq\ ft$

      Total cost $\$3.79 \times 52 \times 102 = \$20,102$

Alternative 2: Precast Concrete

Primary framing   @ $\$1.45/sq\ ft$
  Span factor–0.8
  Load factor–1.8
                                        $\$1.45 \times 0.8 \times 1.8 = \$2.09/sq\ ft$

Secondary framing   @ $\$1.82/sq\ ft$
  Span factor–0.8
  Load factor–1.8
                                        @ $1.82 \times 0.8 \times 1.8$ $= \$2.62/sq\ ft$
                                        $\overline{\$4.71/sq\ ft}$

Locality adjustment
  (0.84 Miami, Fla.) $\$4.71 \times 0.84 = \$3.96/sq\ ft$

      Total cost $\$3.96 \times 52 \times 102 = \$21,003$

Decision: The structural steel will have to be painted, and in Miami's seaside climate it will be repainted frequently. Cost is a stand off and designer is free to accept either system.

  The primary purpose of this exercise is to take the reader through the few simple steps needed to arrive at the cost of a subsystem. The designer in a matter of minutes can determine if a design decision will have adverse cost consequences.

BAY SIZE AND LIVE LOAD ANALYSIS One of the major steel producers has decided to construct an office building for its own use in Richmond, Virginia, having 550,000 to 600,000 sq ft net of open landscaped office space. The suburban site is generous in size but zoning laws limit the building height to 150 feet. The owner's building program calls for a structural steel frame with metal floor deck; the building is to be fireproof, class 1-A. In order to attain maximum flexibility in floor layouts, columns are to have a minimum spacing of 40 feet, and live loads for all floors are to be 125#. User needs require that all occupants be as close to the window wall as possible, to enjoy natural daylight. The building is to be of high quality and have a stainless steel curtain wall.

  The solution to this program has produced eight alternatives that the owner must consider before the final design concept is selected. The first four alternatives are shown in Figure 8-4; this design is a rectangular building with a length-width ratio of 4 to 1. This gives maximum natural light and places all occupants as close to the window wall as is practicable. Alternatives 1 and 2 generate costs on a 40-foot bay size and Alternatives 3 and 4 on a 30-foot bay; live loads vary from 125# to 100#. (To simplify the following calculations, the roof deck assembly with a 35# live load has been omitted.) This is to test the owner's concept of value by showing the cost paid for flexibility. With reduced spans and live loads, less space is needed for the floor-ceiling sandwich and the height of the building is correspondingly reduced.

Alternative 1
40' X 40' bays
125# LL

Alternative 3
30' X 30' bays
125# LL

Service modules

Alternative 2
40' X 40' bays
100# LL

Alternative 4
30' X 30' bays
100# LL

Floor size: 122' X 482'
Bay sizes: 40' X 40' and 30' X 30'
Floor area: 58,804 sq ft net
Number of floors: 10
Total office area: 588,040 sq ft net
Floor-to-floor height: 14' and 13'
Height of building: 140' and 130'
Building perimeter: 1208'

FIG. 8-4 A STRUCTURAL FRAMING SYSTEM WITH VARIOUS LOADS AND BAY SIZES FOR A RECTANGULAR BUILDING FORM

Alternative 1: 40′ × 40′ Bay, 125# Live Load, 14′ Floor to Floor

Primary framing @ $1.29/sq ft
Span factor—1.5
Load factor—1.2

$1.29 \times 1.5 \times 1.2 = \$2.32/\text{sq ft}$

Secondary framing @ $2.03/sq ft
Span factor—1.5
Load factor—1.2

$2.03 \times 1.5 \times 1.2 = \dfrac{\$3.65}{\$5.97/\text{sq ft}}$

Locality adjustment
   (0.80—Richmond, Va.) $\$5.97 \times 0.80 = \$4.78/sq\ ft$

Area each floor (office
space only)

            $122 \times 482 = 58,804\ sq\ ft$

Area of building (office
space only)

            $58,804 \times 10 = 588,040\ sq\ ft$

Total cost of framing assembly

            $\$4.78 \times 588,040 = \$2,810,831$

Alternative 2: 40′ × 40′ Bay, 100# Live Load, 14′ Floor to Floor

Pursuing the same calculations as in Alternative 1, the load factor reduced from 1.2 to 1.0 then:

Total cost of framing assembly
     $\$3.98 \times 588,040 = \$2,340,399$

Alternative 3: 30′ × 30′ Bay, 125# Live Load, 13′ Floor to Floor

Pursuing the same calculations as in Alternative 1, with the span factor reduced from 1.5 to 1.0, then:

Total cost of framing assembly
     $\$3.18 \times 588,040 = \$1,869,967$

Alternative 4: 30′ × 30′ Bay, 100# Live Load, 13′ Floor to Floor

Pursuing the same calculations as in Alternative 1, with span and load factors both reduced to 1.0, then:

Total cost of framing assembly
     $\$2.66 \times 588,040 = \$1,564,186$

There is another factor to be considered. Assume, for ease of calculation, that when the bay span is reduced from 40 to 30 feet, there will be a one-foot reduction in the thickness of the floor-ceiling sandwich, or a total of 10 feet for 10 floors. With a perimeter of 1208 feet and a stainless steel curtain wall as programmed (priced at $16.53/sq ft in Richmond; see Table A-6 in Appendix A for curtain wall costs), then:

$$1208 \times 10 \times \$16.53 = \$199,682$$

A cost benefit of $199,682 would accrue to Alternatives 3 and 4, because of reduction in the area of the building skin as well as a reduction in the cost of the framing assembly resulting from choice of a smaller bay size.

Decision: Hold decision until Alternatives 5 through 8 have been analyzed.

Building Form—Rectangular or Square?

The shape of the office building just described places all building occupants within 60 feet of the window wall, in response to the owner's

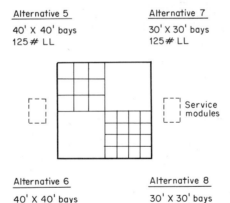

Alternative 5
40' X 40' bays
125 # LL

Alternative 7
30' X 30' bays
125 # LL

Service modules

Alternative 6
40' X 40' bays
100 # LL

Alternative 8
30' X 30' bays
100 # LL

Floor size: 242' X 242'
Bay sizes: 40' X 40' and 30' X 30'
Floor area: 58,564 sq ft net
Number of floors: 10
Total office area: 585,640 sq ft net
Floor-to-floor height: 14' and 13'
Height of building: 140' and 130'
Building perimeter: 968'

FIG. 8-5 A STRUCTURAL FRAMING SYSTEM WITH VARIOUS LOADS AND BAY SIZES FOR A SQUARE BUILDING FORM

request for nearness. This design decision is arbitrary. Is nearness that important? Other alternatives must probe this proximity value and still satisfy essential function at lower cost. If the owner can be persuaded that value is not eroded when 75% of the occupants are within 60 feet of the exterior wall and 85% are within 75 feet, then a new design concept can be pursued with some remarkable economies. This second design, Figure 8-5, is square, not rectangular; it is 242 feet on a side and contains 36 bays, 40' × 40', or 64 bays 30' by 30'. It is the same size and has the same number of bays as the rectangular design.

This next design cost analysis will be concerned with the relationships of curtain wall costs and structural costs for the square form and how these compare with the rectangular form. These comparisons are all tabulated in Table 8-3, and since the costs for the framing assemblies are identical, Alternatives 5 through 8 are repeated here as in Alternatives 1 through 4.

This square building form has a perimeter of 968 lineal feet which is 240 feet less than the 1208 in the rectangular design. This reduction produces substantial savings in the area of curtain wall, and the steel-producer owner wanted the best, in stainless steel. Analyzing the cost of each framing assembly shows that, if the cost of structure is paired with cost savings of curtain wall, the difference in cost between the two is an index of value. Furthermore, quality has been preserved.

TABLE 8-3

OFFICE BUILDING—ALTERNATIVES FOR BAY SIZES AND LIVE LOADS

Alternative	Bay size and live load	Cost of framing assembly	Floor-to-floor height, ft	Perimeter, ft	Savings in curtain wall	Cost of framing assemblies minus curtain wall
			Rectangular building			
1	40' × 40'—125#	$2,810,831	14	1,208	....	$2,810,831
2	40' × 40'—100#	2,340,399	14	1,208	....	2,340,399
3	30' × 30'—125#	1,869,967	13	1,208	$199,682	1,670,285
4	30' × 30'—100#	1,564,186	13	1,208	199,682	1,364,504
			Square building			
5	40' × 40'—125#	2,810,831	14	968	554,736	2,256,095
6	40' × 40'—100#	2,340,399	14	968	554,763	1,785,636
7	30' × 30'—125#	1,869,967	13	968	714,746	1,155,221
8	30' × 30'—100#	1,564,186	13	968	714,746	849,440

For example: it has been demonstrated in Alternatives 3 and 4 that reduced building height contributed to reduced costs of curtain wall. In Alternatives 5 through 8 these cost savings mount substantially higher. At a height of 140 and a reduced perimeter of 240 feet, the savings are:

$$\$16.53 \times 140 \times 240 = \$554,736$$

However, Alternatives 5 and 6 have floor-to-floor heights of 13 feet, not 14, and produce further savings in 10 floors:

$$\$16.53 \times 10 \times 968 = \$160,010$$

and when savings in height are added to savings in perimeter, the total is:

$$\$554.736 + 160,010 = \$714,746$$

Table 8-3 tabulates these design alternatives and cost alternatives, and now a *design cost analysis* can be made with respect to building form and its framing assemblies.

DECISIONS   The architect alone cannot unilaterally make these decisions. They have to do with values: the value of flexibility in floor loading and bay spacing, and the value of human proximity to exterior wall. These decisions can only be made after discussions with the owner. However, the architect should make recommendations to the owner or propose methods for reaching a decision.

PROXIMITY   It is the architect's judgment that there is no loss of value when 75 percent of the building's population is within 60 feet of the window wall. Functional furniture layouts can be made where areas of low human density would be placed on the interior of the building, and those of high density toward the perimeter. The figure of 75 percent can be improved. The savings in curtain wall costs for the square building form are substantial and cannot be ignored.

Recommended Decision: Accept square building form.

FLOOR LOADING   A 125# live load is not typical for an office building. If the owner requires heavy loading for some operations, set aside a special floor or zones within each floor. Essential function would not be impaired.

Recommended Decision: Design for 100# live load.

BAY SIZES   It is agreed, greater flexibility is achieved in an open floor area with fewer columns. Using a 40' × 40' bay with a 100# live load will cost $776,213 more than a 30' × 30' bay with the same load.

Recommended Decision: $776,213 is a high price to pay for flexibility. Is that much flexibility needed? The architect will make studies of typical furniture layouts for several different types of owner operations, each using 40' and 30' bay sizes. The owner can then judge which has better value.

Recommended Decision: Defer until furniture layouts have been approved.

CONCLUSION   Subject to discussions with the owner and pending furniture layout investigations, the architect recommends that the square building form be accepted. Value will not be eroded nor essential function impaired by accepting Alternative 8; it is the least costly. When curtian wall savings are paired with framing assembly costs, Alternative 8 is $1,961,391 or 70% less costly than Alternative 1.

The recommended design of the square building form will produce economies in other building systems, particularly in HVAC, but these will be examined in a subsequent review of *mechanical systems.* Also options in other subsystem selections can have further effect in reducing the cost of the superstructure system. For example: the owner has asked for a 1-A fireproof classification. Under the BOCA building code[3] that is used in the state of Virginia, the classification 1-B is deemed to be the equivalent of 1-A, *provided an automatic fire suppression system* (sprinklers) *is installed.* If an office building is under 150 feet in height—and this one is—it is designer's option whether or not to use the fire suppression system. If the option is taken, fireproofing requirements for structural steel columns and framing assemblies are reduced from a four- to a three-hour rating. This is a cost trade-off. The cost manager will investigate it with the mechanical engineer. Other cost trade-offs will have to be considered; these will be examined later, under Mechanical Systems.

The foregoing discussion has been a representation of effective decision making early in the schematic design phase. Design cost analysis finds best value as it delivers essential function at least cost, and it avoids the cost penalties of wrong decisions that cannot later be rectified during the construction document phase.

[3]BOCA is the acronym for Building Officials and Code Administrators, the organization that administers this model building code.

It is appropriate at this point to interrupt these thoughts and refer to the discussion on professional fees in Chapter 3. The argument was advanced in favor of lump sum fees rather than fees based on a percentage of the dollar amounts of construction contracts. The data in Table 8-3 support that argument. The level of effort that the structural engineer must provide to design, document, specify, and observe in the field for alternative 4 is exactly the same level of effort required for alternative 1; yet the construction cost of the latter is $1,246,645 higher. The structural engineer should be paid a proper amount for services, of course, but should not reap a windfall due to span and load factors. The architect should not pay the engineer an extra percentage on this difference, and the owner should not pay the architect a percentage on the difference plus the latter's markup. In neither case has the fee been earned. Good professional agreements should be negotiated for lump sums with provisions for extra services, just as good construction agreements can be negotiated for lump sums with provisions for extra change orders. Now, back to building systems.

Roofing System

The roofing system includes the roof cover and the roof deck, except for structural decks, which are integral with the superstructure. Roofing systems are classified in three broad divisions: shingles, metal roofing, and built-up with various deck arrangements. A few of these are illustrated in table A-7 in Appendix A.

The essential function of a roofing system is to keep water out of a building. That statement sounds almost naive. But of all the postconstruction problems that architects must confront, water leakage occurs the most often—particularly in the category of built-up roofing. With new energy regulations requiring higher resistance to heat loss in roof decks, these problems can only grow.

SHINGLES   The cost of shingles varies from a low of $1.52 a square foot for wood cedar to a high of $4.30 for Vermont red slate. There are few leakage problems with shingles, but some can be vulnerable to high winds. Selection of shingles, other than for esthetic reasons, is an easy choice between low first cost and performance over time.

METAL ROOFING   If corrugated metals are excluded from consideration the choice is narrowed to two alternatives: copper and lead-coated tin—with variables in how they are joined at the seams: flat, standing, or bat-

FIG. 8-6 ROOFING SYSTEM When the roof dominates an architectural composition, it deserves special consideration. This steep geometry is covered with batten seam lead-coated copper. *(Norbertine Abbey. Photo by Lawrence S. Williams, Inc.)*

ten. The highest in cost is 11-oz copper batten seam at $6.16 a square foot, and 11-oz lead-coated tin is lowest at $3.76.

BUILT-UP ROOFING A five-ply 20-year built-up roof with vapor barrier costs $1.01 a square foot, and a four-ply 20-year roof $0.93. There is no reason, ever, to justify anything less than a 20-year roof; the decrease in value for a 10 or 15-year roof is far greater than the decrease in cost. The real problems in built-up roofing begin on the architect's drawing board where the materials are selected, where the deck structure is determined, where topping, insulation, and flashing are detailed, and finally where the roof drains are located. A dead-flat roof is a dead-flat mistake. The real problems of built-up roofing continue on into the field and depend on whether the roofing was properly applied to the deck, what the weather conditions were at that time, and how the roof was walked on, wheeled over, or poked through after application and before finish of construction. Architects should never select a built-up roofing system unless they have the technical ability to detail and specify it properly, and have the practical know-how to supervise its installation and protect it afterward.

Exterior Walls System

Exterior walls include the outer finish material with decoration or trim as well as backup material. No structural components such as columns or spandrels are included, since these are properly part of the superstructure. Likewise, any finishes, furring, or other materials applied to the inside surface of the exterior wall or its backup are not considered to be a part of the exterior wall system; rather, they are a part of the interior wall finishes system. Fenestration and exterior doors are included as subsystems, since they are largely interchangeable with the basic wall assemblies.

The in-place construction costs for a few selected exterior walls, windows, and exterior doors are found in Appendix A, in Table A-6. Labor and material costs for the components in each system are itemized. The cost of each system is expressed as cost per square foot of wall area.

It has been pointed out that the exterior walls of a building are the most costly of all architectural building systems. During conceptual design, architects must be constantly aware of relative costs as they dip into a palette of various wall materials and make a selection. Exterior wall materials can range from a low of $1.56 a square face foot to a high of $21.34 as tabulated in Table A-4 in Appendix A.

Architects must not only consider the cost of the materials themselves, but also the complexity of the building form when the walls are put together, as well as the area of the wall face, which is a function of building perimeter. The following example of a museum illustrates how a designer may choose between two wall systems and two building forms. A square building is used again as one of the alternatives to emphasize that as the designer moves away from a building form with a one to one length-width ratio, and approaches a one to four or more configuration, the cost of a building constantly increases even though the square footage remains the same.

A UNIVERSITY MUSEUM   One of the universities in St. Louis, Missouri, has decided to build a small museum of about 15,000 square feet gross to house a very important collection of fine arts that has been willed to the university. It is to be a one-story structure with a clear height of 25 feet, and the entire collection is to be skylighted. The building committee has expressed the desire that the exterior of the building be of brick to match the other buildings on campus. The architect, however, was convinced that, since the museum would be all top lighted with no windows in the exterior wall, it would be a grim building in brick. Precast concrete wall

FIG. 8-7 EXTERIOR WALLS SYSTEM—SIMPLE Wall and window; nothing more. Independent from the structural system and articulated for vertical and horizontal expansion and contraction, these walls are truly alive as they respond to thermal forces. *(Nurse's Residence, Temple Medical Center. Photo by Leif Skoogfors.)*

panels with exposed aggregate would be preferable; it would contrast with other campus buildings and call attention to its importance. Also, without windows, some geometry of shape must be introduced to give interest to an otherwise unimpressive form. Figure 8-9 assumes four alternatives that the architect and the building committee will have to choose from. It is true, of course, that the cost of all building systems should be at hand before a decision is made about the exterior wall system. This example, though, is concerned only with wall material and form.

Cost data for the 12″ brick wall alternative were taken directly from the appendix; it was necessary to add the cost of a precast, exposed aggregate wall to the cost of an 8″ concrete block wall to arrive at its total cost. The important and expensive interior wall finishes needed to set off the museum collection are not a part of the exterior wall. In St. Louis, the locality adjustment is 1.05.

It is important to note that the decision about which alternative to select should not be based only on the esthetics of material selection and building form. Rather, the decision should be based on esthetics plus the cost of those things which produce esthetic value. Best value (including esthetics) at least cost, cannot be determined until costs are at hand and design decisions are made.

The design cost analysis continues in Table 8-4. This tabulation now not only gives the price of the four alternatives but also translates that price into the cost per square foot of gross building area. The figures also show how the cost of a museum can go up or down, depending on the

		Building Form	
		(A)	(B)
	Two alternatives, each 15,625 sq ft	125' □ 125'	175' ⌐_⌐ 75' 125' 50'
	Perimeter (lin ft)	500	600
	Area of wall 25' high	12,500	15,000
(1)	4" face brick + 8" block $6.49/sq ft (national) $6.81/sq ft (St. Louis)	$ 85,125	$102,150
(2)	Precast conc. + 8" block $13.81 / sq ft (national) $4.50/sq ft (St. Louis)	$181,250	$217,500

Exterior Walls System

FIG. 8-9 SOME EXTERIOR WALL COSTS IN ST. LOUIS, MISSOURI

FIG. 8-8 EXTERIOR WALLS SYSTEM—COMPLEX This precast concrete wall system also serves as the superstructure system and contains the interior finish system and vertical distribution subsystem for the perimeter HVAC, as well as the sub-frames for all fenestration. Four standard shapes of floor-to-floor units generate a curved facade with surprising economies. *(Headquarters Office Building for Housing and Urban Development. Photo by Ben Schnall.)*

TABLE 8-4

COMPARISON OF EXTERIOR WALL AND PERIMETER COSTS

		(A)	(B)	
(1)		$85,125 $5.45/sq ft	$102,150 $6.54/sq ft	1-B increase over 1-A: $17,025 or 20% $1.09/sq ft
(2)		$181,250 $11.60/sq ft	$217,500 $13.92/sq ft	2-B increase over 2-A: $36,250 or 20% $2.32/sq ft

2-A increase over 1-B: $79,100 or 77% $5.06/sq ft	2-A increase over 1-A: $96,125 or 113% $6.15/sq ft	2-B increase over 1-B: $115,350 or 113% $7.38/sq ft	2-B increase over 1-A: $132,375 or 156% $8.47/sq ft

material selected or the geometry desired. The architect is right: A square brick box is not interesting. But then, neither is a square concrete box interesting (2-A), and it costs $79,100 more than an uninteresting piece of brick geometry (1-B). At any rate, the final design decision will not be based on a hunch, but rather on design cost analysis.

If the above example had been a commercial building rather than a museum, it might be assumed that 60 percent of the exterior wall is precast concrete or brick and 40 percent is curtain wall. Percentages of various wall materials can be calculated in any combination, and windows and doors handled in the same manner. The appendix lists 40 wall, window, and door systems; these were extracted from a list of 148. It is possible for the designer to be quite knowledgeable about the comparative costs of building systems and use them effectively during conceptual design. It is up to the cost manager to sharpen and refine system costs, but the designer should know how to read the cost danger signs associated with design and speak the language of costs fluently.

The Partition System

Partition assemblies include only those parts of the building (exclusive of applied finishes) whose function is to divide interior space.

After exterior walls, partitions are usually the next highest in cost of all the architectural building systems. In searching for the right architectural solution, interior space must be divided up into the required number of individual rooms, and there is little that can be done to change the lineal feet of partitions and the number of doors needed to do this. Selection of partition components is determined by the use of the room, type of construction, and class of occupancy, so again, these set limiting factors on

FIG. 8-10 PARTITION SYSTEM A partition system separates one space from another physically, acoustically, and when desired, visually. It generates privacy and when necessary, security. *(Mercer County Community College. Photo by Lawrence S. Williams, Inc.)*

the range of choice. However, within those ranges prices can vary widely as shown Table A-4 in Appendix A. The price per square foot of partition area runs from $1.48 for ½" drywall on 2" × 4" studs to $11.74 for 12" thick glazed brick and structural tile.

The Interior Wall Finish System

This system includes all applied finishes on partitions and on the interior side of exterior walls.

Generally, this system ranks third in systems cost. It is important that architects know the relative cost of these finishes as they handle interior design. Architectural expression depends on choice of material, texture, and color, as well as of acoustical properties, wearing characteristics, and rate of flame spread. Choice of materials is limitless, and can be as low as $0.26 a square foot for two coats of flat paint to as high as $21.47 for 2" polished red granite as shown in Table A-4 in Appendix A.

135

FIG. 8-11 INTERIOR WALL FINISH SYSTEM—AUSTERE Natural light and texture; not even a coat of paint. *(Norbertine Abbey. Photo by Lawrence S. Williams, Inc.)*

FIG. 8-12 INTERIOR WALL FINISH SYSTEM—LUXURIOUS Wall finishes together with floor finishes and furnishings can create a leisurely comfortable environment. *(Philadelphia Country Club. Photo by Cortlandt Hubbard.)*

The Interior Floor Finishes System

Floor finishes are applied to, but do not include, the structural deck or subfloor.

Here again, architects should know the comparative costs of floor finishes. Just as for interior wall finishes, architectural design and functional requirements will determine floor finishes. They can be as simple as liquid hardeners applied to concrete or as costly as marbles and granites.

The Ceilings System

This system includes finishes applied to the undersurface of decks as well as complete hung ceilings.

Ceilings are the simplest of all building systems. Other than rubbing concrete, there are only three classes of materials to consider: gypsum board, lath and plaster, and acoustical materials. When gypsum board or plaster are used for partitions they are almost always used on the ceilings.

The Conveying System

This building system includes all those equipment assemblies that move people or goods from one place to another, such as:

Elevators	Pneumatic tubes
Escalators	Linen chutes
Cranes	Dumbwaiters

The design documents locate all these conveyors, and the cost manager will assign a lump sum estimate for each assembly.

The Specialties System

This building system is a collection of all the odds and ends needed to make the building function, such as:

FIG. 8-13 SPECIALTY SYSTEM Specialties can range up to the very sophisticated and actually shape architectural form. *(Planetarium, Temple University Physics Building. Photo by Temple University.)*

Toilet partitions   Bulletin boards

Chalkboards   Signs

Fire extinguishers   Flagpoles

These miscellaneous items will be carried as a lump sum during the design phases, and it can vary considerably depending on building type.

The Equipment System

This building system consists of equipment physically attached to the building, such as:

Auditorium seating   Hydraulic dockboards

Library stacks   Venetian blinds

This equipment sometimes is not only attached to the building, but also connected to mechanical and electrical systems, such as are installed in:

Laboratories   Kitchens

Cafeterias   Laundries

FIG. 8-14 FIXED EQUIPMENT SYSTEM   In this building any piece of fixed equipment can be relocated at any other position at any time and have immediate access to a multitude of downfeed services with no disturbance to the floor below. The drainage subsystem has a prefabricated access through the structural deck at any intersection of a 24-inch grid. *(Medical Research Center. Photo by Cortlandt Hubbard.)*

Many times, in order to control quality, these items are let as a separate contract and not left to the general contractor. Equipment costs are carried as a lump sum, and, like specialties, can vary widely in cost depending on building type. Costs can be severely influenced by the quality of equipment. Galvanized metal kitchen equipment performs the same function as stainless steel, but maintenance, useful life, and appearance are extremely different.

ENGINEERING BUILDING SYSTEMS

Chapter 4 and Table 4-1 emphasized the fact that 61 percent of construction costs are in the structural, mechanical, and electrical systems, and this breaks down to approximately 25 percent structural and 36 percent mechanical and electrical. These engineering systems must be kept in mind constantly as architects search for the conceptual form of their buildings and explore alternative designs. Earlier in this chapter a discussion on superstructure emphasized how the cost of that system reacted to architectural decisions. The same is true of HVAC, plumbing, and electrical systems, except that these systems have a large number of subsystems and innumerable components. At best, these subsystems are complex, and they are awkward to monitor as far as costs are concerned. Yet this must be done. Alphonse Dell'Isola tells us that:

> Quite a few years ago, an Italian economist named Vilfredo Pareto (1848–1923), developed the curve known as Pareto's law of distribution. This curve has general application to all areas where a significant number of elements are involved. [See Figure 8-15.] It points out that in any area, a small number of elements (20%) contains the greater percentage of cost (80%). Similarly, a small number of elements will contain the greater percentage of unnecessary costs. Value engineering uses an organized approach to isolate the elements having the greatest bulk of unnecessary costs, with the objective of developing lower cost alternates.[4]

Pareto's law of distribution must be applied to all these engineering disciplines since 60 percent of all construction costs are there. It is here that the cost manager's services are of such great help. All subsystem and component costs are stored in computer memory, and as one element or another is selected it can be objectively analyzed for cost and accepted, or

[4]Alphonse J. Dell'Isola, *Value Engineering in the Construction Industry*, Litton Educational Publishing, Inc., New York, 1975, p. 7. Reprinted by permission of Van Nostrand Reinhold Company.

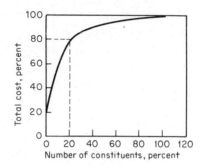

FIG. 8-15 PARETO'S LAW OF DISTRIBUTION

rejected in favor of an alternative preference.

This is when direct, informal communications between all members of the design team is so important. The word *coordination* here means coordination of the design-cost process, not review of a series of drawings.

The HVAC System

The principal subsystems of the heating, ventilating, and air conditioning system are:

Steam System   Air distribution system

Hot water system   Controls and instrumentation

Chilled water system

The design of the distribution system of piping and ductwork, and the location of mechanical spaces greatly influence the cost of HVAC and should be carefully considered during schematic design.

When cost differences between square and rectangular buildings were reviewed (Figures 8-4 and 8-5) it was noted that economies in things other than structure were possible. The square building with less perimeter has less external heat loss or heat gain, giving smaller loads on mechanical equipment. The square building also permits a more efficient and less costly horizontal distribution of horizontal runs of ducts and piping.

The Plumbing System

The principal subsystems of plumbing are:

Domestic water system   Fire protection system

Sanitary drainage system   Plumbing fixtures

Storm drainage system

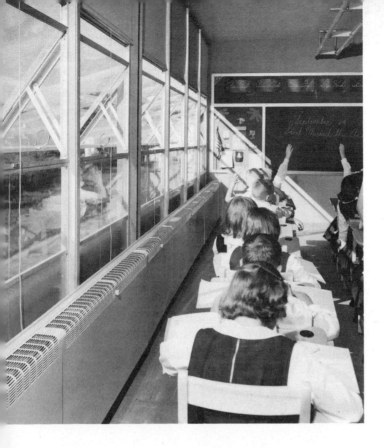

FIG. 8-16 HVAC SYSTEM No air conditioning here and ventilation is not mechanical. The simple heating subsystem also assumes its share of doubling for the interior finish system. When two or more building systems are combined, the same value can be achieved at a lower cost. *(St. Genevieve School. Photo by Cortlandt Hubbard.)*

The sanitary and storm drainage subsystems are activated by gravity and no building can escape the fact that "horizontal" runs must incline at a rate of ¼" to the foot. The subsystems of drainage, air handling, and primary framing compete for position and clearances and cause many problems in interstitial space. The easy design solution is to increase the thickness of the floor-ceiling sandwich, but this has been shown to be very costly. Design cost analysis by ASMEC is essential in apportioning the space.

The fire protection subsystem offers a good opportunity for effective trade-offs among other building systems. When examining the primary and secondary framing assemblies it was shown how fireproofing of structural steel could be reduced by one hour. In addition, under model code regulations and depending on the class of building and type of occupancy, architects are now given far greater freedom than before in the overall design of buildings. Building corridors can be made longer between stairs and exits; size and number of stairs can be reduced; buildings can be made higher; and fire walls can enclose larger areas. Initial costs for plumbing system are higher with a fire protection subsystem, but other system costs will be lower. The extra cost of the fire protection system would be paid back over a period of several years because of a reduction in fire insurance rates. Design cost analysis, seeking better value without loss of essential function, does pay off.

The Electrical System

The principal subsystems of the electrical system are:

Primary service	Controls and instrumentation
Secondary service	Communications system
Branch circuits	Emergency systems
Lighting fixtures	

Heat from lighting fixtures adds substantially to the air conditioning load. By eliminating high overall levels of illumination using ceiling fixtures and placing adequate light on the tasks being performed with local

FIG. 8-17 PLUMBING SYSTEM   How else can it be said? This is plumbing at its best. *(Philadelphia Country Club. Photo by Cortlandt Hubbard.)*

FIG. 8-18 ELECTRICAL SYSTEM There are few buildings that can operate by day or be usable at night without power and illumination. *(Samuel Paley Library. Photo by Lawrence S. Williams, Inc.)*

light sources, both air conditioning load and electrical load are reduced, producing savings in initial and operating costs.

VALUE ENGINEERING

Building systems are the key to cost control, and architects should have more than a speaking acquaintance with their relative costs, as well as those of their subsystems and components. The ability to manipulate design and analyze cost trade-offs among the several systems is greatly enhanced with a knowledge of *value engineering*. Edward Heller defines value engineering this way: "Value engineering is the *conscious* systematic application of a set of techniques that identify needed functions, establish value for them and develop alternatives to perform these functions for minimum cost."[5]

His book is recommended to gain an insight into the theory of value engineering. For a practical application of this theory to building design, Alphonse Dell'Isola's book on value engineering is recommended; he defines value engineering like this:

In simple terms, VE is a systematic approach to obtaining optimum value for every dollar spent. Through a system of investigation, unnecessary

[5]Edward D. Heller, *Value Management*, Addison-Wesley, Reading, Mass., 1971, p. 14.

expenditures are avoided, resulting in improved value and economy. The VE approach is a creative effort directed toward the analysis of functions. It is concerned with the elimination or modification of anything that adds cost to an item without adding to its function. During this process all expenditures relating to construction, maintenance, operation, replacement, etc., are considered.[6]

LIFE-CYCLE COST ANALYSIS

The economics of life-cycle costing are not covered in this book, but when analyzing and selecting building systems, initial costs must be weighed against the cost of performance over time. This is done by life-cycle cost analysis, which has been defined by a task force of the American Institute of Architects as "any technique which allows assessment of a given solution, or choice among alternative solutions, on the basis of considering all relevant economic consequences over a given period of time."[7]

The task force refers to value engineering as a cousin to life-cycle cost analysis. The latter measures benefits or penalties only in dollars; value can include measures other than dollars. The AIA guide to life-cycle cost analysis is excellent, and recommended reading.

PUTTING THE PIECES TOGETHER

This chapter has examined the fifteen individual building systems separately. Their relative importance in terms of cost has been pointed out and the trade-offs between systems emphasized. These building systems are all elements of graphic design. Conceptual design and detailed design, as carried on by ASMEC, are done with a full knowledge of construction costs supplied by the cost manager.

The next chapter pulls these building systems together and views them as a whole, just as ASMEC does. We will follow the cost manager as an estimate is prepared for a hypothetical office building, beginning with the program phase and ending with a detailed cost estimate as the project is ready to go out for bids.

---

[6]Dell'Isola, op. cit., p. 1.

[7]David S. Haviland, ed., *Life Cycle Cost Analysis*, American Institute of Architects, Washington, D.C., 1977, p. 4.

CHAPTER 9

PROCEDURES IN COST CONTROL USING BUILDING SYSTEMS

This chapter will now pursue the cost trail of a hypothetical project from the first phase of programming up to the time it is ready to be bid or negotiated. The architect, using design cost analysis, will work side by side with the engineers and the cost manager as trade-offs are made among the various building systems. Design decisions will fluctuate back and forth as alternatives are considered in terms of best value. Decisions will be made with full confidence because the cost manager is supplying ASMEC with timely, dependable cost information.

Although cost control requires continuous attention, there are three milestone points when the architect is required to produce an estimate. The activities leading up to these milestones may be described as:

- *Searching* for a design cost concept
- *Arriving* at a design cost solution
- *Finalizing* the details of design and cost

The period of searching consists of two parts, programming and schematic design phases; arriving corresponds with design development; and finalizing is accomplished during the construction document phase. Each of these phases has a different set of design data that is used to arrive at a cost estimate, and in each successive phase, as information and data become more quantifiable, the estimate becomes more accurate. In the following project it is assumed that all the necessary programming, drawing, and specifications have been prepared with high professional skill, and we will examine only the cost effects generated by those activities.

PROJECT BACKGROUND

An expanding corporation in St. Louis, Missouri, wishes to consolidate its operations, which are now scattered in various leased locations. To meet their foreseeable needs for the next 10 years, a headquarters office building will be constructed on an eight-acre site, which the corporation now owns. If future growth continues as expected, a twin office tower will be erected on the same site, and the site plan is to be designed to accommodate this future expansion. The eight acres are semiwooded and gently rolling with good drainage. Parking for 250 cars is to be provided within a well-shielded, landscaped environment. Subsurface investigations show no water and excellent foundation material. All required utilities are available along one edge of the site. Zoning and other permits have been received.

The building will require about 190,000 to 200,000 square feet net for office space, and it is desired that each floor have somewhere between 15,000 and 17,000 square feet net. An employees' cafeteria and an executive dining room will be located on the second floor, as the first floor will be reserved for activities that generate conditions of very active public traffic.

The building is to be of outstanding quality in every respect and to project a very stable and positive corporate image. However, in no event is the cost of the building to exceed $55 a square foot gross. A tentative budget of $14,000,000 has been established for all construction costs, and this must be confirmed after the building has been completely programmed.

SEARCHING FOR A DESIGN-COST CONCEPT

Program + design = cost. The building program and the schematic design do set the cost of construction. That has been emphasized all through this book. It is possible for the architect to exercise cost control in these early stages by carrying out the following procedures.

The Program Phase

The architect has now completely programmed the building, and the first task is to confirm the tentative budget of $14,000,000 for the general construction contract. Before any drawings are started, assumptions can be made that establish the building's size, height, form, and perimeter; building systems can be designated and the general level of quality established for materials and components.

Referring to Table A-2 in Appendix A, if the net area of the building is 195,000 square feet, we multiply by 1.25 and arrive at an approximate 244,000 square feet gross. Further, if the area of each floor is set at 20,000 square feet, it would meet the owner's requirement for a net area of 15,000 to 17,000 square feet. Eleven floors and a basement at 20,000 square feet each gives a total of 240,000 square feet gross, and that figure will be used for estimating purposes. A first look at an estimate, using the owner's figure of not more than $55/sq ft, shapes up like this:

240,000 sq ft @ $55	$13,200,000
Site work allowance @ $50,000 per acre	400,000
	$13,600,000
Construction contingencies @ 3%	408,000
Total	$14,008,000

Whoever worked up that budget figure for the owner and set the maximum price per square foot knew how to go about it. However, the architect must not begin to design the building until this figure has been tested still further.

These additional assumptions are made:

- The superstructure for the building will be structured steel with a cellular steel deck. Bay sizes shall be 40′ × 40′ with a 14′ distance from floor to floor.
- The exterior wall of the building shall be of outstanding quality with one-third of the area in reflective insulating glass. The length width ratio is tentatively set at 1.3 to 1.
- It will take about a year to design the building and receive bids, and another two years to construct it, thus placing the midpoint of construction two years away from the present date. That means that two years of inflation will be reflected in the bids, and, at an assumed annual rate of 8 percent, a total of 16 percent must be added to what the building would cost today.

The owner insists on "very high quality" throughout the building as long as it doesn't exceed $55 a square foot, which is the defined economic value desired.

All these program assumptions are noted on a form, as shown in Table 9-1, and the architect then discusses the broad scope of the building and confirms the escalation factor with the cost manager. The next day the cost manager hands the program cost estimate, as shown on Table 9-2, to the architect.

TABLE 9-1

QUESTIONNAIRE ON BASIC BUILDING DATA AND BUILDING SYSTEMS

Please complete this form before calling

Completed analysis will be sent to the following address:

Company Name DESIGN COST ANALYSIS

Attention of THE READER   Phone

Address ANYWHERE   City   State USA   Zip

Building Name VALLEY HEADQUARTERS OFFICE BUILDING

Location ST. LOUIS   City MO   State 63102   Zip

Construction Date   Inflation Factor (if desired)   16   %

Quality: ☒ Superior   ☐ Above Average   ☐ Average   ☐ Minimal

Building Use:

Primary GENERAL OFFICE SPACE	100	% of total area
Secondary		% of total area
Other		% of total area

Please complete all of the following:

Basic Data:

Gross Floor Area (excl. basement)	220,000	Sq. Ft.
Number of Floors (excl. basement)	11	
Area of Ground Floor	20,000	Sq. Ft.
Perimeter at Ground (if known)		Ln. Ft.
Floor to Floor or Eave Height	14	Ln. Ft.
Basement—% of Main Floor	100	%
Approx. Length/width Relationship	1 TO 1.3	

Superstructure:

☒ Steel Frame 40'x40'BAY   ☐ Wood Frame-Commercial
☐ Concrete Frame   ☐ Wood Frame-Residential
☐ Wall Bearing   ☐ Pre Engineered
Other

Exterior Wall: HIGHEST QUALITY INSULATED ALUMINUM   - 2/3
REFLECTIVE INSULATING GLASS   - 1/3

Elevators: ☐ None   Number 6   **Partitions:** ☐ Dry wall   ☐ Block   ☐ Plaster
                                          ∟ METAL - DEMOUNTABLE
                                          Roof Cover: BUILT- UP   20 YEAR

Finishes/Equipment: Check if normal for bldg. use   Otherwise describe below

Interior Finish—Wall	☐ METAL TO MATCH PARTITIONS
—Floor	☐ CARPET 50% VINYL 40% CERAMIC 5% MARBLE 5%
—Ceiling	☐ ACOUSTIC TILE

10,000 SQ.FT. OF   Built-in Equipment   ☐ EMPLOYEE'S CAFETERIA - 250
COMPUTER FlOOR
Htg., Vent. & Air Cond.   ☐ HIGH QUALITY
Plumbing   ☐ " "   Sprinklered 80 %
Electrical   ☐ " "

TABLE 9-2

PROGRAM COST ESTIMATE

System	Total cost, $	Cost per sq ft, $	% of total
Foundations	141,535	0.59	0.9
Floors on grade	49,111	0.20	0.3
Superstructure	3,291,713	13.72	21.6
Roofing	22,895	0.10	0.1
Exterior walls	2,705,705	11.27	17.7
Partitions	1,877,854	7.82	12.3
Wall finishes	170,357	0.71	1.1
Floor finishes	517,238	2.16	3.4
Ceiling finishes	403,752	1.68	2.6
Conveying systems	823,287	3.43	5.4
Fixed equipment	796,000	3.32	5.2
HVAC	2,145,703	8.94	14.0
Plumbing	755,277	3.15	4.9
Electrical	1,573,988	6.56	10.5
Total	15,274,415	63.65	100.0

Above cost is based on current wages and prices for the zip code area 63102 and includes inflation of 16.0%.

The Program Cost Estimate   The bottom line of Table 9-2 comes as a staggering jolt. Something must be wrong. Even without site work the total cost of the building is over 15 million dollars and over $63 a square foot, or 15% above the allowable $55.

A scan of the various systems shows that the superstructure and exterior walls systems are high, as are floor and interior wall finishes systems. The cost manager notes that the specialties system has been combined with the fixed equipment system, as nothing is really known about either at this program stage. But the cost manager goes on to say that all system costs are too high. The level of quality for the building was overstated by the architect when stipulating materials and quality in the questionnaire. A figure of $28 per square face foot for the exterior wall area had been allowed, but apparently this level of quality cannot be sustained. Structural spans are too great; mechanical and electrical systems must be followed closely as they develop during schematic design.

The cost manager advises the architect that $8 a square foot can be taken out of the estimate without reducing the size of the building if the architect maintains a simple building form and closely supervises the quality of each building system. At this point the architect should make clear to the owner that to achieve the building within the budget, there has to be give and take between the two of them. The building program

149

and the quality of building systems will have to be adjusted to arrive at the cost objectives.

The Schematic Design Phase

The architect has set the basic size and form of the office building as shown in Figure 9-1. The building still has 20,000 square feet gross for each floor, but has grown to a total area of 244,000 square feet with the addition of a penthouse. Bay sizes have been reduced to 30′ × 30′ from 40′ × 40′ in the program estimate, and floor-to-floor height reduced to 13′ from 14′.

Three alternatives will be explored. Each alternative will be accompanied by a set of drawings and an outline set of specifications, describing the changes to building systems for that particular alternative.

ASMEC will be making many design and cost decisions as they examine the possible trade-offs among the several systems. ASMEC must also react to client requests that affect costs during this conceptual stage.

FIG. 9-1 VALLEY HEADQUARTERS OFFICE BUILDING

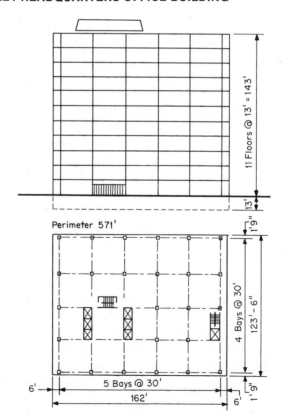

The cost manager is very active during these explorations, and for every sketch of architectural and engineering alternatives, there is a computer sketch of the cost alternatives.

TABLE 9-3

SCHEMATIC COST ESTIMATE NO. 1

Description	Labor, $	Material, $	Total, $	$/sq ft	
Foundations	75,161	47,227	122,388	0.50	
Floors on grade	24,901	25,521	50,422	0.21	
Superstructure	1,065,591	2,025,629	3.091,220	12.67	•
Roofing	25,747	29,627	55,374	0.23	
Exterior walls	832,462	1,487,491	2,319,953	9.51	•
Partitions	430,888	859,356	1,290,244	5.29	•
Wall finishes	190,126	344,770	534,896	2.19	•
Floor finishes	186,469	448,754	635,223	2.60	•
Ceiling finishes	170,138	154,211	324,349	1.33	•
Conveying systems	267,796	610,512	878,308	3.60	•
Specialties	115,942	244,279	360,221	1.48	
Fixed equipment	208,833	490,882	699,715	2.87	
HVAC	1,080,842	930,545	2,011,387	8.24	•
Plumbing	303,622	342,785	646,407	2.65	•
Electrical	772,800	748,160	1,520,960	6.23	•
Construction total	5,751,318	8,789,749	14,541,067	59.60	

Note: Above cost is based on current wages and prices for the zip code area 63102 and includes markups for overhead and profit, taxes and insurance, general conditions, and sales tax on materials. It also includes an inflation factor of 16.0%.

Source: Dodge Building Cost Services (McGraw-Hill Information Systems Company) with Wood & Tower Inc., *1979 Dodge Construction System Costs,* McGraw-Hill, New York, 1978.

Schematic Alternative 1   Table 9-3 shows the cost estimate for this alternative. It is prepared in greater detail than the program estimate. This summary sheet breaks down the total cost into cost of labor and cost of materials, and further details of each building system are also given by the cost manager so that each system can be examined by ASMEC. This will be shown in Table 9-4.

Cost Estimate No. 1 not only indicates the project location by zip code and the inflation factor of 16 percent over two years, but also calls attention to the hidden costs included in the estimate to cover markups, taxes, general conditions, and insurance. These hidden costs are very substantial, as we shall see later on.

The estimate for construction costs is now down to $59.60 per square foot, a very satisfactory start in the right direction, but with a long way still to go. The principal differences between this estimate and the preced-

TABLE 9-4

SCHEMATIC COST ESTIMATE NO. 1 WITH COST DETAILS OF BUILDING SYSTEMS

Description	Quantity	Unit	Labor, $	Material, $	Total, $
Floor finishes					
Ceramic tile	11000	sq ft	23,989	20,691	44,680
Vinyl asbesto tile	66000	sq ft	31,151	60,750	91,901
Computer floor	10000	sq ft	27,830	103,919	131,749
Carpeting	12710	sq yd	52,953	186,504	239,457
Painting	31610	sq ft	14,920	3,373	18,293
Marble flooring	11000	sq ft	35,626	73,517	109,143
Total			186,469	448,754	635,223
Ceiling finishes					
Plaster	22000	sq ft	46,189	14,087	60,276
Paint ceiling	26000	sq ft	14,387	2,775	17,162
Acoustical tile	198000	sq ft	109,562	137,349	246,911
Total			170,138	154,211	324,349
Conveying systems					
Cab allowance	7	each	12,193	32,139	44,332
Doors, guides, controls, etc.	1	LP SM	82,921	201,482	284,403
Elevator, medium speed	6	each	153,692	338,701	492,393
Freight elevator, electric	1	each	18,990	38,190	57,180
Total			267,796	610,512	878,308
Specialties					
Toilet partitions	1	LP SM	13,342	60,379	73,721
Toilet accessories	1	LP SM	2,600	3,900	6,500
Misc specialties	1	LP SM	100,000	180,000	280,000
Total			115,942	244,279	360,221
Fixed equipment					
Dock leveler	1	each	175	3,284	3,459
Dock leveler foundation	1	each	1,064	755	1,819
Dock bumpers	2	each	44	123	167
Interior communications allowance	1	LP SM	75,000	175,000	250,000
Kitchen equipment	1	LP SM	32,550	106,720	139,270
Fixed equipment	1	LP SM	100,000	205,000	305,000
Total			208,833	490,882	699,715

Source: Dodge Building Cost Services (McGraw-Hill Information Systems Company) with Wood & Tower Inc., *1979 Dodge Construction Systems Costs,* McGraw-Hill, New York, 1978.

ing one are shown by dots located next to the square-foot cost of those building systems affected.

Looking at the highlights of this estimate, it is noted that the superstructure costs have been reduced below the program estimate by about a dollar a square foot because of the decreased bay size. Exterior wall costs have been reduced by three dollars a face square foot (quality) and wall area reduced (quantity) as floor heights have been reduced to 13 feet. This drops the wall system cost from $11.27 to $9.51 per square foot gross, a substantial saving.

The architect, in working with the owner, has generated more open-space planning and reduced the number of lineal feet of interior partitions, resulting in substantial savings in the partition system. On the other hand, the owner has told the architect that marble floors and walls are desired for all elevator lobbies from the first to the eleventh, and this has pushed up costs for these two systems.

Specialties and fixed equipment systems have now been separated and itemized based on information given in the drawings and specifications and have increased more than a dollar a square foot over the program allowance.

The three mechanical-electrical systems have all advanced in costs because of information contained in the outline specifications.

It must be thoroughly understood that, at this time and based on this meager information, these construction costs are not absolute; they are, however, well-informed. The value here is in cost comparisons, system by system. Marble is beautiful and easily maintained, but the owner must be informed that this level of quality is too high; keep it in the first-floor lobby, but use vinyl wall covering elsewhere.

The architect must never stop with one design solution, even if the design is esthetically and functionally satisfactory. Best value must be sought and sought again, and this is done through alternative approaches.

Details of Alternative 1 Along with each schematic cost estimate the cost manager produces a set of construction costs of all the components that make up each system. It is very easy for the designer to examine the printout shown in Table 9-4 and see how design decisions are affecting the cost of a building. This is only one sheet of many system details, but it does raise these questions in the eyes of the designer:

Why all that marble flooring? Over one hundred thousand dollars . . . and the wall finish system shows on another page that marble walls are costing $424,000 in addition.

A lay-in acoustical tile ceiling could reduce ceiling costs, but the architect considers it esthetically undesirable.

An elevator is needed to service the cafeteria on the second floor. The basement is no place for a cafeteria, and the owner has reserved the first floor for all those offices having continuous and direct contact with the public. The cafeteria is forced to the second floor with some very awkward service problems as a result and over $60,000 in costs for that elevator alone.

The owner's requirements shown in the outline specifications for miscellaneous specialties must be examined; $280,000 is far too high.

Under fixed equipment the special interior communications allowance must hold until better information is available, and the food-service consultant must talk to the cost manager and verify that lump sum for kitchen equipment.

ASMEC, as it reviews these detailed cost figures in the early stages of design, will apply the principles of value analysis and life-cycle costing to each building system and its principal components.

Schematic Alternative 2   This alternative has changed none of the essential elements of building form and architectural design, but it has explained some cost reductions in a few building systems and, most importantly, has investigated a poured-in-place, reinforced-concrete superstructure in place of structural steel. The bottom line shows an overall cost saving of $2.54/sq ft over Alternative 1, even though the concrete frame is more expensive than steel.

TABLE 9-5

SCHEMATIC COST ESTIMATE NO. 2
(dollars)

Description	Labor, $	Material, $	Total, $	$/sq ft
Foundations	75,161	47,227	122,388	0.50
Floors on grade	24,901	25,521	50,422	0.21
Superstructure	1,925,129	1,400,846	3,325,975	13.63 ●
Roofing	25,747	29,627	55,374	0.23
Exterior walls	832,462	1,242,532	2,074,994	8.50 ●
Partitions	430,888	859,356	1,290,244	5.29
Wall finishes	86,686	95,694	182,380	0.75 ●
Floor finishes	161,486	413,053	574,539	2.35 ●
Ceiling finishes	170,138	154,211	324,349	1.33
Conveying systems	267,796	610,512	878,308	3.60
Specialties	115,942	244,279	360,221	1.48
Fixed equipment	208,833	490,882	699,715	2.87
HVAC	1,080,842	930,545	2,011,387	8.24
Plumbing	303,622	342,785	646,407	2.65
Electrical	734,720	589,120	1,323,840	5.43
Construction total	6,444,353	7,476,190	13,920,543	57.06

Note: Above cost is based on current wages and prices for the zip code area 63102 and includes markups for overhead and profit, taxes and insurance, general conditions, and sales tax on materials. It also includes an inflation factor of 16.0%.

Source: Dodge Building Cost Services (McGraw-Hill Information Systems Company) with Wood & Tower Inc., *1979 Dodge Construction Systems Costs*, McGraw-Hill, New York, 1978.

This is a superficial examination of concrete costs, based on averages. The cost undoubtedly could be further reduced after examining in detail the many concrete framing and floor systems that are available. In this instance allowance has been made for an underfloor duct system to accommodate power and telephone lines. The cost manager advises that, by the time construction is started, it appears there will be a severe shortage of form carpenters that will slow down the rate of construction. The decision is made to stay with structural steel.

The architect has made another study of the exterior curtain wall and the cost manager advises that the estimate can be reduced to $25 per square foot of wall area. The architect so advises the owner who is very reluctant to make the change. The architect agrees the more expensive wall is far better, in performance and appearance.

The wall and floor finish systems have eliminated the marble in all floors except the first and substituted carpet and vinyl wall covering saving $1.65 per square foot.

A revised illumination concept has reduced electrical cost by 80 cents, and the cost manager has made suggestions to the mechanical engineers which should effect some economies in HVAC and plumbing.

Schematic Alternative 3   This is the final schematic design concept that is presented to the owner. It is based on a revised design and earlier explorations made in Alternatives 1 and 2.

In this solution the design has taken advantage of the rolling site, and all dining facilities have been moved to the ground floor, which was the former basement level; the dining area now opens up to a terrace at grade level. Although the site plan was completely revised to do this, the design now eliminates the service elevator, and access to and from the kitchen area is greatly simplified.

ASMEC, after long discussions with the cost manager, made final decisions for the schematic design, resulting in the cost estimate shown in Table 9-6.

The final square-foot cost of $54.54 was made possible by these decisions:

1.   Move dining facilities to grade level.
2.   Use structural steel frame.
3.   Use better curtain wall at $28/sq ft.
4.   Reduce amount of interior partitions still further.
5.   Omit freight elevator.
6.   Adjust specialties and fixed equipment.
7.   Reduce cost of HVAC and plumbing systems.

TABLE 9-6

SCHEMATIC COST ESTIMATE NO. 3

Description	Labor, $	Material, $	Total, $	$/sq ft
Foundations	75,161	47,227	122,388	0.50
Floors on grade	24,901	25,521	50,422	0.21
Superstructure	1,065,591	2,025,629	3,091,220	12.67 ●
Roofing	25,747	29,627	55,374	0.23
Exterior walls	832,462	1,487,491	2,319,953	9.51 ●
Partitions	363,888	686,831	1,050,719	4.31 ●
Wall finishes	86,686	95,694	182,380	0.75
Floor finishes	161,486	413,053	574,539	2.35
Ceiling finishes	170,138	154,211	324,349	1.33
Conveying systems	244,626	561,805	806,431	3.31 ●
Specialties	90,942	194,279	285,221	1.17 ●
Fixed equipment	183,833	440,882	624,715	2.56 ●
HVAC	949,124	927,148	1,876,272	7.69 ●
Plumbing	321,995	292,783	614,778	2.52 ●
Electrical	734,720	589,120	1,323,840	5.43
Construction total	5,331,300	7,971,301	13,302,601	54.54

Note: Above cost is based on current wages and prices for the zip code area 63102 and includes markups for overhead and profit, taxes and insurance, general conditions, and sales tax on materials. It also includes an inflation factor of 16.0%.

Source: Dodge Building Cost Services (McGraw-Hill Information Systems Company) with Wood & Tower Inc., *1979 Dodge Construction Systems Costs,* McGraw-Hill, New York, 1978.

The final cost estimate, exclusive of site work details but with a lump-sum allowance, now looks like this:

Construction cost	$13,302,601
Site work allowance	400,000
	$13,702,601
Construction contingencies @ 3%	411,078
Total	$14,113,679

In round numbers this is close enough to the budget for the schematic design phase. Further reductions are to be expected in the later stages. The important thing to remember about this schematic design is that it was initiated knowing that costs were on the high side, and concluded with the sure knowledge that the architect was in range of the right figure. When the designer develops more information and details about the building, the level of confidence in the cost estimate will be even higher.

ARRIVING AT A DESIGN-COST SOLUTION

In the design development phase, the final schematic concept is firmed up and completed. Floor-to-floor heights have been reduced from 13′ 0″ to 12′ 6″. Architectural and engineering systems are set and principal components selected. This is final design and it must be frozen; in broad terms, no changes are to be made during the construction documents stage; the details only may be shifted about and refined.

In the design development cost estimate shown in Table 9-7, the only significant change in the cost estimate for the building has been in the partition system. Some of the partitions eliminated in the schematic solution had to be restored. The cost of the building has now increased to $55.06 a square foot. This is a great disappointment and extreme care must be taken to pull these costs down in the construction document phase.

The architect is still not out of trouble; the site costs that have now been established are based on drawings and specifications rather than a lump-sum allowance. Landscaping is extensive, a fountain has been added, and placing the dining facility at grade required retaining walls and more excavation.

The total cost estimate now shapes up like this:

Construction cost	$13,430,751
Site work	$ 690,000
	$14,120,751
Construction contingencies @ 3%	$ 423,622
Total	$14,544,373

The total construction cost is still more than a half million dollars over the budget. But the architect can enter into the next phase, knowing that 4 or 5 percent can be taken out of this total if architectural detailing is watched carefully and the engineering systems closely monitored. The cost manager's participation and guidance is essential as the work moves ahead.

DESIGN COST ANALYSIS

Since the office building has been completely programmed and its architectural and engineering systems set in their final configurations, we can now say again: Program + design = cost.

TABLE 9-7

DESIGN DEVELOPMENT COST ESTIMATE
(dollars)

Description	Labor, $	Material, $	Total, $	$/sq ft
Foundations	75,161	47,227	122,388	0.50
Floors on grade	24,901	25,521	50,422	0.21
Superstructure	1,065,591	2,025,629	3,091,220	12.67
Roofing	25,747	29,627	55,374	0.23
Exterior walls	832,462	1,487,491	2,319,953	9.51
Partitions	405,888	794,981	1,200,869	4.92●
Wall finishes	86,686	95,694	182,380	0.75
Floor finishes	161,486	413,053	574,539	2.35
Ceiling finishes	170,138	154,211	324,349	1.33
Conveying systems	244,626	561,805	806,431	3.31
Specialties	90,942	184,279	275,221	1.13●
Fixed equipment	183,833	428,882	612,715	2.51●
HVAC	949,124	927,148	1,876,272	7.69
Plumbing	321,995	292,783	614,778	2.52
Electrical	734,720	589,120	1,323,840	5.43
Construction total	5,373,300	8,057,451	13,430,751	55.06

Description	Quantity	Unit	Labor, $	Material, $	Total, $
General site work					
Clear site	1	LP SM	30,000	20,000	50,000
Excavation	1	LP SM	25,000	25,000	50,000
Bituminous paving	1	LP SM	75,000	100,000	175,000
Walks	1	LP SM	13,000	17,000	30,000
Retaining walls	1	LP SM	12,000	18,000	30,000
Fountain	1	LP SM	9,000	11,000	20,000
Landscaping allowance	1	LP SM	50,000	100,000	150,000
Site drainage	1	LP SM	40,000	60,000	100,000
Site electrical	1	LP SM	20,000	30,000	50,000
Miscellaneous site work	1	LP SM	17,000	18,000	35,000
			291,000	399,000	690,000
Site work total			291,000	399,000	690,000

Note: Above cost is based on current wages and prices for the zip-code area 63102 and includes markups for overhead and profit, taxes and insurance, general conditions, and sales tax on materials. It also includes an inflation factor of 16.0%.

Source: Dodge Building Cost Services (McGraw-Hill Information Systems Company) with Wood & Tower Inc., *1979 Dodge Construction Systems Costs,* McGraw-Hill, New York, 1978.

TABLE 9-8

CONSTRUCTION COST TRAIL

(dollars per square foot)

	1	2	3	4	5	Decision summary 5
	Program, $	*Schematic design, $*			*Design development, $*	
Foundations	0.59	[0.50]	✓	✓	✓	0.50
Floors on grade	0.20	[0.21]	✓	✓	✓	0.21
Superstructure	13.72	12.67	13.63	[12.67]	✓	12.67
Roofing	0.10	[0.23]	✓	✓	✓	0.23
Exterior walls	11.27	9.51	8.50	[9.51]	✓	9.51
Partitions	7.82	5.29	✓	4.31	[4.92]	4.92
Wall finishes	0.71	2.19	[0.75]	✓	✓	0.75
Floor finishes	2.16	2.60	[2.35]	✓	✓	2.35
Ceiling finishes	1.68	[1.33]	✓	✓	✓	1.33
Conveying systems	3.43	3.60	✓	[3.31]	✓	3.31
Specialties	3.32	1.48	✓	1.17	[1.13]	1.13
Fixed equipment		2.87	✓	2.56	[2.51]	2.51
HVAC	9.94	8.24	✓	[7.69]	✓	7.69
Plumbing	3.15	2.65	✓	[2.52]	✓	2.52
Electrical	6.56	6.23	[5.43]	✓	✓	5.43
Total	63.65	59.60	57.06	54.54	[55.06]	55.06
Site work						2.83

Table 9-8 illustrates how cost control has been applied during the five program and design stages we have just gone through. The first column is a display of the program estimate, and the second column shows the first schematic estimate. The subsequent columns show where costs were changed from the preceding alternatives. A check mark indicates no change. In this way an overview is given of the trade-offs that are possible within each system. ASMEC has made decisions and the client has made decisions. Final system decisions are shown in boxes that locate just when and where they were made. The Design Development Estimate is recapped in the last column and is the final decision summary that closes out that phase of the work.

The task of following the cost trail of each building system through all its changes and studying the implications of each computer printout is tedious and taxes one's patience. Architects generally don't enjoy this constant auditing and adjusting, but there is no need for them to do it. Once the architect knows the principles of cost control, it becomes the province of the cost manager to perform the mechanics.

159

This design cost analysis of the Valley Headquarters Office Building will now proceed to the final working-drawing and specification stage.

FINALIZING THE DETAILS OF DESIGN AND COST

It is during the construction document phase that the cost manager shifts from estimating construction costs by building systems to the detailed quantity take-off method. Beginning when the working drawings are about half finished and continuing until the drawings and specifications are almost complete, the cost manager itemizes all quantities and cost of labor and materials by building trades, just as the contractor does. This detailed analysis is translated into building system costs and other information arrays that will be useful to the architect during the bidding and construction periods.

Table 9-9 is a final construction cost estimate, summarizing costs by building systems. This summary is in the same form as the others, except that site work is now included in the construction total, and the costs for mechanical and electrical systems are broken down into subsystem and component costs.

The summary can be scanned for its principal differences from the design development cost estimate. The building costs have now been cut below $55 a square foot to $53.26, and when the site work is included the construction costs for the entire project was $55.78. The total project cost now reads:

Construction costs	$13,610,785
Construction contingencies @ 3%	408,324
Total	$14,019,109

That final figure is right on the target budget of $14 million. At this point it might be said that the author is suspect, that he set up a fictitious budget and then proceeded to adjust and juggle figures until they came out where he wanted them. Not so. The budget is realistic for a real office building, and the author adjusted and juggled *the design* until their costs came out where he wanted them. That is exactly what ASMEC should do on every project: adjust the design and cost simultaneously, control both until they give best value, and then finalize the solution.

The computer printouts seen here are a small fraction of the inches and inches of paper thickness (and computer hours) required to arrive at the final answer. The cost manager at Wood and Tower worked with the author over a period of several weeks, as systems, subsystems, and components were traded off, revised, taken out, or reinserted.

TABLE 9-9

FINAL CONSTRUCTION COST ESTIMATE BY BUILDING SYSTEMS

Description	Labor, $	Material, $	Total, $	$/sq ft
	Site work			
General site work	193,148	195,550	388,698	1.59
Roads, walks, and parking	53,543	53,441	106,984	0.44
Site plumbing	21,382	23,927	45,309	0.19
Site electrical	19,842	30,167	50,009	0.20
Site lighting	9,294	15,913	25,207	0.10
Site work total	297,209	318,998	616,207	2.53
	Office building			
Foundations	81,359	56,581	137,940	0.57
Floors on grade	25,845	31,026	56,871	0.23
Superstructure	950,405	1,942,623	2,893,028	11.86
Roofing	23,830	36,273	60,103	0.25
Exterior walls	408,714	1,832,116	2,240,830	9.18
Partitions	414,871	808,745	1,223,616	5.01
Wall finishes	80,740	105,701	186,441	0.76
Floor finishes	132,341	379,144	511,485	2.10
Ceiling finishes	166,737	158,380	325,117	1.33
Conveying systems	242,131	569,142	811,273	3.32
Specialties	60,373	105,477	165,850	0.68
Fixed equipment	121,299	257,115	378,414	1.55
HVAC	111,619	330,892	442,511	1.81
Hot water system	98,190	210,980	309,170	1.27
Chilled water system	25,810	203,745	229,555	0.94
Air distribution system	360,409	572,116	932,525	3.82
Fuel systems	6,890	20,756	27,646	0.11
Plumbing	115,000	252,200	367,200	1.50
Domestic water system	18,542	26,635	45,177	0.19
Sanitary drainage	12,831	12,184	25,015	0.10
Storm drain system	13,971	21,424	35,395	0.15
Fire protection	6,509	13,802	20,311	0.08
Plumbing fixtures	28,185	92,537	120,722	0.49
Sprinkler system	87,056	73,874	160,930	0.66
Secondary service	23,329	69,305	92,634	0.38
Branch circuits	174,872	89,199	264,071	1.08
Lighting fixtures	112,693	463,129	575,822	2.36
Motor and control work	41,983	52,354	94,337	0.39
Communications systems	139,297	78,278	217,575	0.89
Miscellaneous electrical	1,854	41,160	43,014	0.18
Building total	4,087,685	8,906,893	12,994,578	53.26
Construction total	4,384,894	9,225,892	13,610,785	55.78

Source: Dodge Building Cost Services (McGraw-Hill Information Systems Company) with Wood & Tower Inc., *1979 Dodge Construction Systems Costs,* McGraw-Hill, New York, 1978.

The project is now ready to go out for bids. Let us review other cost data that is now available in many other forms.

GROUP SYSTEM SUMMARY

Once the cost manager has the array of all labor and material costs for the building stored in computer memory, that information can be called out in many forms.

Table 9-10 presents the building systems arranged in groups. All estimates will now show the site work system included in total construction costs.

TABLE 9-10

GROUP SYSTEM SUMMARY

Description	Labor, $	Material, $	Total, $	$/sq ft
Site work				
General site work	193,148	195,550	388,698	1.59
Roads, walks & parking	53,543	53,441	106,984	0.44
Site plumbing	21,382	23,927	45,309	0.19
Site electrical	19,842	30,167	50,009	0.20
Site lighting	9,294	15,913	25,207	0.10
Total	297,209	318,998	616,207	2.53
Architectural & structural				
Foundations	81,359	56,581	137,940	0.57
Floors on grade	25,845	31,026	56,871	0.23
Superstructure	950,405	1,942,623	2,893,028	11.86
Roofing	23,830	36,273	60,103	0.25
Exterior walls	408,714	1,832,116	2,240,830	9.18
Partitions	414,871	808,745	1,223,616	5.01
Wall finishes	80,740	105,701	186,441	0.76
Floor finishes	132,34	379,144	511,485	2.10
Ceiling finishes	166,737	158,380	325,117	1.33
Total	2,284,842	5,350,589	7,635,431	31.29
Specialties & equipment				
Conveying systems	242,131	569,142	811,273	3.32
Specialties	60,373	105,477	165,850	0.68
Fixed equipment	121,299	257,115	378,414	1.55
Total	423,803	931,734	1,355,537	5.56
HVAC				
HVAC	111,619	330,892	442,511	1.81
Hot water system	98,190	210,980	309,170	1.27
Chilled water system	25,810	203,745	229,555	0.94

HVAC (Cont.)			
Air distribution system	360,409	572,116	932,525	3.82
Fuel systems	6,890	20,756	27,646	0.11
Total	602,918	1,338,489	1,941,407	7.96
Plumbing			
Plumbing	115,000	252,200	367,200	1.50
Domestic water system	18,542	26,635	45,177	0.19
Sanitary drainage	12,831	12,184	25,015	0.10
Storm drain system	13,971	21,424	35,395	0.15
Fire protection	6,509	13,802	20.311	0.08
Plumbing fixtures	28,185	92,537	120,722	0.49
Total	195,038	418,782	613,820	2.52
Process plumbing			
Sprinkler system	87,056	73,874	160,930	0.66
Total	87,056	73,874	160,930	0.66
Electrical			
Secondary service	23,329	69,305	92,634	0.38
Branch circuits	174,872	89,199	264,071	1.08
Lighting fixtures	112,693	463,129	575,822	2.36
Motor & control work	41,983	52,354	94,337	0.39
Communications systems	139,297	78,278	217,575	0.89
Miscellaneous electrical	1,854	41,160	43,014	0.18
Total	494,028	793,425	1,287,453	5.28
Construction total	4,384,894	9,225,891	13,610,785	55.78

Source: Dodge Building Cost Services (McGraw-Hill Information Systems Company) with Wood & Tower Inc., *1979 Dodge Construction Systems Costs,* McGraw-Hill, New York, 1978.

With this grouping of system costs and with the subtotal costs for the mechanical-electrical work, it is quite simple for ASMEC to trace subsystem and component costs *as a broad picture* during design cost analysis.

SYSTEM COMPONENT ANALYSIS

The next sequence of cost information in going from the general to the specific is shown in Table 9-11, *System Component Analysis.*

Where the group system summary gave a broad picture of each building system, component analysis gives a *detailed picture.* Table 9-11 shows the cost and quantities of materials for each of the components of three building systems: the superstructure, roofing, and exterior walls.

It is information like this made available to ASMEC that permits the design team to use value analysis during the construction document phase. Each line item must be examined for value as well as cost, and there are many pages of line items, particularly in the mechanical-electrical systems.

TABLE 9-11

SYSTEM COMPONENT ANALYSIS

Description	Total cost, $ dollars	Quantity	Unit	$/unit
Superstructure				
Struct steel columns, beams, girts	1,343,660	1,270	tons	1,058.00
Spray-on fireproofing	174,005	209,000	sq ft	0.83
Cellular metal deck, 3″	791,567	224,000	sq ft	3.53
Flat slab forms	12,732	4,000	sq ft	3.18
Slabs, mesh reinforcement	94,789	228,000	sq ft	0.42
Slab, reinforcement	4,241	7,300	lbs	0.58
Slab, concrete	230,569	2,812	cu yd	81.99
Steel trowel floor finish	102,390	224,000	sq ft	0.46
Stairs, steel pan w/conc	56,697	550	riser	103.09
Landing, steel pan w/conc	37,054	1,600	sq ft	23.16
Stair rail, raked, double pipe	16,832	750	ln ft	22.44
Corrugated galv deck, 20 GA	25,092	20,000	sq ft	1.25
Insulated at penthouse floor	3,400	4,000	sq ft	0.85
Total	2,893,028			
Roofing				
Polystyrene insulation	18,000	20,000	sq ft	0.90
Built-up roofing	18,692	20,000	sq ft	0.93
Flashing	3,163	950	ln ft	3.33
Gravel stop w/facia	3,526	710	ln ft	4.97
Wood blocking	1,795	950	ln ft	1.89
Wood cant	1,328	950	ln ft	1.40
Roof walkways	899	95	ln ft	9.46
Roof accessories	12,700	1	item	12,700.00
Total	60,103			
Exterior walls				
Insulated metal siding	18,612	3,180	sq ft	5.85
Exterior block, 8″	10,137	3,050	sq ft	3.32
Curtain wall, complete	2,198,336	78,512	sq ft	28.00
Aluminum entrance, complete	1,856	40	sq ft	46.40
Vehicular doors, rolling steel	1,070	80	sq ft	13.37
Vehicular doors, paint	65	160	sq ft	0.41
Misc. iron doorframe	597	560	lb	1.07
Alum sash	6,860	620	sq ft	11.06
Plate glass, ¼″	3,297	620	sq ft	5.32
Total	2,240,830			

Source: Dodge Building Cost Services (McGraw-Hill Information Systems Company) with Wood & Tower Inc., *1979 Dodge Construction Systems Costs,* McGraw-Hill, New York, 1978.

TABLE 9-12

CREW DAY ANALYSIS

Work activity	Quantity	Unit	Standard crew	Crew days
Superstructure				
Structural steel columns, beams, girts	1,270	tons	1 HE,5 SI,1 OL	334.2
Spray-on fireproofing	209,000	sq ft	1 PS	696.7
Cellular metal deck, 3″	224,000	sq ft	2 SI	711.1
Flat slab forms	4,000	sq ft	3 CP,1 LA	14.4
Slabs, mesh, reinforcement	228,000	sq ft	1 RI	175.4
Slab, reinforcement	7,300	lbs	1 RI	7.9
Slab, concrete	2,812	cu yd	1 LA,2 CM	160.7
Steel-trowel floor finish	224,000	sq ft	1 CM	527.1
Stairs, steel pan w/conc	550	riser	1 HE,3 SI	26.2
Landing, steel pan w/conc	1,600	sq ft	1 SI	57.1
Stair rail, raked, double-pipe	750	ln ft	1 SI	21.4
Corrugated galvanized deck, 20-GA	20,000	sq ft	1 SI	40.0
Insulation at penthouse floor	4,000	sq ft	1 RF	9.5
Roofing				
Polystyrene insulation	20,000	sq ft	1 RF	16.7
Built-up roofing	20,000	sq ft	1 RF	57.1
Flashing	950	ln ft	1 SM	6.3
Gravel stop w/facia	710	ln ft	1 SM	6.6
Wood blocking	950	ln ft	1 CP	5.8
Wood cant	950	ln ft	1 CP	3.7
Roof walkways	95	ln ft	4 CP,1 LA	0.6
Roof accessories	1	item	4 RF	9.9
Exterior walls				
Insulated metal siding	3,180	sq ft	4 SI	7.1
Exterior block, 8″	3,050	sq ft	4 BL,3 LA	5.9
Curtain wall, complete	78,512	sq ft	1 GL,2 SI	713.7
Aluminum entrance, complete	40	sq ft	1 GL,2 SI	0.7
Vehicular doors, rolling steel	80	sq ft	2 SI	0.8
Vehicular doors, paint	160	sq ft	1 PA	0.2
Miscellaneous iron door frame	560	lbs	1 SI	0.8
Aluminum sash	620	sq ft	1 SI	8.9
Plate glass, 1/4″	620	sq ft	1 GL	11.1

Source: Dodge Building Cost Services (McGraw-Hill Information Systems Company) with Wood & Tower Inc., *1979 Dodge Construction Systems Costs,* McGraw-Hill, New York, 1978.

CREW DAY ANALYSIS

Table 9-12 takes the same three building systems we have just examined but this time demonstrates how much labor and which crafts are required to install each component—not how much material.

Taking the quantities of materials shown in Table 9-11, this estimate itemizes the crew days in a way that is unique in cost estimating.

Component analysis plus crew day analysis combine to give a powerful tool for the management of construction. They are useful in processing change orders and monthly requisitions for payment, as well as providing a ready check on whether the project is properly staffed for efficient and speedy construction.

LABOR RESOURCES REQUIRED

Table 9-13 displays the total worker-days required by each of the construction trades to complete the building.

This summary must be used very carefully, as it is based on the national average productivity of one hypothetical worker. Productivity varies by the individual worker, by the trade, by the geographical region and also according to union or nonunion jurisdiction. However, it is use-

TABLE 9-13

LABOR RESOURCES REQUIRED

Craft	Abbr.	Worker-days
Asbestos worker	AW	226.4
Bricklayer	BL	262.2
Carpenter	CP	4,854.8
Cement mason	CM	1,106.2
Electrician	EL	3,371.2
Glazier	GL	725.5
Laborer	LA	2,593.8
Lather	LH	263.0
Oiler	OL	412.8
Operating engineer, hoisting	HE	1,146.3
Operating engineer, excavation	EO	505.5
Painter	PA	154.9
Pipefitter	PF	1,014.9
Plasterer	PS	959.7
Plumber	PL	1,862.6
Reinforcing ironworker	RI	309.6
Roofer	RF	122.9
Sheet metal worker	SM	1,453.3
Structural ironworker	SI	5,826.3
Teamster	TM	42.4
Tile setter	TS	398.6
Waterproofer	WP	20.3
		27,633.2

Source: Dodge Building Cost Services (McGraw-Hill Information Systems Company) with Wood & Tower Inc., *1979 Dodge Construction Systems Costs,* McGraw-Hill, New York, 1978.

ful to know the estimated number of typical worker-days or years required to produce a building. Assuming good weather and continuous employment at 220 worker-days a year, this project would require 126 worker-years.

The Local Public Works Development Act requires this estimate when setting priorities and selecting projects to receive federal funds.

TRADE SUMMARY

The summary presented in Table 9-14 shows cost distribution by construction trades rather than by building systems. This is the traditional, detailed method of preparing cost estimates, using the format set forth in the Uniform Construction Index (UCI). This format will be used by the contractors in preparing their bids, and the successful bidder will submit a schedule of values in similar format to the architect for approval.

It is obvious, however, that, no matter how necessary these cost data may be for bidding and construction, they are of little use to the professional designer. On the other hand, the cost manager must have this information, specific in details and quantities, before it is translated into the cost language of building systems.

TRADE COMPONENT ANALYSIS

Table 9-15 is a page taken at random from many pages that itemize in detail the quantities of each component together with unit and total costs.

The total cost of each component includes both labor and material. For example, under *Roofing and sheet metal* are shown the quantities and the unit and total costs for five separate components, which altogether total $56,081 for these trades. This total is transferred to the *Trade summary*, Table 9-14, where it is apportioned between labor and material.

Remember, it is now, when materials and labor are actually needed, that market conditions in both make themselves felt, often painfully. In the region of the project, extreme shortages can suddenly develop—in cement or pipe fitters or plywood—and costs can rise much faster than the inflation factor that was worked into all our computations. The cost manager alone can stay on top of these aberrations, the architect does not know and does not want to know. The cost manager wants to know and does know: That is the business of cost management.

TABLE 9-14

TRADE SUMMARY

Description	Labor, $	Material, $	Total, $
Concrete paving	11,106	4,729	15,835
Excavating and grading	61,460	93,917	155,377
Demolition	7,500	1,500	9,000
Bituminous paving	30,371	37,964	68,335
Concrete	319,061	355,656	674,717
Waterproofing	4,500	4,064	8,564
Cement finish	110,832	9,406	120,238
Resilient floors	32,277	66,096	98,373
Stone work	23,500	64,250	87,750
Pavers	8,576	8,856	17,432
Elevated floors	13,522	67,694	81,216
Carpeting	56,794	210,849	267,643
Metal siding	4,982	13,630	18,612
Glass and glazing	2,188	1,109	3,297
Sash	1,565	5,295	6,860
Curtain wall	392,929	1,807,263	2,200,192
Metal deck	258,086	558,573	816,659
Roofing and sheet metal	21,754	34,327	56,081
Structural steel	317,500	1,026,160	1,343,660
Miscellaneous iron	36,267	82,114	118,381
Masonry	25,035	13,849	38,884
Carpentry	2,076	1,946	4,022
Lath and plaster	173,657	71,388	245,045
Hollow metal	5,519	8,233	13,752
Hardware	0	8,961	8,961
Acoustical work	98,000	137,200	235,200
Ceramic quarry tile, terrazzo	65,800	54,699	120,499
Painting	26,047	7,526	33,573
Movable partitions	291,715	725,730	1,017,445
Toilet partitions and accessories	7,773	30,777	38,550
Miscellaneous specialties	62,932	92,450	155,382
Overhead doors	282	788	1,070
Dock levelers	530	3,495	4,025
Elevators	242,131	569,142	811,273
Equipment	120,000	253,000	373,000
Landscaping	90,228	65,049	155,277
Fire protection	87,056	73,874	160,930
HVAC	602,918	1,338,489	1,941,407
Plumbing	216,420	442,709	659,129
Electrical	523,164	839,505	1,362,669
Site piping	27,417	29,991	57,408
Insulation	1,424	3,638	5,062
Construction total	4,384,894	9,225,891	13,610,785

Source: Dodge Building Cost Services (McGraw-Hill Information Systems Company) with Wood & Tower Inc., *1979 Dodge Construction Systems Costs,* McGraw-Hill, New York, 1978.

TABLE 9-15

TRADE COMPONENT ANALYSIS

Description	Total Cost, $	Quantity	Unit	$/unit
Metal siding				
Insulated metal siding	18,612	3,180	sq ft	5.85
	18,612			
Glass and glazing				
Plate glass, ¼″	3,297	620	sq ft	5.32
	3,297			
Sash				
Aluminum sash	6,860	620	sq ft	11.06
	6,860			
Curtain wall				
Curtain wall, complete	2,198,336	78,512	sq ft	28.00
Aluminum entrance, complete	1,856	40	sq ft	46.40
	2,200,192			
Metal deck				
Cellular metal deck, 3″	791,567	224,000	sq ft	3.53
Corrugated galvanized deck,				
20-GA	25,092	20,000	sq ft	1.25
	816,659			
Roofing and sheet metal				
Polystyrene insulation	18,000	20,000	sq ft	0.90
Built-up roofing	18,692	20,000	sq ft	0.93
Flashing	3,163	950	ln ft	3.33
Gravel stop, w/facia	3,526	710	ln ft	4.97
Roof accessories	12,700	1	item	12,700.00
	56,081			

Source: Dodge Building Cost Services (McGraw-Hill Information Systems Company) with Wood & Tower Inc., *1979 Dodge Construction Systems Costs,* McGraw-Hill, New York, 1978.

ESTIMATE SUMMARY

This cost analysis is one that an architect rarely sees. Table 9-16 takes a hard look at all those costs other than the bare bones of construction. And they are startling. Some of these represent market conditions reflected in overhead and profit; others, such as taxes and escalation, reflect economic conditions, and insurance and bonds are mechanisms that protect contractors and owners from risks and liabilities. Some of these are fixed and quantifiable at the time of bidding; some are not and require keen assessment and judgment.

TABLE 9-16

ESTIMATE SUMMARY

Description		Labor, $	Material, $	Total, $
Base amounts		3,324,158	7,905,432	11,229,590
Taxes & insurance	22.0%	341,319	0	341,319
Sales tax	5.0%	0	193,584	193,584
Overhead & profit	3.0%	0	0	199,253
				734,156
General contractor				
Bond	1.0%	0	0	30,800
Overhead & profit	12.0%	0	0	320,964
Labor escalation	16.0%	159,593	0	159,593
Material escalation	16.0%	0	209,325	209,325
				720,682
HVAC and plumbing				
Bond	1.0%	0	0	22,576
Overhead & profit	17.0%	0	0	317,586
Labor escalation	16.0%	87,258	0	87,258
Material escalation	16.0%	0	170,405	170,405
				597,825
Electrical				
Bond	1.0%	0	0	12,374
Overhead & profit	17.0%	0	0	174,542
Labor escalation	16.0%	55,987	0	55,987
Material escalation	16.0%	0	85,629	85,629
				328,532
Constructon total, including extended markups				13,610,785
Final total, including nonextended markups				13,610,785

Note: The markup is included in each component extension. The amount is already in the construction total and is shown only for reference.
Source: Dodge Building Cost Services (McGraw-Hill Information Systems Company) with Wood & Tower Inc., *1979 Dodge Construction Systems Costs,* McGraw-Hill, New York, 1978.

The figures made for the Valley Headquarters Office Building show that the sticks and stones of construction cost $11,229,590, and that markups in all categories amount to $2,381,195, or 21% of all labor and materials.

When these items are exposed to view it makes the architect and the engineer consider very carefully how the owner's dollars are expended in their designs. For every dollar spent on the tangibles, one-quarter more is automatically needed to cover the intangibles.

TABLE 9-17

SYSTEM COMPONENT ANALYSIS WITH: QUANTITY CONVERSION TO METRIC AND DOLLAR CONVERSION TO FRENCH FRANC

Description	Total cost, $	Quantity	Unit	$/unit
Superstructure				
Structural steel columns, beams, girts	5,858,356	1,152,119	kg	5.08
Spray-on fireproofing	758,662	19,416	sq m	39.07
Cellular metal deck, 3″	3,451,231	20,810	sq m	165.84
Flat slab forms	55,519	372	sq m	149.24
Slabs, mesh reinforcement	413,279	21,181	sq m	19.51
Slab, reinforcement	18,491	3,311	kg	5.58
Slab, concrete	1,005,279	2,150	cu m	467.57
Steel-trowel floor finish	446,418	20,810	sq m	21.45
Stairs, steel pan w/conc	247,203	550	riser	449.46
Landing, steel pan w/conc	161,553	149	sq m	1,084.25
Stair rail, raked, double pipe	73,391	229	m	320.48
Corrugated galvanized deck, 20-GA	109,393	1,858	sq m	58.88
Insulation at penthouse floor	14,824	372	sq m	39.85
Total	12,613,599			
Roofing				
Polystyrene insulation	78,480	1,858	sq m	42.24
Built-up roofing	81,497	1,858	sq m	43.86
Flashing	13,785	290	m	47.53
Gravel stop w/facia	15,373	216	m	71.17
Wood blocking	7,824	290	m	26.98
Wood cant	5,788	290	m	19.96
Roof walkways	3,916	29	m	135.03
Roof accessories	55,372	1	item	55,372.00
Total	262,035			
Exterior walls				
Insulated metal siding	81,144	295	sq m	275.06
Exterior block 8″	44,204	283	sq m	156.20
Curtain wall, complete	9,584,743	7,294	sq m	1,314.06
Aluminum entrance, complete	8,087	4	sq m	2,021.75
Vehicular doors, rolling steel	4,665	7	sq m	666.43
Vehicular doors, paint	286	15	sq m	19.07
Miscellaneous iron door frame	2,616	254	kg	10.30
Aluminum sash	29,917	58	sq m	515.81
Plate glass, ¼″	14,373	58	sq m	247.81
Total	9,770,035			

Source: Dodge Building Cost Services (McGraw-Hill Information Systems Company) with Wood & Tower Inc., *1979 Dodge Construction Systems Costs,* McGraw-Hill, New York, 1978.

INSTANTANEOUS CONVERSIONS

One of the advantages of using a computer for estimating is being able to convert from U.S. Standard units of measurement to the metric system at the push of a button. The units shown in the metric conversion table in the appendix are all built into the computer estimating program. In the years ahead the construction industry will slowly change to metric, and so will the design professions. The start has already been made.

For those professionals whose projects are located around the world, the computer can automatically convert costs to any foreign currency base at the rate of exchange current on any given day.

Table 9-17 is exactly the same as Table 9-11, except that all units are expressed in the metric system and unit and total costs expressed in French francs, current at the time of this writing.

CHAPTER 10

DESIGN COST ANALYSIS DURING PROGRAM AND DESIGN

The purpose of this chapter and the one following is to demonstrate cost control as of a series of cost-related activities under the direction of the architect, using the resources and advice of a cost manager. The ASMEC design team, of course, is involved in every decision relating to cost, but the architect, as prime contractor, has final responsibility and accountability. When laying out a project, architects draw upon many sources. For example: In designing a large theater or concert hall, there are many guidelines, code references, and checklists that are followed to provide safety for the occupants, excellent sight lines from any seat in the house, comfort for the spectator (through proper width, spacing, and alignment of seats), and finally acoustical perfection. This last can be attained only by engaging a specialist in the very difficult field of acoustics. The architect here is rigorously constrained by technical needs and must not at any time let design considerations override them or the result can be failure. Similarly, the architect in achieving cost control, follows guidelines and checklists, and a specialist should be engaged in the very difficult field of construction cost management. The architect must not, at any time, override these *cost* constraints, or again the result can be failure.

Checklists and cost managers do not control, or even dominate, the design of any project: the architect does. Cost information and checkpoints of application are made available to architects so that they can creatively manipulate design solutions that not only perform well and have outstanding visual and human esthetics, but also can be built within the financial limits imposed on them.

A cost control checklist consists of a sequential series of cost-related activities and decisions performed by ASMEC, the owner, and the contractor during the many phases of a project from start-up, through design and construction, and on to occupancy and operation. These cost activities are not to be confused with any other checklist of professional activities. A cost control checklist is relatively small and is limited to those elements that are directly or indirectly related to the cost of construction. Also, it must be understood, a checklist is just that—a guideline. It is not an exact, "how-to" procedure that assures perfection. Each item on the list must be examined, and, if found relevant to a specific project, modified or adapted to a design-cost solution. Finally, the checklists that will follow are only an aerial map of some difficult terrain; to hold a project on course a navigator will be needed to estimate drift and to take some fine readings—and that is a cost manager.

We have examined the many possible arrangements for having a building designed and having it constructed. And, as with a cost checklist, there is no universal format that fits all design-build conditions. Some assumptions have been established that shape the lists to follow. It is assumed that:

- The owner is a private, nongovernmental entity.
- A small building committee has been formed that can make rapid decisions for the owner.
- An architectural firm that will use outside engineering consultants has been engaged for the project.
- A cost manager will be available for advice at any time during the start-up and programming phases of the work.
- The architect will prepare the building program.
- The design-build process will be a traditional, linear one of program, design, bid, build, and occupy.

- Escalation of construction costs will be high and constant.
- There will be one general contractor, the lowest bidder, who will construct the work.

The checklists based on these assumptions can be easily modified to fit any other set of conditions.

Figure 10-1 shows a matrix of how the cost-related elements of the checklist will be examined under the direction of the architect. This chap-

---

FIGURE 10-1

MATRIX OF COST-RELATED ACTIVITIES

Architect ●→ during | with

	Start-up	Program	Schematic design	Design development	Construction doc.	Bid	Building construction	Post construction
Own staff		X	X	X	X	X	X	X
Cost manager		X	X	X	X	X	X	
Engineers			X	X	X	X	X	X
Owner	X	X	X	X	X	X	X	X
Contractor						X	X	X

Chapter 10 ⟵————⟶ ⟵ Chapter 11 ————————⟶

---

ter will be concerned only with those activities dealing with start-up, programming and design. The following chapter, for the first and only time in this book, will look beyond design and follow through to construction and completion of the work. These latter phases will include construction documents, bidding, construction itself, and postconstruction activities.

Within each phase, the checklist will consider each activity, direct or indirect, that the architect will manage when interacting with ASMEC, the owner, and the contractor. The degree of effort and the timing of interactions will vary within each phase, and from phase to phase. Activities within each box of the matrix are not complete in themselves; they are synergetic, each reinforcing and influencing the other. If the architect's direction of these activities is cogent and timely, then the cost effectiveness of ASMEC will be greater than the sum of its parts.

START-UP PHASE

This phase is critical. Initial understandings between architect and owner set the climate and tone for all events to follow. The architect, after much striving and probably under severe competitive strain, is now anxious to enter into a contract and get under way. The owner, however, has many concerns and will eventually want to have answers to four specific questions: How much will the building cost to construct? When will it be ready for occupancy? What services will the architect provide? What will be the total professional fee? It is best to meet these questions at the outset, if at all possible; if not, then a framework must be constructed where these answers can be found at an early date. The architect must consider the following elements of cost with the owner and also with other principals in the firm.

With the Owner

1. Does the owner have a fixed cost for construction that is not to be exceeded? If so, does the owner have a total project cost pro forma? Is it available?

   Does the owner have in mind a minimum size for the facility to meet foreseeable needs? If so, is this compatible with the stated maximum dollars for construction?

   Does the owner expect the architect to establish the cost of the project? When? After programming? After the design phases? Are there any outside limits to these explorations?

2. Will the method of financing, or locked-in financial constraints, influence design interpretation or predetermine the method of contracting for construction?

   Does the owner have the financial capability to carry the project through to completion? Will payment of the architect's fee be deferred and contingent upon the owner obtaining a financial commitment based on the architect's design? If so, why undertake the commission?

3. Does the owner have a fixed time limit set for occupancy? Or for completion of construction documents ready for bidding? Is there any flexibility in either date? How much?

   If possible, arrive at a general consensus on the design and construction schedules.

4. Stipulate the type of construction contract to be used. Is the architect free to exercise other options to reflect market conditions at the time of bidding? How will this affect the architectural fee?

   Multiple contracts require more time, attention, and office expense than do single, general contracts. Other forms of construction contracts have a marked influence on architectural and engineering production costs and require a different fee structure.

5. Define the scope of professional services to be given under the professional agreement. As a minimum, this will include:
   a. Structural, mechanical, and electrical engineering consultants.
   b. Cost consultant.

   Itemize other services required and when they are needed; these might include interior design, special consultants, or a continuous on-site representative from the architect's office.

6. Receive the owner's approval of all consultants and specialists who will be involved in the project. It is not always necessary, but the owner should be aware of all the professionals engaged by the architect, and approval of them should be a matter of record.

7. Confirm consultant fees beyond routine services. Some projects have special engineering problems requiring additional fees beyond the ordinary. Verify with consultants before setting architectural fee with the owner.

8. Compute an architectural fee adequate to cover defined services and generate a reasonable profit. Architectural and engineering services should be reimbursed at a level commensurate with services of high professional quality and a well-paid staff. Allowances must be made for design contingencies, lag-time, and other aberrations that occur on every job; these costs hover anywhere between 5 and 10 percent. Reasonable profit is hard to define, but reasonable people argue that, on projects without high risk or high technology, reasonable profit lies somewhere between 14 and 18 percent of total in-house expenses plus all outside services.

9. Execute the Owner-Architect Agreement. It is the author's conviction that every architectural firm should have four people of proven ability always on retainer: an attorney, an accountant, an insurance counselor, and a public relations advisor. If the agreement is prepared by the owner, if it has any disturbing clauses, or if it is not routine, have an attorney review it before signing.

10. When discussions on the above items have been concluded, and the agreement is signed, prepare a memorandum of understanding covering these points, and send a copy to the owner. The agreement does not cover all shades of meaning and nuances of understanding; a memorandum can, and it should become the first entry of a continuing record.

With Principals or Partner(s)

1. If the architect has partners or other principals in the firm, an agreement should not be signed until those others have had the opportunity to review and comment on it. All principals know full well that great effort has been expended to get the commission, but having won it, they should pool their knowledge and examine the agreement for flaws. This collective advice is needed, as well as that of the attorney, on all but routine, minor contracts. Months of effort and steady cash flow will be needed to meet a new series of deadlines, and these must be balanced with other commitments in the office.

2. Set a time schedule for all phases of the project.

3. Estimate staff requirements for each phase.

4. Establish office budget to execute commission.

A Hypothetical Start-up Case Study

Following is a communication from a college to an architect announcing the award of a commission to design a library. Every architect would like to receive such an announcement. It is a gem of a commission, the fee is satisfactory, and the architect is to prepare the building program and be responsible for the interior design as well. It is little short of carte blanche. The architects are anxious to see the building committee and get started.

TO: The Architect

FROM: The College

RE: Proposed Library

This is to announce that your firm has been selected to design our new College Library. The following seven statements represent the background for this project, and, with your concurrence, we will instruct our attorney to draw up an agreement which will reflect these conditions.

1. We wish to build a small library to replace the present one on the campus. Our Librarian says she will require about 11,400 square feet net of usable space to meet her needs, and the Director of Physical Plant assures us that $59.00 a gross square foot is ample for the cost of construction, assuming average quality for materials and equipment.

2. We have reserved two acres of land in an ideal location with all required utilities under an adjacent roadway. Since our present central steam plant is taxed to capacity, it will not be available for this project.

3. We want your services to cover a single, general contract for construction, including library stacks and fixed equipment. We also want you to handle the library interiors, for which an allowance of $70,000 has been made to supplement some of the old furnishings we expect to re-use.

4. Further, since we want all services and responsibilities to be under your direction, we want you to take on the programming of the building as well as its design.

5. We expect to pay 7% for architectural services, including all consultants, and will reimburse you in reasonable amounts for programming and interior design.

6. Contracts for all these services will be dated 1 March 19—, and the building must be ready to receive books no later than 1 July 19—, all within 16 months.

7. An anonymous donor has provided us with $1,150,000 which we consider ample for construction and fees. If actual costs exceed this amount, you will be required to reprogram, redesign, and rebid the project until it falls within the budget, at no additional cost to us.

Please confirm this understanding, and be ready to discuss it with the Building Committee within three days.

After reading that memorandum over several times and studying it carefully, it clearly comes through as a bear trap rather than a gem. The owner has stated the size of a building, its quality, and its probable cost per square foot. A furniture allowance has been stipulated together with ample fees provided they all fall within a total cost limitation of $1,150,-000. In addition, a very tight time schedule has been imposed on a design-bid-build operation so the library will be ready for the fall term of the college.

No allowance has been made for construction contingencies or escalation of building prices. The cost consultant advises that another $5 a square foot will be needed for a library of average quality.

The memorandum is very precise in what it says, but it does not hang together as a whole. This will be a very demanding client who is very firm in expressing the conditions for a contract, but the level of quality the client expects to get may not fit the dollars available. A cost consultant must be engaged and that fee added to the architectural fee.

All these figures and constraints must be analyzed quickly. Hard facts must be ready for that meeting with the building committee. If the library is to be held within the set budget, the college must be informed of just what that $1,150,000 will buy. The following memorandum was prepared with one specific recommendation among three proposed alternatives.

TO: The College

FROM: The Architect

RE: Proposed Library

Our preprogram budget analysis, shown on Attachment No. 1, (Table 10-1) indicates that total projected costs for your Library will exceed funding of $1,150,000 by about $82,000. The reasons are:

- The unit cost per gross square foot, for a library of average quality constructed in your particular location, will be close to $64, rather than $59, at today's prices.

- In order to assure that this Project will remain within budget (and not have to be rebid and upset the date for occupancy), we have engaged a cost consultant at a fee of $5,500, which must be added to the normal architectural fee.

- A contingency of 3% must be allowed to cover unforeseeable costs during construction.
- Allowance for escalation of prices over today's building cost index is a mandatory line item in a budget, and it adds significantly to the cost of construction. The current rate of increase is 9 percent per year.

There are three alternatives open to you:

1. *Reduce the quality of the building:* Still enclose the same amount of space, but reduce its quality by $4 a sq ft (to $60) and reduce new furniture allowance by $15,000. The revised budget for this alternative is shown on Attachment No. 2. (Table 10-2)

2. *Reduce programmed space requirements* by at least 1,000 square feet. This will bring the project within range of your budget, but leave you with a facility not much better than your present building. This alternative is not recommended.

3. *Raise additional funds* to supplement those now available.

With your understanding and approval, we are prepared to move ahead on Alternative No. 1. We will generate an austere solution having high functional and esthetic qualities, but doing without some amenities.

Every effort will be made to complete the project by 1 July 19—

The following schedule is needed:

Begin		1 March 19—	Cumulative Time
Complete	programming	15 March 19—	2 weeks
Complete	schematic design	15 April 19—	6 weeks
Complete	design development	15 May 19—	10 weeks
Complete	contract documents	7 July 19—	17 weeks
Complete	bid/award	1 August 19—	5 months
Complete	construction	1 July 19—	16 months

This is a very close schedule for a single design-bid-build contract. It will require that you authorize us to place contracts for fabrication and delivery of structural steel, as well as critical components of HVAC and electrical systems, upon completion of the design development phase. This material will be assigned to the low bidder to prevent any delays in his contract.

We request that the date for completion be set for 1 August 19—, as the Library can still be made operational by mid-September.

A note of caution: Eight of the construction trades have agreements expiring in the Spring of 19—. This could cause delays that no one can control.

TABLE 10-1

COLLEGE LIBRARY PREPROGRAM BUDGET

Building and furnishings
1.	Construction contract (15,000 sq ft gross @ $64.00)		$ 960,000
2.	Interiors contract (lump sum)		70,000

Professional services
3.	Programming (3 × time card costs not to exceed)	$ 5,000	
4.	Architecture and engineering (7% of 1 above)	67,200	
5.	Interiors (lump sum)	7,000	
6.	Cost manager (lump sum)	5,500	
7.	Subtotal		84,700

Miscellaneous
8.	Survey (roads and utilities, on hand)	000	
9.	Survey (topography and trees)	900	
10.	Test borings (lump sum)	1,500	
11.	Subtotal		2,400

Additional costs
12.	Price escalation (up to midpoint of construction—1 + 4 above—11 months @ 9% per year)	84,744	
13.	Construction contingencies (3% of 1 + 4 above)	30,816	
14.	Subtotal		115,560
15.	Total (construction costs and fees)		$1,232,660

When the architect met with the building committee the session proved to be a difficult one. But, at its conclusion, everyone agreed it had been a frank and realistic exchange about the procedures of design and the cost of construction.

First the committee examined the program budget (Table 10-1) which was some $82,000 above available funds. No one disagreed with the architect's estimate for the total gross square footage of the library, but the Director of Physical Plant was visibly upset when told that his figure of $59 a square foot would produce a building of low quality rather than average. (See Table A-3 in Appendix A.) When pressed, he admitted that the planning committee had been carrying that figure for over a year before the Board of Trustees approved construction of the library. Escalation during that year had indeed added another $5 a square foot.

Similarly, no one could disagree with the amounts added for future

TABLE 10-2

REVISED PREPROGRAM BUDGET

Buildings and furnishings			
1.	Construction contract (15,000 sq ft gross @ $60.00)		$ 900,000
2.	Interiors contract (lump sum)		55,000
Professional services			
3.	Programming (3 × time card costs not to exceed)	$ 5,000	
4.	Architecture and engineering (7% of 1 above)	63,000	
5.	Interiors (lump sum)	6,000	
6.	Cost manager (lump sum)	5,500	
7.	Subtotal		79,500
Miscellaneous			
8.	Survey (roads and utilities, on hand)	000	
9.	Survey (topography and trees)	900	
10.	Test borings (lump sum)	1,500	
11.	Subtotal		2,400
Additional costs			
12.	Price escalation (up to mid-point of construction—1 + 4 above—11 months @ 9% per year)	79,448	
13.	Construction contingencies (3% of 1 + 4 above)	28,890	
14.	Subtotal		108,338
15.	Total (Construction costs and fees)		$1,145,238

escalation and construction contingencies. But when the mathematics for these allowances were spread out on paper they were all amazed at the $108,000 figure, or 11 percent of construction costs.

One of the college trustees who served on the building committee strongly protested the extra fee for a cost consultant and insisted that, since the architect's fee was a substantial $67,200, the architect should absorb the extra charge. But the architect held firm, explaining that the estimated net profit for the firm was somewhere between $11,000 and $12,000, and that this would be cut in half if the consultant fee were absorbed.

It made no sense at all to trade a million dollars of liability exposure for a $6,000 bill. Moreover, if the project were to exceed the funds and had to be rebid, the college could not possibly meet its date of occupancy.

A cost consultant was absolutely essential to help keep costs within the budget. If any savings could be made in construction costs, they would be transferred to the interiors allowance, which had been cut back. The architect offered to consolidate fees for all professional services (Items 3-4-5-6) into one lump-sum fee of $83,000, but the consultant fee would not be absorbed.

The building committee next turned to the revised budget (Table 10-2), and the architect went down the list of revisions item by item, explaining how the library could be constructed within the budget, and again the offer was made to combine all professional fees into one lump sum of $78,000.

The librarian, who had been patiently listening to the discussion on how to reduce costs, finally could contain herself no longer. In a low but steely voice she reminded the building committee that for well over a year, the library planning committee had labored to produce a building of which the college could be proud, and now in two hours the quality of construction was to be reduced and the furnishings allowance slashed by over 20 percent. Quality worth $75,000 had been removed from the building and replaced with some fancy economic projections that had absolutely nothing to do with library needs. She demanded that the committee go back to the Board of Trustees and request a delay in the project until another $75,000 could be raised; they would get along with the old library for a while longer. After an awkward silence, the architect reminded the committee of another fact they should consider. The economy could accelerate at a faster rate than at present. Even if it didn't, and it took a year to raise another $75,000, that gain would be wiped out by inflation of construction costs. Therefore, it would be better to proceed at once and maintain the present schedule.

Deliberations proceeded, and, after some uncomfortable moments now and then, the committee made a final decision to have an agreement drawn between the college and the architect based on the revised preprogram budget, not to exceed $1,150,000, with all professional services combined into one lump sum of $78,000, and with the time for occupancy extended by one month, for a total of 17 months.

The conclusion to be drawn from this case study is very simple: If, at the outset of any project, there is any anticipated bad news, the owner should know about it then, rather than later. Bad news includes adverse impacts on cost, quality, or time. The owner must be told the facts realistically, intelligently, and forthrightly. That is design cost analysis at its best.

PROGRAM PHASE

This phase produces the literary design of a building, determines its size and quality, sets date of occupancy, and establishes the range of its construction costs. Final cost delineation will depend on how graphic design interprets the building program. The following cost activities and decisions are required during this phase.

With the Owner

1. Ascertain the limits of authority of the building committee. Can it make final decisions for the owner? Whose signature is required to approve procedures, documents, and building design?

2. Establish a value profile for the project. In broad, general terms, discuss first the level of quality the owner desires, the relationships of the building and its site to the region about it, the public services it will require, and the load it will place on the existing community infrastructure. Does the owner intend to meet only the minimum legal requirements with respect to community and environmental impacts, or shall the design of the facility go beyond this and contribute positively to both, whenever possible? Second, a dialogue is needed to define the quality of all building systems in general terms and set the relative values for low initial construction costs and low annual operating costs.

   Will the owner place any constraints on design esthetics? Is the architect free to generate style and select building materials? Is there an image to be conveyed? Are human esthetics and amenities a consideration? Review the balance between efficiency and ease of maintenance, and warmth of atmosphere and personal comfort.

3. Establish owner requirements. Does the owner have long-range plans beyond the scope of the present project? Will the building be added to? Upwardly or outwardly? Is flexibility or convertibility required? To what degree? What should be the approximate useful life of the building? How much emphasis shall be placed on low life-cycle costs? What particular attitude, if any, does the owner have with respect to developing the lowest possible energy budget?

4. Establish user needs with the building committee, with those directing departments or other group spaces, with individuals working in or using particular rooms, and with those responsible for cleaning

and maintaining all spaces. Set up a building program beginning with the principal parts of building and site, breaking these down to the level of the single units of space, and describing the functional relationships among all the elements. The building program should describe the size, activities and operations, environmental requirements, and specific human needs for each unit of space.

5. Establish time limits for building design and construction. Allowances must be made for unanticipated but inevitable delays caused by lack of decisions and approvals, strikes in the construction trades, shortages of building materials, and stretched-out delivery of manufactured products.

6. Agree on an approximate cost range for a building of the programmed size and quality. Recognize that the accuracy factor at this stage is plus or minus 12 or 13 percent, and that program size and quality may have to be adjusted downward to bring the final design solution within the limits of funds committed for construction.

7. Present to the owner a written Program Report covering the above six items. Receive the owner's written approval and authorization to proceed into the *schematic design* phase.

With Architectural Staff

1. Review all legal restrictions. Examine all zoning laws and building codes; environmental, energy, and safety regulations; and special provisions of art commissions, city planning commissions, and other boards of review. Arrange to file necessary applications and schedule public hearings. Anticipate any impediment that will prevent timely construction of the building.

2. Gather information from the owner, perform background research and investigations, seek out relevant data, and program the building at all levels. In areas of high technology, check out specific program elements with consulting engineers.

3. Generate total net square feet for all programmed units of space. Convert net areas to gross areas of space.

4. Prepare a written Program Report consisting of the following:
   a. Value profile
   b. Owner requirements

    c. Building program based on user needs

    d. Time schedules to design and construct

    e. Construction cost estimate (including escalation but excluding site work)

    f. Project estimate (if required)

With the Cost Manager

1. Review the project background. Discuss the value profile, enumerate owner requirements, and review the quality of the building program.

2. Pinpoint the building location.

3. Establish quality and types of building systems and project probable material selections.

4. Confirm the time allowed to design and construct.

5. Estimate the probable rate of annual escalation.

6. Confirm the ratio of gross to net square feet.

7. Confirm whether the project is to be constructed using union or non-union labor.

8. Reveive advice and guidance from time to time on construction costs. Prepare a program estimate allowing for escalation up to the mid-point of construction, and, if required, a total project estimate.

An Example of Detailed Programming in Canada

The following examples are used to illustrate how one large public-building owner has approached the problem of writing a building program. The Public Works Department of Canada has prepared a building user's manual known as the *Project Brief System*.[1] This is a very knowledgeable and thorough document from which have been extracted a few examples of programming at various levels.

Table 10-3 illustrates a sample criteria sheet for Level 1: Facility Spaces; this illustrates a format that considers the building as a whole and how it relates to its surrounding community. Note that the descriptions

[1]*Project Brief System*, Department of Public Works, Ottawa, Canada, September 1978.·

TABLE 10-3

FACILITY SPACES CRITERIA SHEET

LEVEL 1: FACILITY SPACES
TITLE: 2 NEWTOWN FEDERAL BUILDING

0.1.	The Newtown Federal Building is required to provide space for the Department of Manpower and Immigration, and the Unemployment Insurance Commission. The primary activities will be clerical and processing of large volumes of mail. Parts of the building will also be used for community activities during nonoffice hours. Maximum occupancy 220 persons.	FUNCTIONAL DESCRIPTION
1.1. 1.2.	Massive architectural statements should be avoided in keeping with the local small-scale adjacent built environment. etc.	QUALITATIVE CRITERIA
2.1. 2.2.	The building shall be oriented towards the adjacent municipal buildings. etc.	LOCATIONAL CRITERIA
3.1. 3.2.	The building shall have a minimum net usable area of 30,000 square feet. etc.	QUANTITATIVE CRITERIA
4.1.1. 4.1.2. 4.9.1. 4.9.2.	Structure The structure shall be designed for floor loadings as specified in the National Building Code. (For exception see Unit spaces Numbers 12 and 24). etc. Fire protection Fire protection shall be provided by an ordinary hazard sprinkler system throughout the building, a standpipe system, and fire extinguishers, all in accordance with DPE Mechanical Design Standard MDS-2. etc.	TECHNICAL CRITERIA

Source: *Project Brief System,* Department of Public Works, Ottawa, Canada, September 1978.

are divided into headings of function, quality, location, quantity, and technical information.

Level 2: Group Spaces, combines the cluster and group spaces discussed in Chapter 7. Note that the descriptions shown in Table 10-4 are divided into the same five headings used for Facility Spaces.

TABLE 10-4

GROUP SPACES CRITERIA SHEET

LEVEL 2: GROUP SPACES TITLE: 2 UNEMPLOYMENT INSURANCE COMMISSION OFFICES		
0.1.	The Unemployment Insurance Commission offices will be used primarily for the electronic data processing of insurance claims with some interviewing of claimants. Maximum occupancy 15 employees, 10 visitors.	FUNCTIONAL DESCRIPTION
1.1. 1.2.	The offices shall conform to, and not exceed the standard of quality of other similar offices in this community. etc.	QUALITATIVE CRITERIA
2.1. 2.2.	The offices shall be located adjacent to the main building entrance. etc.	LOCATIONAL CRITERIA
3.1. 3.2.	The offices, which will include unit spaces 1 to 6, shall have a minimum net usable area of 4500 square feet. etc.	QUANTITATIVE CRITERIA
4.0.	(see Unit Space Level for technical criteria which deviate from those at the Building level).	TECHNICAL CRITERIA

Source: Project Brief System, Department of Public Works, Ottawa, Canada, September 1978.

The last criteria sheet deals with unit spaces, or individual rooms, as shown in Table 10-5. The descriptions follow the same format as the two higher levels.

The method of arriving at the information on the criteria sheets is explained in Figure 10-2. User needs are carefully collected at each level and then converted to criteria for each space at that level. The resultant criteria become the "program" for that space. At its best, this represents very careful and detailed programming for complex buildings. However,

TABLE 10-5

UNIT SPACES CRITERIA SHEET

LEVEL 3: UNIT SPACES TITLE: 2 INTERVIEW ROOM		
0.1.	A room in which recipients of unemployment insurance will discuss their job-seeking efforts with an employment officer. Maximum occupancy 3 persons.	FUNCTIONAL DESCRIPTION
1.1. 1.2.	The room shall be conducive to confidential discussion of a personal nature. etc.	QUALITATIVE CRITERIA
2.1. 2.2	The room shall be directly accessible from the main entrance lobby and from the waiting room (unit space 1). etc.	LOCATIONAL CRITERIA
3.1. 3.2.	The room shall have a minimum area of 100 square feet. etc.	QUANTITATIVE CRITERIA
4.4.1. 4.4.2.	Finished floors The floor shall have a sound-absorbing finish. etc.	TECHNICAL CRITERIA

SOURCE: *Project Brief System,* Department of Public Works, Ottawa, Canada, September 1978.

it must be said once again: buildings can be underprogrammed and over-programmed. The architect must judge, for each particular instance, how much consideration and detail is required to define a space properly.

SCHEMATIC DESIGN PHASE

It is during this conceptual stage of design that basic decisions are made. The final schematic design will unalterably set the framework of solution and cost, and it will form a limiting boundary within which all future decisions must be made. Creativity and intuition are turned loose. The design team sifts through many alternatives *in search of that solution* which is most responsive to the building program and which generates best value. A good design decision can simultaneously create a bad cost decision. In order to prevent design decisions with unfavorable cost con-

FIGURE 10-2

CONVERSION OF USER NEEDS TO CRITERIA

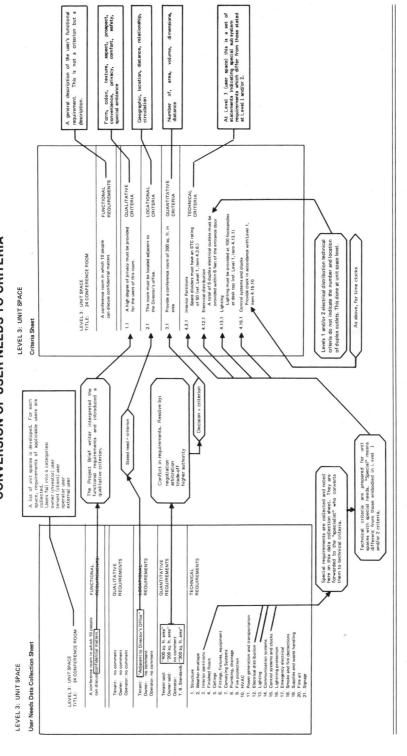

191

sequences, ASMEC must consider all of the following cost activities before the final design is selected.

With Architectural Staff

1. Using the format shown on the endpapers of this book, prepare a control schedule for the project. This must undergo a final scrutiny by the best minds in the office; as much experience as possible should go into its composition. Lag-time must be recognized as a reality when setting hard dates that must be maintained. It must be remembered that, when architects finish their drawings and other documents, it takes additional time for the engineering drawings and documents to catch up. Hard dates should take these discrepancies into account. Set up coordinating procedures that will keep all design professionals on a concurrent basis, or will alert the design team when they are not.

2. Prepare an environmental impact analysis. Satisfy all regulating jurisdictions that quantifiable impacts on the site itself, and the community surrounding it, are acceptable as designed. Confirm that the project control schedule has made an accurate forecast of the time frame required for this activity, as many public hearings and delays can be expected.

3. Establish spatial, functional, and pedestrian and vehicular traffic relationships within the building and on the site.

4. Investigate *design-cost alternatives* as required. In broad terms, test various building configurations, sited in diversified ways. Always search for the optimum solution at least cost. Analyze and compare different building systems for each configuration and set the quality of those systems. Examine each alternative configuration for: (a) total floor area needed to achieve essential functions and relationships; (b) efficiency of the ratio of net to gross floor area; (c) efficiency of ratio of perimeter wall area to gross floor area; and (d) complexity of architectural detailing and of individual building systems.

5. Set energy standards for building configuration, site orientation, and exterior wall and roofing systems.

6. Continuously review project control schedule to assure that all activities are progressing satisfactorily.

7. Using value analysis, select the final schematic design that best

responds to the building program and owner requirements, that minimizes impact on site and community, and that gives best value within the limits of available funds.

8. Run a legal check on the final design and confirm that there are no building code, zoning, or other regulatory violations.

9. Prepare a Schematic Design Report consisting of the following:
   a. Architectural and engineering drawings
   b. Architectural and engineering outline specifications
   c. Alternatives examined and reasons for selecting the final design
   d. Time schedule to design and construct, and form of construction contract
   e. Environmental impact statements
   f. Energy analysis and budget
   g. Construction cost estimate (including escalation but excluding site work)
   h. Construction contingency (3 percent)
   i. Project cost estimate (if required)

10. After approval of the Schematic Design Report by the owner, obtain any approvals and permits from regulating agencies necessary to insure that there will be no future delays to construction. If all clearances cannot be obtained, receive the owner's specific instructions to proceed in spite of the difficultieis.

11. After approval of the Schematic Design Report, it becomes the document on which design development will subsequently be based. No changes to the basic concept illustrated in the report shall be made by the owner without additional compensation.

With the Cost Manager

1. Initiate a construction market survey. Anticipate conditions that might prevail at time of bidding. Investigate the availability of building materials, labor, and fabricated components needed by the schematic design. Using the checklist of market conditions itemized at the end of Chapter 6, prepare a report of favorable and unfavorable conditions that will influence ASMEC as they make design decisions.

2. Confirm the probable rate of annual escalation.

3. Establish ASMEC. Set up formal and informal communication networks among architect, engineers and construction manager. Contin-

uously analyze the various alternatives. Advise which systems produce better value. Analyze floor areas and perimeters of the different alternatives. When compatible with design objectives advise on how to reduce complexities in building systems and architectual detailing.

4. As the ASMEC design sketches appear, prepare cost estimates to accompany each sketch. Investigate cost trade-offs among building systems and material selection.

5. Select final schematic design solution. Prepare a construction-cost estimate including escalation of costs up to the midpoint of construction. Carry outside the construction estimate separate lump-sum line items for site development work and for construction contingencies in the amount of 3 percent.

6. Confirm mechanical and electrical engineering estimates for annual cost of energy consumption.

7. Review and revise project estimates if required.

With All Engineering Consultants

1. Review the architect-engineer agreements. Reach an understanding on the cost of construction, mutual responsibilities and obligations, insurance, time for completing each phase of the project, required staff commitments, and the fee for the work.

2. Execute the agreements.

3. Review the project background. Supply copies of the Program Report. Outline the general principles to be followed in the value profile and owner requirements. Point out specific engineering requirements of the building program and of site development. Supply copies of the Project Control Schedule and describe the procedures expected from ASMEC. Outline the role of the cost manager and the methods of cost estimating, using building systems, subsystems, components, and materials.

4. Establish the quality level of engineering systems.

5. As the architect develops alternative designs, consultants should respond with an alternative engineering system for each design. Seek out best fit at least cost as engineering systems are integrated with architectural systems. Maintain continuous dialogue with construction cost manager. When ASMEC agrees on the final design alterna-

tive, make final selection of engineering systems, verify their costs, and produce final designs.

6. Engineering consultants must prepare schematic drawings and outline specifications. Reports giving the rationale for selecting particular systems and their principal subsystems will also be needed.

7. Verify that all engineering systems meet building code and other applicable regulations.

With the Structural Engineer

1. Analyze subsurface conditions at the site. If conditions are complex engage a soils engineering specialist. Have adequate borings and test pits made to map the depth and composition of various strata, or voids, and the presence and level of water, if any. The idea of avoiding subsurface investigations to save money is not negotiable. Foundations must be accurately designed to meet positively defined soil bearing values. Foundation costs can range from nominal to very expensive; approximate costs must be estimated during schematic design.

2. Examine the design-cost alternatives available in structural steel, reinforced concrete, precast, etc. Hypothesize optimum systems of span-and-grid combinations required by each of the architect's schematic alternatives, as well as the owner's requirements for flexibility, expansibility, and convertibility.

3. Based on the final architectural design alternative, select the final structural system and assemblies of all subsystems. Coordinate with mechanical, horizontal, and vertical distribution subsystems.

4. Position all column and other vertical support assemblies.

With Mechanical and Electrical Engineers

1. Investigate all public utilities and easements under and adjacent to the site. Assure that capacities are adequate and that connections can be made.

2. Analyze all energy requirements for the building and set the energy budget or energy constraints in accordance with federal and state regulations. Determine if energy demand will necessitate the use of non-

depletable energy resources. Estimate annual cost of energy consumption.

3. Lay out general horizontal and vertical distribution subsystems. Coordinate with structural engineer and architect to develop the least dimension for the floor-ceiling sandwich.

4. Locate and roughly size all mechanical spaces and shafts.

With Special Consultants

Analyze building program, outlining the need for special services such as acoustics, traffic and parking, food services, stage lighting, etc. Advise architects and engineers of area, volume, or energy load requirements that they must provide.

With the Owner

1. Maintain continuous communications with the owner, and review progress of all architectural and engineering work periodically. This will vary with the size and complexity of the project and with the owner's personal curiosity or anxiety. Some architects prefer to work in seclusion during the conceptual stage of design and present only the final design solution to the owner. Other architects prefer little or no engineering advice at this time, and still others insist it is too early to develop a serious cost estimate.

   It is recommended here, that, much practice to the contrary, architects seek immediate advice from engineers and other consultants; that they prepare a serious schematic cost estimate with the help of a cost manager; and that they stay in constant communication with the owner. When the final schematic design is presented to the owner, it should be replete with engineering know-how and cost information. If the owner is seeing all this for the first time it may come as a complete surprise. Of course the surprise may delight and please the owner in every way, but more often it results in many changes and revisions or outright rejection, with accompanying delays and loss of goodwill.

2. Present the Schematic Design Report to the owner for approval. Explain that escalation costs have been included in the construction cost estimate, and that the cost of site work is being carried as a separate lump-sum item until the design development phase. Also

explain that a separate line item is being carried for construction contingencies in the amount of 3 percent of all construction costs. This will be used to cover unanticipated extras during construction, such as excavation and foundation problems. It should also be pointed out that it is not possible to produce a perfect set of construction drawings and specifications, and that a contingency item is needed to cover such document inaccuracies.

Review the time schedule to design and construct the building, and confirm the type of construction contract. Explain the steps taken to produce an energy-conscious design and meet the requirements of the energy budget. Review the design procedures followed to minimize impacts on the site and community.

3. Receive written approval of the Schematic Design Report, or make satisfactory revisions to gain such approval.

4. Receive authorization to proceed into the *design development* phase with the understanding that any deviations from the basic schematic design concept will require new designs resulting in changes in building cost, time schedules, and professional fee.

If public agency approvals have not yet been received, this should be brought to the attention of the owner. If there is a possibility of a turndown, perhaps work should be delayed until receipt of approval.

DESIGN DEVELOPMENT

This design phase takes the *schematic design* and hones it, refines it, harmonizes all its building systems, and analyzes all its costs until it *arrives at a final solution* that can be constructed with available funds. ASMEC continues all its control functions as it considers the following cost activities.

With Architectural Staff

1. Constantly compare the development of design documents with the building program, owner requirements, and value profile.

2. Constantly monitor the progress control schedule and assure that architect, engineer, and consultant activities are synchronized.

3. Confirm that site orientation, building configuration, and design of

the exterior walls and roofing systems produce an energy-efficient building.

4. Assign approximate length of useful life to all building systems.

5. Consider the options, and finalize the quality of all building systems. Simplicity of design and low cost of maintenance and operation shall be considered, as well as appearance, performance, and useful life. Seek recommendations from the cost manager.

6. Coordinate and carefully integrate architectural systems with engineering systems.

7. Make extensive area analysis of each group of functionally related spaces in the building. Eliminate all waste space. Design decisions to add space for esthetic reasons or for generous amenities are quite valid if they were acknowledged in the value profile. Additional areas, when added, should always be done with a full knowledge of the costs involved. It must be a conscious cost decision as well as a design decision.

8. Assure that proper consideration has been given to all human and environmental factors in the design of each unit space, as described in the building program.

9. Search the design for conflicts among building systems. Generate dimensional tolerances that will assure a good fit when detailed in the construction documents phase.

10. Using value analysis, complete the final design and compute its construction cost. Initiate a design-cost freeze.

11. Once again, run a legal check to assure that there are no code, zoning, or regulatory violations.

12. Set up a plan for operational procedures and responsibilities that will apply during construction. This must be carefully defined in the general conditions and specifications of the construction agreement.

13. Prepare a Design Development Report consisting of the following:
    a. Project description and facts package
    b. Renderings and models
    c. Architectural and engineering drawings
    d. Architectural and engineering preliminary specifications
    e. Area and volume calculations
    f. Advance plan for construction procedures.
    g. Energy analysis and budget

    h.   Construction cost estimate (including escalation and site work)

    i.   Construction contingency

    j.   Cash flow chart

    k.   Project cost estimate (if required)

    l.   Energy and other operating and maintenance costs (if required)

14.   After approval by the owner, obtain the required approvals and permits from all regulatory agencies.

With the Cost Manager

1.   ASMEC, as a design team, now comes into full operation. As the architect and engineers develop their designs and details up through the final solution, the construction manager continually analyzes the building systems and subsystems and maintains a running total cost of all systems. ASMEC in this development stage is shifting subsystems here and there, making trade-offs to keep total costs within allocated funds.

2.   Since the engineering systems contribute so heavily to construction costs, the construction manager will expect adequate drawings and outline specifications from the engineers in order to estimate the cost of the many subsystems.

    It is the architect's responsibility to actively monitor the engineers and assist the construction manager in this regard. During this phase much effort and many drawings are required from the engineers that usually are deferred to the construction documents stage. Time must be scheduled to develop this information. The accuracy of a cost estimate is directly proportional to the information at hand. System analysis and trade-offs cannot be made until principal subsystem and component designs are at hand.

3.   Monitoring the cost of subsystem design assists in integrating all building systems and helps to eliminate costly extras in the field during construction. For example: The thickness of the floor-ceiling sandwich is initially set by the architect, working with the structural and mechanical engineers. The thinner the sandwich, the less costly the building, particularly if it is high rise. When the sandwich is pinched too thin, it is said that conflicts occur between the structural and HVAC systems. Not so. There is a conflict between *subsystems*, between a beam in the primary or secondary framing subsystems and a duct in the air distribution subsystem. As the construction manager

calls for more information on subsystem design, more of these conflicts emerge, and ASMEC can solve these problems at an early date.

4. Continue to update market conditions expected at the time of bidding, and confirm annual escalation costs.

5. When the building design is finalized, prepare a design development estimate, including cost escalation up to the midpoint of construction and all site development costs. Continue to carry a separate line item for construction contingencies in the amount of 3 percent.

6. Confirm mechanical and electrical engineering estimates for the annual cost of energy consumption.

7. Prepare an annual estimate of costs for maintaining and operating all building systems, if required.

8. Develop a projected cash flow (pay-out) chart of the owner's monthly project construction costs.

With All Engineers and Consultants

1. Constantly review the Progress Control Schedule.

2. Continuously analyze subsystem design, and make trade-offs where suitable. Work with the cost manager, and supply adequate drawings and any information needed to develop a knowledgeable cost estimate. Constantly examine subsystems and components for useful life, quality, complexity, and cost to operate.

3. Using value analysis, finalize all system and subsystem configurations, select principal components, and merge them with architectural and other engineering systems. Resolve subsystems conflicts at the level of detail set for design development.

4. Prepare design development engineering drawings and preliminary specifications.

5. Verify that all engineering systems meet building code and other applicable regulations.

With the Structural Engineer

1. Finalize foundation design.

2. Locate and size all principal assemblies of vertical support, primary framing, secondary framing, and floor decks.

With the Mechanical Engineer

1. Finalize location of vertical and horizontal distribution subsystems. Confirm that clearances with interstitial spaces are adequate for future detailing.

2. Locate and size mechanical spaces, chases, and risers.

3. Develop the concept of an energy-efficient building. Apply the latest technologies of mechanical and electrical conservation, of mechanical and electrical reclamation, and of energy management after the building is in use. Prepare an energy report explaining how these principles will be employed in the building.

4. Confirm the energy budget.

5. Prepare an estimate of the annual cost of energy consumption. Review it with the cost manager.

With the Owner

1. Periodically review the evolving design concept, as well as its accompanying cost analysis, as it approaches its final stage.

2. Confirm projections on useful life.

3. Submit the Design Development Report for approval. Carefully explain each of the elements of the report in detail. It is most important that the owner understand these documents fully. This is the building the owner is buying. This is the final and unalterable graphic design that interprets the building program. This is what it will cost to construct, and this is what it will cost to maintain and operate. Some owners never know what the building will be like until they can walk into it. Renderings and models help, but some owners cannot visualize in three dimensions by looking at two-dimensional, small-scale drawings. It is important therefore, that the owner understand and be comfortable with the design, and be made well aware that it cannot be changed without great expense.

4. Receive written approval of the Design Development Report, or make revisions to gain such approval.

5. Receive authorization to proceed into the construction documents phase.

END OF THE DESIGN STAGE

The design stage truly includes the three phases of program, schematic design, and design development, and together they have set the cost of construction.

Program + Design = Cost

That is what this book has been all about. Its purpose has been to show how to achieve, under the sensitive direction of ASMEC, a cost estimate which is constantly dependable throughout the design stage. That is design cost analysis.

At the end of the design stage, the construction estimate should be within plus or minus 5 percent of its objective. As the project moves into and through the construction documents phase, that 5 percent should be reduced to one or two points on either side of the target. Of course the design process doesn't actually stop until the building is constructed, but *design cost analysis,* as defined here, stopped when the design freeze was initiated at the end of the design development phase.

However, the final chapter will follow the cost trail through to its conclusion in the postconstruction activities.

CHAPTER 11

DESIGN COST ANALYSIS FROM CONSTRUCTION DOCUMENTS TO THE PERIOD OF POSTCONSTRUCTION

This chapter is a checklist of cost-related activities and decisions associated with working drawings and specifications, bidding, construction, and, finally, postconstruction. Put in another way, these are architectural procedures in accountancy—monitoring the owner's construction dollars over a considerable period of time.

Professional responsibilities and liabilities run high during these phases. It is here where errors and omissions are born in the construction documents. It is here where architects have to work with builders with whom they have no contractual relationships. It is here where architects are placed squarely in the middle in all dollar transactions between the owner and the contractor. These are all very precarious positions. Architects must proceed prudently, be aware of pitfalls, and document the financial record thoroughly every step of the way. Following are some guidelines through the fiduciary thicket.

CONSTRUCTION DOCUMENTS PHASE

The end of the design development phase is a significant milestone in the progress of professional activities toward the realization of the project. At this time, final decisions have been made on the

- Esthetics of a design solution
- Scope of program requirements
- Functional relationships of the program
- Level of quality for all building systems
- Areas and volumes of the building
- Construction cost estimate of the project

These defined values and quantities must now be converted into a legal instrument, a set of construction documents, that will be used to construct the building and establish its final cost. Basic design decisions are transformed into working drawings and specifications that graphically convey a message that is instantly readable, biddable, and buildable.

Emphasis now shifts from conceptual design to detailed design; from esthetics to technology; from intuition to management and organization; from artistic sensitivity to hard-headed construction capability.

As this translation of design takes its final form, ASMEC constantly seeks best value at least cost in the minutiae of detail. This is done by maintaining the desired level of quality while giving positive consideration to achieving the

- Least quantity of labor and materials while still satisfying functional requirements
- Least complexity in the assembly of subsystems and components while still satisfying esthetic requirements
- Highest technologies possible during construction and operations
- Practicalities needed to deal with the real world of the marketplace

The following cost-related activities are associated with the construction documents phase.

With Architectural Staff

1. Constantly monitor progress of the work, using the project control schedule, and assure that architect, engineer, and consultant activities are synchronized. Confirm the project completion date.

204

2. Begin architectural drawings and specifications. Coordinate these documents with each other and with the engineering and consultant documents. The greatest source of claims brought against errors- and omissions-insurance is faulty document coordination by design professionals. The importance of coordination cannot be over-stressed; it is the key ingredient of quality control. Review the Quality Assurance Checklist in Figure B-6 in Appendix B.

3. Schedule regular meetings of ASMEC and maintain cost surveillance over all building systems.

4. Constantly compare the development of construction documents with the building program, owner requirements, and value profile.

5. Using value analysis, examine subsystem and component selections for complexity, quality, and useful life. Resolve any conflicts among subsystems.

6. When documents are about 50 percent complete, initiate detailed quantity takeoff with the cost manager.

7. Prepare the final plan for the operational procedures that will apply during construction. Determine what alternatives and cash allowances, if any, will be included in the bidding documents.

8. Complete all drawings and specifications with general and supplemental conditions. Finalize all bidding documents. Check for accuracy and coordinate.

9. Prepare final area and volume calculations.

10. Make a final legal check, and verify that required approvals will be issued by all regulatory agencies having jurisdiction.

11. Prepare a Construction Documents Report, consisting of the following:
    a. Bidding documents:
       (1) Instructions to bidders
       (2) Bid form
       (3) Form of construction agreement
       (4) Conditions of the contract
       (5) Drawings and Specifications
    b. Cost Estimates:
       (1) Cost of construction
       (2) Cost of alternatives
       (3) Construction contingency
       (4) Project cost estimate (if required)

    (5)   Costs of operations and maintenance (if required)

    (6)   Final cash flow chart

  c. Final energy analysis and budget

  d. Area and volume calculations

  e. List of items not in contract

With the Cost Manager

1. Continue to update market conditions expected at the time of bidding, and confirm expected escalation in costs up to the midpoint of construction.

2. From time to time analyze architectural and engineering drawings and specifications. Advise on possible cost reductions or greater value.

3. When the construction documents are approximately 50 percent complete, execute a detailed quantity take-off and prepare a progress estimate as a check against the design development cost estimate.

4. Confer with engineers and consultants. Cooperate and arrive at agreement on the costs of their building systems.

5. Review and estimate the cost of alternatives, if any. Review all cash allowances.

6. Before the completed documents go out for bid prepare a detailed check estimate to serve as final verification of the project budget. This will be included in the final Construction Documents Report. It will also serve as a check on the reasonableness of bids and the schedule of values, when submitted by the contractor.

7. Prepare estimates for construction contingencies, cash flow during construction, and, if required, an estimate of total project maintenance and operations costs.

8. Confirm mechanical and electrical engineering estimates for the annual cost of energy consumption.

With Engineers and Consultants

1. Constantly check the progress of work, using the Project Control Schedule.

2. Using value analysis, examine engineering subsystems and components for complexity, quality, and useful life. Resolve any conflicts among subsystems.

3. Initiate a detailed quantity take-off of engineering systems by the cost manager when the drawings and specifications are approximately 50 percent complete. Cooperate with the cost manager and confirm the estimated costs for all engineering systems and subsystems.

4. Prepare the final engineering drawings and specifications. Check for accuracy with each other and with architectural and other consultant documents.

5. Verify that all engineering systems meet building codes and all other applicable regulations.

6. Prepare the final energy analysis and budget.

7. Prepare the final estimate of the annual cost of energy consumption. Review it with the cost manager.

With the Owner

1. From time to time as progress warrants, review the construction documents and cost estimate with the owner. Keep the owner continuously informed.

2. Review any changes that may have occurred since approval of the Design Development Report, and point out any costs associated with them.

3. Review any alternatives and cash allowances that may become a part of the bidding documents.

4. Review specific items not in the contract. These may be items supplied by the owner or under another contract. Be specific, as these often raise difficult problems as the building nears completion. Items not in the contract do not appear in the construction estimate; they are shown in the project estimate.

5. Receive instructions on insurance, bonds, and amendments or additions to the general conditions of the contract from the owner or the owner's legal counsel or insurance agent.

6. Finalize the form of construction agreement and the procedures to be used during construction.

7. Receive written approval of the Construction Documents Report, or make revisions to gain such approval.

8. Receive approval of the list of bidders. Establish a time interval for bidding. Select the time and place for bid opening.

9. Receive authorization to call for bids.

End of Construction Documents Phase

The Construction Documents Report stands as the final measure of excellence in architectural and engineering services. The design has now crystallized, the documents set forth how the building is to be assembled, and the cost of construction has been estimated. These three elements are essential for professional excellence, and knowledge of costs is indispensable. From this point forward, as implementation shifts from the design professionals to the contractor and subcontractors, not a single move will be made at any time until the cost of that activity is determined and agreed upon.

The next phase to be examined is bidding and award of contract. That phase will be a battle of dollars among contractors, and the lowest proffered cost of construction will capture the prize.

THE BIDDING PHASE

Receiving and processing bids, selecting the low bidder, and executing a construction agreement between the owner and low bidder is serious business. Procedures must be flawless and these can vary from state to state. The essential principle for architects to remember is that they are design professionals and not lawyers. Architects assist and advise owners, and owners, with the help of legal counsel, execute the agreement and arrange for many other details at the same time. It should also be noted that some lawyers engaged by owners are not knowledgeable in the field of building construction and may require some advice and assistance.

The assumption for this checklist stated that the owner was to be a private, non-governmental entity. Public agencies each have their own set of procedures, and bids are opened publicly, with bidders invited to sit in and observe as the bids are opened. The bidding procedures described here are private and closed and represent only the author's opinion about how bidders should be selected and contracts awarded.

On most public works, the bid of any contractor who can supply the necessary bonds will be given consideration. This practice can lead to a diverse set of bidders, some of whom are extremely capable and some not. In private work this is to be avoided at all costs, and, in a list of bidders, the candidates should all be of about the same calibre and have approximately the same capabilities. Union bidders should not be asked to compete with non-union bidders. The size of a project influences selection; bidders should be equipped, experienced, and bonded to handle projects of the given magnitude; they should feel comfortable and competent with the scale of the work. Architects should know, from past personal experience or prequalification, that bidders have the financial capacity and stable organization to carry out the job. A bidder, to whom, as low bidder the owner would not award a contract, should never be on the list. If the number two bidder is a good friend of the owner, or if the number two bidder offers to drop down to a couple thousand dollars below number one, do not advise acceptance. The award should go to the low bidder without exception; have this understanding with the owner when the list is being prepared. When the architect consistently follows this policy over time, contractors come to know it and put forth their best efforts to bid the sharpest price possible.

The following cost-related activities take place during the bidding phase.

With Architectural Staff

1. Hold a prebid conference with the bidders soon after the project has gone out for bids. Make a presentation with models and renderings, and show the overall view of the project not afforded by working drawings. Point out the conditions they will be running into—favorable and unfavorable. Spell out those architectural and engineering measures that can make construction easier, faster, or less expensive. Enumerate procedures the architect will use while the building is under construction. Solicit questions from the bidders.

2. Tabulate bids immediately after opening, and send copies to all bidders.

3. Analyze the bids and alternates. Call in the cost manager, engineers, and consultants if necessary.

With the Owner

1. Receive all bids up to the final hour of acceptance, as stated in the instructions to bidders. The owner may, after advice from the architect, elect to receive bids after that hour because of some irregularity. Bids are being put together almost up to the hour of opening, and someone may be stalled in a traffic jam while trying to make delivery.

A few minutes delay may be found acceptable. However, the architect's advice should usually be to open no bids until they have all been received, and to reject late bids. No bid should be accepted after the others have been opened; word travels fast.

2. Open and examine the bids for conformance with instruction to bidders.

3. Tabulate the bids and alternates. Determine the low bidder. Most times this is simple, occasionally not. If there are no alternates, the low bidder is apparent; if there are alternates, the low bidder will be one of several persons. Alternates should be prioritized in rank order of acceptance, and the bidders should know this. In any event, it is the privilege of all owners to award the contract as they see fit; and it is also the architects' responsibility to insist on high ethical standards as they advise the owners on awards of contract.

4. Notify the low bidder immediately.

5. If rigid cost control procedures have been followed, it will rarely be necessary to negotiate with the low bidder to bring construction costs in line with available funds. If it is necessary, call in the cost manager and negotiate, but only with the low bidder.

6. Assist the owner in preparing the agreement with the low bidder, now called the contractor. The construction documents are identified, signed, and made a part of the agreement. Also assist the owner in arranging for required bonds, filing the waiver-of-liens, photographing the site, and making any other special arrangements peculiar to the project. If there are delays in signing the agreement, advise the owner to write a letter of intent to the contractor, so that he is alerted as to the approximate date when construction forces must be mobilized.

   The bidding document stipulate the maximum time that a contractor's bid remains in effect. Long delays in accepting a bid can work a hardship on the contractor and may even discourage bidding. Execute the agreement as soon as possible.

7. Return to the bidders the bid bonds or other form of security that guaranteed execution of contract. Timing of this will vary. Sufficient protection is afforded the owner if bonds or securities of the three low bidders are held until the agreement is signed, with all others returned soon after bid opening.

8. Notify the owner to place all insurance required by the conditions of the contract.

CONSTRUCTION PHASE

When a project goes into construction the contractor's organization and the architect's organization begin a long series of business interactions, and if the architect has one or more representatives assigned to the site, interaction can be continuous. The owner, however, meets the contractor only rarely. All orders from the owner to the contractor are issued through the architect who is the owner's representative during construction, but there are certain legal limits placed on this authority. There is no contractual link between the architect and contractor, and their roles and relationships are stipulated in the general conditions. If the construction agreement is to be changed in any way, only the owner can order it, not the architect. If construction is to be stopped because of inferior workmanship or for other causes, only the owner can order the work stopped, not the architect. When the building is completed, only the owner can order its acceptance, not the architect.

Since every professional activity will now be associated directly or indirectly with the cost of construction, cost control now becomes more important than ever. The phases of cost estimating are over. Construction will now deal only in hard dollars, not estimates, and the architect assumes the burden of professional liability in the event of a wrong decision or improper activity. In short, the architect can be held personally responsible for the mismanagement of the construction dollar.

The National Society of Professional Engineers, in their *Quality Control Manual*, has this to say about construction administration:

> Construction contract administration may be the most difficult of all professional practice. There is an evolution of an attitude in which society readily accepts litigation to resolve differences which places the A/E in a position of having to practice defensively.
>
> The design professional must be very alert in this area of service. No matter how masterful and ingenious the design professional has been in the design of a project, he can lose everything, including the confidence and respect of his client, if the construction administrator does not clearly understand or discharge his responsibilities.[1]

To prevent this from happening, the general conditions of the contract should be studied in great detail and the following cost-related activities executed carefully:

---

[1]Victor O. Schinnerer & Company, Inc., *Guidelines for Development of Architect/Engineer Quality Control Manual*, National Society of Professional Engineers, 1977, p. 11.

With Architectural Staff and Contractor

1. Receive copies of all required permits from the contractor.

2. Receive, for the owner, all bonds and certificates of insurance required by the construction agreement from the contractor.

3. Write a "proceed" letter to the contractor authorizing the start of work but calling attention to the fact that no subcontractor may enter onto the site until after formal approval by the architect.

4. Provide the contractor with certificates of all insurance carried by the owner on the project.

5. Call for an indoctrination meeting of all principals of the architectural, engineering, and contracting organizations who will have responsibilities during construction. Issue to all parties a Field Procedure Manual outlining the procedures to be followed by all A-E personnel during construction. Develop understandings with the contractors as to how their construction procedures will dovetail with those of the A-E. Under no circumstances should it be suggested or implied that the architect can prescribe the contractor's construction means, methods, techniques, sequences, or procedures. Under no circumstances undertake to specify conditions of human safety at the site. Arrange communication procedures between A-E and contractor, and designate the individual who will be responsible for maintaining them. This indoctrination meeting is important. It is the opening dialogue between designers and builders, and it can establish a cooperative and friendly climate for the long road ahead.

6. Approve subcontractors one by one, as set forth in Chapter 5, using the form in Figure B-2 in Appendix B.

7. Receive shop drawings from the contractor. Process and approve them, as described in Chapter 5 and in Figure B-8 in Appendix B. Remember, shop drawings are not part of the contract documents; they are drawings of convenience to the contractor, prepared by the contractor or subcontractors to show how the design and working drawings are to be implemented.

8. Receive samples of materials and components; review field-constructed samples; process and approve.

9. Review and act upon all specified test reports on architectural materials, equipment, and systems.

10. As conditions and events require, visit the site, schedule meetings,

and observe the status of construction in general and architectural systems in particular. Be alert to any potential hazards or threats to safety. Exercise every "reasonable care, skill and diligence" to determine that the work is being constructed in accordance with the contract documents. Prepare an objective field report in writing for each visit, deal only with the facts and eliminate any personal opinions.

11. If defective work is discovered, it should be called to the attention of the contractor and remedial action requested. Deal only with the contractor and his superintendent on the site. The architect can reject work not in compliance with the contract documents but cannot stop work on any part of the project, except in an extreme, life-threatening emergency.

12. If, as a result of field observations or contract procedures, it can be determined that the project is falling behind the progress schedule, meetings must be arranged between the contractor and the owner where the architect can draw specific attention to this deficiency. If it can be demonstrated that delays have not been caused by the contractor, then the schedule must be revised in terms as favorable to the owner as possible. If delays have been caused by the contractor or subcontractor, then ways must be found to bring the project up to speed. In any event, the owner must be continuously informed about delays.

13. Each month, when the contractor submits an application for payment, ascertain as closely as possible that the quantities of completed work and acquired materials are as stated in the application. Obtain the corresponding information from engineers and consultants on their respective systems. Check against the schedule of values previously submitted; withold items covering any defective work, deduct specified retainage, and issue a certificate of payment to the owner. Check the certificate of payment with the cost manager if necessary. Elaborate projects can generate tricky and complex applications for payment. It must always be clear that the balance yet to be paid the contractor, plus the retained percentage, is sufficient to complete and pay for all remaining construction. Contractors sometimes do go bankrupt, and bonding companies then do have to complete the work; but architects must be able to demonstrate that, to the best of their knowledge and belief, overpayments have never been made.

After the work is 50 percent complete, retainage may or may not be reduced. Consent of surety may be necessary first; if so, the contractor must obtain it.

14. No change can be made in the construction contract that involves cost or time without a formal change order signed by the owner and the architect. The best change order is one that is initiated before the actual change is made. Also, the increase or decrease in dollars or time should be agreed to in advance by owner and contractor. The least satisfactory change order is one where the change is ordered by the owner (on the advice of the architect) and its cost is not known or not agreed to by the contractor, but remains to be settled at some later date. This is done by methods set forth in the general conditions, or perhaps, eventually by litigation. The very worst condition arises when the architect permits a change to be made without a formal change order, or when some necessary additional item is traded—by reducing the cost of something else—without the owner's knowledge. There is no change in contract cost here, but there *is* a change in value.

Perfect contract documents are seldom seen. Change orders are necessary. Three percent of the construction contract has been budgeted for construction contingencies, and a change order is a contingency. The condition that requires a change order should be met head-on as soon as it is discovered; this must not be delayed. Drawings and specifications may be necessary, and the contractor must submit a price for the work. If the price is out of line, then negotiate, using the cost manager if necessary; but arrive at a price, agreed-upon by owner and contractor. Prepare the change order, sign it, have the owner sign it, and order the contractor to make the change. Pay for the change, using contingency funds.

That is the way to process a change order. There will be some bruises along the way; negotiating a change order can be difficult—even shattering. However, the owner's confidence in the architect will not suffer where the owner has been properly briefed in setting up a contingency fund, and understands that extras are to be expected. If the change was caused by an A-E error, certainly the owner should not have to pay a higher fee to the architect because of increased costs. Of course, the owner may press a claim against the architect for the added cost of an error or omission, and that is why most architects carry professional liability insurance. It must be repeated: The greatest single cause for claims against design professionals can be traced to lack of coordination in the construction documents. Better coordination means fewer change orders.

15. When minor alterations or clarifications of the construction documents are needed, that do not change cost or time, a field order can be issued. Field orders can be authorized by the architect on his own initiative.

16. It is absolutely essential to keep meticulous records during the construction phase of the project. Refer to Figure B-7 in Appendix B, and study when to write and when *not* to write for the record.

17. Inspect the building for completeness. Prepare a punch list of work yet to be done or to be corrected.

18. Prepare a certificate of substantial completion with written acceptance by the owner and the contractor.

19. Prepare record drawings based on information supplied by the contractor. Do not use the phrase "as built drawings," which implies that the architect has *precisely located* each part of the work, including those parts buried underground or otherwise not visible—behind partitions and between floors.

20. Receive from the contractor:
    a. Guarantees and bonds
    b. Certificates of inspection
    c. User's manual showing how to operate all equipment and maintain all visible surfaces

21. Make a final inspection of the project with owner, engineers, and consultants.

22. Receive from the contractor:
    a. Release of liens
    b. Consent of surety (if required)
    c. Final application for payment
    d. Statement that all construction work has been completed in accordance with the contract documents

23. Issue the final certificate of payment.

With the Cost Manager

1. Review the schedule of values received from the contractor. Compare line items with those in the final construction documents cost esti-

mate. Make sure that there were no accelerated payments during the first stages of construction. Approve, or request revisions.

2. Review the contractor's progress schedule of the work. Since the architect cannot control or direct the contractor in matters of sequence or procedure, the schedule must be accepted as submitted. The scheduled completion date, however, is stated in the agreement with the owner, and the contractor is obligated to meet it. During construction, the schedule should be updated from time to time to reflect actual history and current realities.

3. Review the projected cash-draw chart received from the contractor to estimate the monthly applications for payment. Compare this with the schedule of values and the progress schedule, and check against the original cash-draw estimate prepared by the cost manager. No changes need be requested nor approvals given. The estimate is approximate only; payments will be based on work actually installed.

4. Review and comment on the contractor's application for payment and the accuracy of change orders when requested by the architect. Assist in negotiations with the contractor if necessary.

With Engineers and Consultants

1. Attend the indoctrination meeting with the architect and the contractor's representatives.

2. Review the capabilities and performance records of subcontractors submitted for approval by the contractor responsible for engineering systems.

3. Review the progress schedule submitted by the contractor, and determine how engineering system schedules are to be interlocked with all other systems.

4. Receive shop drawings from the architect; process and return them. Review engineers' responsibilities and liabilities. Establish procedures to gain approvals in the shortest possible time.

5. Receive samples of materials and components; review field-constructed samples; process and approve.

6. Review and act upon all specified test reports on engineering materials, equipment, and systems.

7. Attend job meetings scheduled by the architect and visit the site as conditions and events require to observe the status of the engineer-

ing systems. If any potential hazards or threats to safety are observed on those parts of the work associated with engineering systems, report the condition to the architect immediately. Prepare an objective field report in writing for each visit, and transmit it to the architect. Deal only with the facts and eliminate any personal opinion.

8. If defective work is discovered, it should be called to the attention of the architect immediately.

9. If, as a result of field observations or contract procedures, it can be determined that the installation of engineering systems is falling behind the progress schedule, that condition and the reasons for it shall be reported to the architect.

10. Review the contractor's monthly application for payment and advise the architect as to whether the amounts requested for engineering systems properly reflect the value of work set in place.

11. Assist the architect in preparing change orders and field orders if any engineering systems are involved.

12. Keep a meticulous record of all engineering transactions with the client, the contractor, and other parties involved in the work.

13. Inspect engineering systems upon completion. Prepare a punch list of work yet to be done or to be corrected.

14. Make a final inspection of the project with the architect and the owner.

With the Owner

1. Keep the owner informed of the progress of work at all times. Invite the owner's representative to attend all regular and special meetings. Send the owner minutes of meetings and other memoranda and correspondence relevant to the owner's interests. Notify the owner if a project is running behind schedule (or might do so later on), and state reasons for the delay.

2. Notify the owner to place all insurance required under the contract.

3. Upon receipt of certificates of payment from the architect, the owner shall make payments to the contractor promptly.

4. Approve change orders when submitted by the architect.

5. Review conditions leading to defective work if it should occur, and take steps to correct them.

6. When the architect issues a certificate of substantial completion, the owner will approve it in writing and share the responsibilities of maintenance, heat, utilities, and insurance, as stated in the certificate.

7. The owner will accompany the architect and engineer when they make final inspection of the building.

8. The owner will receive from the architect all guarantees, certificates, release of liens, and all other relevant material for the owner's files.

9. The architect should assist the owner in arranging for a certificate of occupancy, if necessary.

10. The owner accepts the building and makes final payment to the contractor.

THE POSTCONSTRUCTION PHASE

When defects in a building show up, the owner is quick to call the architect and ask that they be remedied. During the shakedown period, when an owner first occupies a building, many operating difficulties can occur. Some unsophisticated building owners, using untrained personnel can do much to abuse a building, and it is the architect's difficult task to separate mismanagement of operation from actual defects in any of the building systems.

However, defects do occur in materials and workmanship, and reputable contractors and subcontractors correct them when requested if it can be clearly demonstrated that they are at fault. Too often the immediate reaction to a building defect is to say it is a "design error," and, of course, it sometimes is. So, an all-inclusive general statement can be made, going something like this: "When a defect is discovered in a building within a year after substantial completion, it shall be corrected by the party who caused the defect, or, failing that, arbitration or litigation will establish who is responsible and the amount of damages involved."

Contrary to popular opinion, except for certain special guarantees, the general contractor does not guarantee the building for a period of one year after completion; rather, the general conditions require that he correct all defects or any work not installed in accordance with the contract documents that *may be discovered* within that one-year period. A professional inspection may find defects that are quite small and unnoticed by maintenance personnel. Small defects can grow into large defects when unattended.

Accordingly, the architect should perform the following cost-related activities:

With Owner, Architectural Staff, and Engineers

1. Eleven months after substantial completion, schedule a meeting with the owner to evaluate the building and its operations.
2. Inspect architectural and engineering systems, and search for defects in materials, equipment, and workmanship.
3. If defects are found, have the owner give written notice to the contractor, requesting correction.

APPENDIXES
CONTENTS

APPENDIX A

CONSTRUCTION COST INFORMATION

TABLE A-1

LOCALITY ADJUSTMENTS

	GENERAL	LABOR	MATERIAL
ABILENE, TEXAS	0.78	0.65	0.90
AKRON, OHIO	0.93	0.99	0.88
ALBANY, NEW YORK	0.96	0.98	0.93
ALBURQUERQUE, NEW MEXICO	0.85	0.85	0.84
AMARILLO, TEXAS	0.80	0.74	0.86
ANCHORAGE, ALASKA	1.32	1.34	1.29
ATLANTA, GEORGIA	0.85	0.80	0.91
ATLANTIC CITY, NEW JERSEY	0.92	0.97	0.87
AUSTIN, TEXAS	0.79	0.72	0.86
BALTIMORE, MARYLAND	0.93	0.90	0.96
BARTLESVILLE, OKLAHOMA	0.87	0.79	0.95
BILLINGS, MONTANA	0.89	0.87	0.92
BIRMINGHAM, ALABAMA	0.83	0.81	0.85
BISMARK, NORTH DAKOTA	0.89	0.77	1.01
BLOOMINGTON, INDIANA	0.92	0.89	0.95
BOISE, IDAHO	0.89	0.92	0.86
BOSTON, MASSACHUSETTS	1.02	1.03	1.02
BREMERTON, WASHINGTON	0.99	1.05	0.93
BRIDGEPORT, CONNECTICUT	0.93	0.91	0.96
BROWNSVILLE, TEXAS	0.65	0.40	0.90
BUFFALO, NEW YORK	0.98	1.06	0.91
BURLINGTON, VERMONT	0.92	0.89	0.95
BUTTE, MONTANA	1.04	1.12	0.96

Source: Dodge Building Cost Services (McGraw-Hill Information Systems Company) with Wood & Tower Inc., *1979 Dodge Construction Systems Costs,* McGraw-Hill, New York, 1978.

TABLE A-1 (*Cont.*)

LOCALITY ADJUSTMENTS

	GENERAL	LABOR	MATERIAL
CAMDEN, NEW JERSEY	0.96	1.00	0.92
CAMP HILL, PENNSYLVANIA	0.86	0.89	0.83
CHARLESTON, SOUTH CAROLINA	0.75	0.57	0.93
CHARLESTON, WEST VIRGINIA	0.95	0.91	0.99
CHARLOTTE, NORTH CAROLINA	0.74	0.60	0.88
CHARLOTTESVILLE, VIRGINIA	1.00	0.93	1.07
CHATTANOOGA, TENNESSEE	0.84	0.76	0.91
CHERRY HILL, NEW JERSEY	0.96	1.04	0.88
CHEYENNE, WYOMING	0.96	0.90	1.02
CHICAGO, ILLINOIS	0.99	1.01	0.97
CHILLICOTHE, MISSOURI	0.73	0.54	0.92
CINCINNATI, OHIO	0.98	1.02	0.93
CLARKSBURG, WEST VIRGINIA	0.89	0.87	0.90
CLEVELAND, OHIO	1.06	1.10	1.02
COLORADO SPRING, COLORADO	0.90	0.82	0.98
COLUMBIA, SOUTH CAROLINA	0.70	0.49	0.92
COLUMBUS, OHIO	0.95	0.94	0.97
DALLAS, TEXAS	0.86	0.82	0.90
DAVENPORT, IOWA	0.91	0.86	0.96
DENVER, COLORADO	0.88	0.90	0.87
DES MOINES, IOWA	0.96	0.87	1.05
DETROIT, MICHIGAN	1.11	1.06	1.16
DOTHAN, ALABAMA	0.74	0.54	0.95

TABLE A-1 (*Cont.*)

LOCALITY ADJUSTMENTS

	GENERAL	LABOR	MATERIAL
DULUTH, MINNESOTA	0.86	0.90	0.83
EL PASO, TEXAS	0.75	0.67	0.84
ERIE, PENNSYLVANIA	0.89	0.92	0.86
EVANSVILLE, INDIANA	0.92	0.91	0.92
GAINSVILLE, FLORIDA	0.87	0.63	1.12
GARY, INDIANA	0.96	0.98	0.93
HARRISBURGH, PENNSYLVANIA	0.84	0.89	0.79
HARTFORD, CONNECTICUT	0.92	0.95	0.90
HATTIESBURG, MISSISSIPPI	0.76	0.69	0.84
HONOLULU, HAWAII	1.20	1.04	1.36
HOUSTON, TEXAS	0.87	0.86	0.87
INDIANAPOLIS, INDIANA	0.93	0.94	0.93
JACKSON, MISSISSIPPI	0.73	0.68	0.78
JACKSONVILLE, FLORIDA	0.82	0.76	0.88
JEFFERSON CITY, MISSOURI	0.92	0.89	0.94
KANSAS CITY, MISSOURI	0.96	0.97	0.94
LANSING, MICHIGAN	1.00	1.04	0.95
LAS VEGAS, NEVADA	1.05	1.14	0.96
LEXINGTON, KENTUCKY	0.83	0.75	0.91
LITTLE ROCK, ARKANSAS	0.79	0.71	0.87
LOS ANGELES, CALIFORNIA	1.08	1.19	0.98
LOUISVILLE, KENTUCKY	0.89	0.89	0.89
LUBBOCK, TEXAS	0.85	0.74	0.97

TABLE A-1 (*Cont.*)

LOCALITY ADJUSTMENTS

	GENERAL	LABOR	MATERIAL
MADISON, WISCONSIN	0.87	0.89	0.84
MANCHESTER, NEW HAMPSHIRE	0.85	0.78	0.92
MANSFIELD, OHIO	0.81	0.82	0.81
MARSHALLTOWN, IOWA	0.80	0.72	0.87
MEDFORD, OREGON	0.99	1.01	0.98
MEMPHIS, TENNESSEE	0.86	0.83	0.89
MIAMI, FLORIDA	0.84	0.85	0.84
MILES CITY, MONTANA	0.95	0.85	1.04
MILWAUKEE, WISCONSIN	0.98	0.99	0.97
MINNEAPOLIS, MINNESOTA	1.04	0.92	1.16
MOBILE, ALABAMA	0.85	0.83	0.86
MONROE, LOUISIANA	0.84	0.75	0.93
NAPLES, FLORIDA	0.69	0.51	0.88
NASHVILLE, TENNESSEE	0.80	0.72	0.88
NASSAU-SUFFOLK, NEW YORK	1.08	1.15	1.01
NEW ORLEANS, LOUISIANA	0.87	0.85	0.90
NEW YORK CITY, NEW YORK	1.17	1.16	1.17
NEWARK, NEW JERSEY	0.98	1.05	0.91
NORFOLK, VIRGINIA	0.85	0.75	0.95
OKLAHOMA CITY, OKLAHOMA	0.87	0.83	0.92
OMAHA, NEBRASKA	0.98	0.91	1.05
ORANGEBURG, SOUTH CAROLINA	0.66	0.43	0.88
ORLANDO, FLORIDA	0.86	0.76	0.97

TABLE A-1 (*Cont.*)

LOCALITY ADJUSTMENTS

	GENERAL	LABOR	MATERIAL
PASCO, WASHINGTON	0.98	1.00	0.96
PEORIA, ILLINOIS	0.97	0.98	0.95
PHILADELPHIA, PENNSYLVANIA	0.97	0.98	0.96
PHOENIX, ARIZONA	0.95	0.97	0.92
PITTSBURGH, PENNSYLVANIA	1.01	1.08	0.93
PITTSFIELD, MASSACHUSETTS	0.90	0.88	0.93
PORTLAND, MAINE	0.84	0.75	0.92
PORTLAND, OREGON	1.02	1.04	1.00
PRESCOTT, ARIZONA	0.96	0.97	0.95
PROVIDENCE, RHODE ISLAND	0.90	0.88	0.92
RALEIGH, NORTH CAROLINA	0.76	0.61	0.91
RAPID CITY, SOUTH DAKOTA	0.83	0.73	0.93
READING, PENNSYLVANIA	0.93	0.91	0.95
RENO, NEVADA	1.10	1.08	1.12
RICHLAND, WASHINGTON	0.98	1.00	0.96
RICHMOND, VIRGINIA	0.80	0.70	0.89
ROCHESTER, NEW YORK	0.93	0.97	0.89
ROCK SPRINGS, WYOMING	1.04	0.97	1.11
SACRAMENTO, CALIFORNIA	1.12	1.24	1.00
SAINT LOUIS, MISSOURI	1.05	1.06	1.05
SALEM, MASSACHUSETTS	0.97	0.96	0.97
SALISBURY, MARYLAND	0.78	0.58	0.98
SALT LAKE CITY, UTAH	0.90	0.93	0.88

TABLE A-1 (*Cont.*)

LOCALITY ADJUSTMENTS

	GENERAL	LABOR	MATERIAL
SAN ANTONIO, TEXAS	0.78	0.74	0.81
SAN DIEGO, CALIFORNIA	1.07	1.17	0.97
SAN FRANCISCO, CALIFORNIA	1.22	1.31	1.13
SAN JOSE, CALIFORNIA	1.13	1.19	1.07
SAN JUAN, PUERTO RICO	0.85	0.43	1.26
SAVANNAH, GEORGIA	0.82	0.70	0.93
SCHENECTADY, NEW YORK	0.93	0.96	0.90
SEATTLE, WASHINGTON	1.03	1.08	0.99
SELMA, ALABAMA	0.82	0.76	0.88
SHREVEPORT, LOUISIANA	0.85	0.79	0.92
SIOUX FALLS, SOUTH DAKOTA	0.89	0.79	0.99
SPOKANE, WASHINGTON	0.99	1.00	0.98
SPRINGFIELD, ILLINOIS	0.91	0.91	0.91
SPRINGFIELD, MASSACHUSETTS	0.88	0.91	0.86
STAMFORD, CONNECTICUT	0.94	0.88	1.01
SYRACUSE, NEW YORK	0.97	0.96	0.99
TALLAHASSEE, FLORIDA	0.83	0.68	0.98
TAMPA, FLORIDA	1.03	1.01	1.05
TERRA HAUTE, INDIANA	0.93	0.90	0.96
TOPEKA, KANSAS	0.90	0.87	0.93
TRAVERSE CITY, MICHIGAN	0.86	0.84	0.89
TRENTON, NEW JERSEY	0.97	1.02	0.91
TULSA, OKLAHOMA	0.83	0.78	0.89

TABLE A-1 (*Cont.*)

LOCALITY ADJUSTMENTS

	GENERAL	LABOR	MATERIAL
TUSCALOOSA, ALABAMA	0.79	0.73	0.85
TUSCON, ARIZONA	0.96	0.98	0.93
TYLER, TEXAS	0.78	0.63	0.93
WASHINGTON, D.C.	1.01	0.97	1.05
WATERBURY, CONNECTICUT	0.90	0.88	0.93
WICHITA, KANSAS	0.93	0.88	0.97
WILMINGTON, DELAWARE	0.94	0.99	0.89
WILMINGTON, NORTH CAROLINA	0.77	0.57	0.97
WINCHESTER, VIRGINIA	0.93	0.89	0.98
YAKIMA, WASHINGTON	1.00	1.02	0.97
YOUNGSTOWN, OHIO	0.97	1.04	0.90
ZANESVILLE, OHIO	0.95	0.88	1.02
EDMONTON, ALBERTA	0.95	0.97	0.92
HALIFAX, NOVA SCOTIA	0.85	0.69	1.01
MONTREAL, QUEBEC	0.89	0.87	0.91
OTTAWA, ONTARIO	0.96	0.95	0.98
QUEBEC CITY, QUEBEC	0.89	0.86	0.91
REGINA, SASK.	0.91	0.89	0.94
TORONTO, ONTARIO	1.00	1.04	0.96
VANCOUVER, B.C.	0.97	1.08	0.87
WINDSOR, ONTARIO	0.97	1.00	0.94
WINNIPEG, MANITOBA	0.90	0.88	0.92

TABLE A-2

ACCEPTABLE GROSS TO NET AND NET TO GROSS RATIOS FOR VARIOUS BUILDING TYPES

Building type	Gross to net ratio	Net to gross ratio
Administrative	150%	67%
Apartment	156	64
Auditorium	142	70
Bank	140	72
Biology	161	62
Chemistry	170	59
Church	142	70
Classroom	152	66
Courthouse	162	61
Department store	123	81
Dining hall	138	72
Dormitory	154	65
Engineering	164	61
Fraternity	160	63
Garage	118	85
Gymnasium	142	70
Hospital	183	55
Hotel	158	63
Laboratory	171	58
Library	132	76
Office building	125	80
Restaurant	141	70
Science	167	60
Service	120	83
Student union	172	59
Warehouse	108	93

TABLE A-3*

AVERAGE BUILDING COSTS

BUILDING TYPE: SHOPPING CENTERS

BUILDING SYSTEM	LOW AVERAGE $/SF	% TOT	AVERAGE $/SF	% TOT	HIGH AVERAGE $/SF	% TOT
FOUNDATIONS	$ 1.22	6.1%	$ 1.30	5.5%	$ 1.34	4.8%
FLOORS ON GRADE	1.32	6.6	1.42	6.0	1.46	5.2
SUPERSTRUCTURE	3.84	19.1	4.10	17.4	4.24	15.1
ROOFING	0.58	2.9	0.64	2.7	0.66	2.4
EXTERIOR WALLS	3.32	16.5	3.54	15.0	3.80	13.5
PARTITIONS	0.70	3.5	0.76	3.2	0.82	2.9
WALL FINISHES	0.52	2.6	0.56	2.4	1.10	3.9
FLOOR FINISHES	0.90	4.5	0.98	4.2	1.06	3.8
CEILING FINISHES	0.98	4.9	1.06	4.5	2.10	7.5
CONVEYING SYSTEMS	0.0	0.0	0.0	0.0	0.0	0.0
SPECIALTIES	0.56	2.8	0.60	2.5	1.70	6.1
FIXED EQUIPMENT	0.0	0.0	0.0	0.0	0.56	2.0
HVAC	1.64	8.1	2.64	11.2	2.84	10.1
PLUMBING	2.34	11.6	2.50	10.6	2.68	9.6
ELECTRICAL	2.22	11.0	3.44	14.6	3.70	13.2
GROSS BUILDING COST	$ 20.14	100%	$ 23.54	100%	$ 28.06	100%

Source: Dodge Building Cost Services (McGraw-Hill Information Systems Company) with Wood & Tower Inc., *1979 Dodge Construction Systems Costs*, McGraw-Hill, New York, 1978.
*Gross Building Cost in this table is equivalent to Construction Cost as used in this book.

TABLE A-3 (*Cont.*)

AVERAGE BUILDING COSTS

BUILDING TYPE: COMMUNITY HALLS AND CENTERS, SOCIAL CENTERS

BUILDING SYSTEM	LOW AVERAGE $/SF	% TOT	AVERAGE $/SF	% TOT	HIGH AVERAGE $/SF	% TOT
FOUNDATIONS	$ 1.74	5.1%	$ 1.88	5.1%	$ 1.94	4.7%
FLOORS ON GRADE	1.62	4.7	1.74	4.7	1.82	4.4
SUPERSTRUCTURE	6.94	20.3	7.44	20.3	7.68	18.7
ROOFING	1.04	3.0	1.12	3.1	1.16	2.8
EXTERIOR WALLS	5.68	16.6	6.08	16.6	6.52	15.9
PARTITIONS	2.50	7.3	2.68	7.3	2.88	7.0
WALL FINISHES	1.26	3.7	1.36	3.7	1.44	3.5
FLOOR FINISHES	2.02	5.9	2.18	5.9	2.34	5.7
CEILING FINISHES	1.82	5.3	1.96	5.3	2.10	5.1
CONVEYING SYSTEMS	0.0	0.0	0.0	0.0	0.0	0.0
SPECIALTIES	0.26	0.8	0.28	0.8	0.32	0.8
FIXED EQUIPMENT	1.04	3.0	1.12	3.1	3.23	7.9
HVAC	3.24	9.5	3.40	9.3	3.72	9.1
PLUMBING	1.86	5.4	2.02	5.5	2.16	5.3
ELECTRICAL	3.22	9.4	3.44	9.4	3.68	9.0
GROSS BUILDING COST	$ 34.24	100%	$ 36.70	100%	$ 40.99	100%

TABLE A-3 (*Cont.*)

AVERAGE BUILDING COSTS

BUILDING TYPE: CORPORATE OFFICE BUILDINGS

BUILDING SYSTEM	LOW AVERAGE $/SF	LOW AVERAGE % TOT	AVERAGE $/SF	AVERAGE % TOT	HIGH AVERAGE $/SF	HIGH AVERAGE % TOT
FOUNDATIONS	$ 2.72	6.0%	$ 2.88	6.0%	$ 3.08	5.5%
FLOORS ON GRADE	0.66	1.5	0.70	1.5	0.74	1.3
SUPERSTRUCTURE	9.00	20.0	9.14	19.0	9.76	17.6
ROOFING	0.96	2.1	1.04	2.2	1.12	2.0
EXTERIOR WALLS	7.80	17.3	8.04	16.7	9.60	17.3
PARTITIONS	3.28	7.3	3.72	7.7	3.98	7.2
WALL FINISHES	2.50	5.5	2.62	5.5	2.05	3.7
FLOOR FINISHES	1.82	4.0	1.44	3.0	2.10	3.8
CEILING FINISHES	1.22	2.7	1.30	2.7	1.38	2.5
CONVEYING SYSTEMS	0.66	1.5	0.72	1.5	1.30	2.3
SPECIALTIES	0.66	1.5	0.78	1.6	1.50	2.7
FIXED EQUIPMENT	0.76	1.7	0.82	1.7	1.90	3.4
HVAC	6.60	14.6	8.00	16.7	8.70	15.7
PLUMBING	2.76	6.1	3.00	6.3	3.24	5.8
ELECTRICAL	3.70	8.2	3.80	7.9	5.06	9.1
GROSS BUILDING COST	$ 45.10	100%	$ 48.00	100%	$ 55.51	100%

TABLE A-3 (*Cont.*)

AVERAGE BUILDING COSTS

BUILDING TYPE: UNIVERSITY AND COLLEGE CLASSROOM BUILDINGS

BUILDING SYSTEM	LOW AVERAGE		AVERAGE		HIGH AVERAGE	
	$/SF	% TOT	$/SF	% TOT	$/SF	% TOT
FOUNDATIONS	$ 1.72	3.1%	$ 1.82	3.0%	$ 1.88	2.8%
FLOORS ON GRADE	0.74	1.3	0.80	1.3	0.82	1.2
SUPERSTRUCTURE	9.06	16.5	10.78	18.0	11.10	16.4
ROOFING	0.90	1.6	0.98	1.6	1.40	2.1
EXTERIOR WALLS	6.38	11.6	6.84	11.4	7.30	10.8
PARTITIONS	2.84	5.2	3.06	5.1	3.26	4.8
WALL FINISHES	1.62	3.0	1.74	2.9	1.86	2.8
FLOOR FINISHES	1.20	2.2	1.28	2.1	2.02	3.0
CEILING FINISHES	1.18	2.2	1.26	2.1	1.65	2.4
CONVEYING SYSTEMS	0.84	1.5	0.90	1.5	0.96	1.4
SPECIALTIES	1.86	3.4	2.00	3.3	4.00	5.9
FIXED EQUIPMENT	5.32	9.7	5.70	9.5	7.10	10.5
HVAC	9.52	17.4	10.18	17.0	10.90	16.1
PLUMBING	4.60	8.4	4.92	8.2	5.26	7.8
ELECTRICAL	7.04	12.8	7.52	12.6	8.04	11.9
GROSS BUILDING COST	$ 54.82	100%	$ 59.78	100%	$ 67.55	100%

TABLE A-3 *(Cont.)*

AVERAGE BUILDING COSTS

BUILDING TYPE: LABORATORY BUILDINGS

BUILDING SYSTEM	LOW AVERAGE $/SF	% TOT	AVERAGE $/SF	% TOT	HIGH AVERAGE $/SF	% TOT
FOUNDATIONS	$ 2.26	5.2%	$ 2.42	3.8%	$ 2.50	3.7%
FLOORS ON GRADE	0.84	1.9	0.90	1.4	0.92	1.4
SUPERSTRUCTURE	6.20	14.3	10.94	17.1	11.16	16.5
ROOFING	0.96	2.2	1.02	1.6	1.06	1.6
EXTERIOR WALLS	4.36	10.0	6.80	10.6	7.28	10.8
PARTITIONS	3.06	7.1	3.28	5.1	3.52	5.2
WALL FINISHES	1.80	4.1	1.94	3.0	2.06	3.0
FLOOR FINISHES	1.28	2.9	1.36	2.1	1.46	2.2
CEILING FINISHES	1.24	2.9	1.34	2.1	1.44	2.1
CONVEYING SYSTEMS	0.86	2.0	0.92	1.4	0.98	1.4
SPECIALTIES	1.88	4.3	2.02	3.2	2.16	3.2
FIXED EQUIPMENT	3.57	8.2	5.10	8.0	5.46	8.1
HVAC	6.06	14.0	10.76	16.8	11.50	17.0
PLUMBING	3.92	9.0	6.34	9.9	6.78	10.0
ELECTRICAL	5.10	11.8	8.76	13.7	9.36	13.8
GROSS BUILDING COST	$ 43.39	100%	$ 63.90	100%	$ 67.64	100%

TABLE A-3 (*Cont.*)

AVERAGE BUILDING COSTS

BUILDING TYPE: GENERAL HOSPITALS

BUILDING SYSTEM	LOW AVERAGE $/SF	LOW AVERAGE % TOT	AVERAGE $/SF	AVERAGE % TOT	HIGH AVERAGE $/SF	HIGH AVERAGE % TOT
FOUNDATIONS	$ 2.48	3.6%	$ 2.66	3.3%	$ 2.74	3.2%
FLOORS ON GRADE	0.42	0.6	0.44	0.6	0.46	0.5
SUPERSTRUCTURE	9.38	13.6	10.06	12.6	10.36	12.1
ROOFING	1.42	2.1	1.54	1.9	1.58	1.8
EXTERIOR WALLS	6.06	8.8	6.48	8.1	6.68	7.8
PARTITIONS	6.96	10.1	7.44	9.3	7.66	8.9
WALL FINISHES	1.64	2.4	1.76	2.2	2.82	3.3
FLOOR FINISHES	1.70	2.5	1.82	2.3	2.88	3.4
CEILING FINISHES	1.60	2.3	1.72	2.2	2.14	2.5
CONVEYING SYSTEMS	2.10	3.0	2.24	2.8	2.32	2.7
SPECIALTIES	1.70	2.5	1.80	2.3	1.86	2.2
FIXED EQUIPMENT	4.66	6.8	4.98	6.2	5.14	6.0
HVAC	12.18	17.7	15.28	19.1	16.75	19.6
PLUMBING	7.00	10.1	8.82	11.0	9.08	10.6
ELECTRICAL	9.70	14.1	12.78	16.0	13.16	15.4
GROSS BUILDING COST	$ 69.00	100%	$ 79.82	100%	$ 85.63	100%

TABLE A-3 (*Cont.*)

AVERAGE BUILDING COSTS

BUILDING TYPE: COLLEGE AND UNIVERSITY LIBRARIES

BUILDING SYSTEM	LOW AVERAGE $/SF	LOW AVERAGE % TOT	AVERAGE $/SF	AVERAGE % TOT	HIGH AVERAGE $/SF	HIGH AVERAGE % TOT
FOUNDATIONS	$ 2.12	3.5%	$ 2.26	3.5%	$ 2.32	3.2%
FLOORS ON GRADE	0.86	1.4	0.90	1.4	0.94	1.3
SUPERSTRUCTURE	12.74	21.2	13.54	21.2	13.94	19.4
ROOFING	1.16	1.9	1.22	1.9	1.28	1.8
EXTERIOR WALLS	8.10	13.5	8.58	13.4	10.30	14.4
PARTITIONS	2.78	4.6	2.96	4.6	3.16	4.4
WALL FINISHES	0.98	1.6	1.06	1.7	1.12	1.6
FLOOR FINISHES	1.40	2.3	1.48	2.3	1.58	2.2
CEILING FINISHES	1.86	3.1	1.98	3.1	2.12	3.0
CONVEYING SYSTEMS	0.96	1.6	1.02	1.6	1.08	1.5
SPECIALTIES	2.18	3.6	2.26	3.5	4.20	5.9
FIXED EQUIPMENT	5.88	9.8	6.42	10.1	8.13	11.3
HVAC	9.62	16.0	10.22	16.0	10.94	15.2
PLUMBING	3.54	5.9	3.78	5.9	4.04	5.6
ELECTRICAL	5.82	9.7	6.20	9.7	6.62	9.2
GROSS BUILDING COST	$ 60.00	100%	$ 63.88	100%	$ 71.77	100%

TABLE A-4

AVERAGE SYSTEM COSTS

The following table gives the low, mid and high costs for the system types shown. The next section provides detailed costs for individual systems.

By showing the range of costs associated with each type of system, this table enables the user to quickly conceptualize the cost implications of his selection. All units are expressed in costs per square foot.

EXTERIOR WALLS	L	M	H
Wood Siding	1.56	2.20	2.56
Galvanized Iron Siding	1.99	2.26	2.78
Aluminum Sidings	2.07	2.37	2.82
6" to 12" CMU	2.54	2.88	3.82
Stuccos on Sheathing/Lath/Insul.	2.81	3.02	3.56
Galbestos	3.12	3.70	4.61
Aggregate Finished Plywood	3.15	3.21	3.55
4" to 12" Adobe Brick	3.56	4.44	5.64
8" to 12" CMU Split Faced	3.69	4.30	4.87
Porcelain Enamel Panel	3.76	4.40	4.97
4" to 10" Poured Concrete	5.33	6.31	6.90
Curtain Walls - Metal & Glass	5.93	14.14	21.34
10" Brick Cavity (w & w/o insul.)	7.26	7.66	8.25
8" to 12" Face & Common	6.90	8.25	9.95
Precast Concrete Panel	7.82	9.82	10.93
6" to 12" Glass Block	9.22	9.65	10.17
Stone & CMU Backup	11.80	12.20	12.60

Source: Dodge Building Cost Services (McGraw-Hill Information Systems Company) with Wood & Tower Inc., *1979 Dodge Construction Systems Costs,* McGraw-Hill, New York, 1978.

TABLE A-4 (*Cont.*)

AVERAGE SYSTEM COSTS

ROOFING	L	M	H
Elastomeric Membrane	1.25	1.60	1.86
Corrugated Galvanized Iron	1.38	2.56	2.76
Asphalt Shingle	1.65	1.76	1.79
Wood Shingle	1.52	2.10	2.12
Asbestos Shingle	1.83	1.89	2.63
Concrete Tile	2.33	2.38	2.43
Slate Tile	2.62	3.24	4.30
Clay Tile	3.06	3.30	3.64
Copper, Lead, Terne Roofs	3.76	5.36	6.16
Built-Up Roofing On:			
Wood Decking	1.28	1.33	1.69
Lightweight & Insulating Concrete	1.86	2.22	2.33
Poured Gypsums & Tees,			
Formboards	2.20	2.46	2.74
Metal Deckings	2.37	2.88	3.71
Precast Concrete Decking	3.72	5.82	7.04

PARTITIONS			
Drywall	1.48	1.95	2.63
Drywall Laminated	2.32	2.57	2.69
4" to 8" CMU	2.28	2.49	3.07
Drywall Shaft (Elevator)	2.20	2.50	2.63
Lath & Plaster	2.91	3.59	3.78
CMU (Sound Block)	2.82	3.05	3.37
Gypsum Block & Plaster	3.40	3.52	3.79
CMU & Gypsum Board (Furred)	3.78	4.05	4.34
6" to 12" CMU & Glazed CMU	3.54	5.77	6.26
CMU Plastered	3.73	4.33	4.63
12" CMU (Unreinf. - Reinf.)	3.85	4.56	5.85
Struct. Glazed Tile (1 & 2 Faced)	5.42	6.68	7.72
6" to 12" Poured Concrete	5.69	7.14	8.16
Struct. Glazed Tile & Plaster (One side)	6.00	6.50	7.64
Glazed Tile, Gypsum Board (Studs)	6.42	8.12	8.41
Concrete Wall & Gypsum Board			
(Furred)	6.20	6.42	6.87
Glazed Brick & Tile	9.05	11.41	11.66

TABLE A-4 (*Cont.*)

AVERAGE SYSTEM COSTS

	L	M	H
INTERIOR WALL FINISHES			
Painting	.26	.33	.45
Staining	.41	.47	.53
Papering	.57	1.76	2.22
Fabrics, Composition Covering	.92	2.07	2.96
Elastomeric Coating	1.91	2.24	2.37
Plastic Panel	1.40	1.50	1.65
Pre-Finished Plywood	1.67	2.21	4.01
Plaster	2.00	2.14	2.35
Ceramic	2.58	3.13	3.36
Solid Wood Boards	3.05	3.13	4.29
Brick Veneer	3.30	3.50	3.83
Slate	9.20	9.80	10.77
Marble & Travertine	11.13	13.17	16.17
Limestone	11.08	12.15	13.97
Granite	14.00	19.11	21.47
FLOOR FINISHES			
Hardeners, Liquids & Aggregate	.20	.72	1.16
Resilient	.73	1.72	2.78
Carpeting	1.05	1.78	2.72
Concrete Topping	1.11	1.46	1.61
Creosote Block	1.69	1.85	2.00
Fir & Pine	2.00	2.47	2.55
Ceramic & Quarry	2.32	3.69	5.04
Oak	2.34	2.86	3.00
Maple	2.46	3.60	4.54
Terrazzo	3.44	4.37	5.02
Brick Paving	3.93	4.60	4.91
Computer Pedestal (Raised)	6.35	6.80	7.09
Slate	6.98	7.50	8.06

TABLE A-4 (*Cont.*)

AVERAGE SYSTEM COSTS

CEILINGS	L	M	H
Rubbed Concrete Ceiling	.25	.81	.93
Gypsum Board (Direct & Hangers)	.82	1.57	1.76
Acoustical (Direct & Suspended)	1.31	4.59	7.14
Plaster (Direct & Suspended)	1.53	2.20	2.36

TABLE A-5

SUPERSTRUCTURE

PRIMARY AND SECONDARY FRAMING ASSEMBLIES

In determining the cost of the framing system, the cost of primary framing (that framing which transfers the load to the columns) is considered separately from the secondary framing (that framing which transfers segments of the deck load to the primary framing).

NOTE: Bearing walls, where used, take the place of the primary framing assembly (including columns) and directly support the secondary framing assembly.

PRIMARY FRAMING ASSEMBLY AVERAGE COSTS

One or more of the framing assemblies listed below are used in practically all modern structural systems.

The cost figures given below are based on an average 30-foot column spacing and 100 pounds per square foot live load. Following these are tables that adjust for the relative cost effect of varying spans and floor loads for each of the framing assemblies.

Source: Dodge Building Cost Services (McGraw-Hill Information Systems Company) with Wood & Tower Inc., *1979 Dodge Construction Systems Costs,* McGraw*Hill,* New York, 1978.

TABLE A-5 (*Cont.*)

SUPERSTRUCTURE

PRIMARY FRAMING ASSEMBLIES AVERAGE COSTS
BASED ON 30' COLUMN SPACING (900 SF OF AREA)

	LABOR	MATERIAL	TOTAL
WOOD TIMBER			
24" x 24" Fir (1440 BF)	$520.00	$ 820.00	$1,340.00
Cost/SF	0.57	0.92	1.49
LAMINATED WOOD			
16" x 30" Laminated (1200 BF)	420.00	1,440.00	1,860.00
Cost/SF	0.47	1.60	2.07
STRUCTURAL STEEL			
18 WF 96 Beam (2880 LBS)	360.00	806.00	1,166.00
Cost/SF	0.40	0.89	1.29
REINFORCED CONCRETE			
Concrete Beam 12" x 24"			
Formwork (150 SF)	340.00	159.00	499.00
Concrete (2.22 CY)	60.00	88.00	148.00
Reinf. Steel (1200 LBS)	270.00	285.00	555.00
Finishing (beam top) (30 SF)	8.00		8.00
	678.00	532.00	1,210.00
Cost/SF	0.75	0.59	1.34

TABLE A-5 (*Cont.*)

SUPERSTRUCTURE

	LABOR	MATERIAL	TOTAL
PRECAST CONCRETE			
12" x 20" Concrete Beam	$395.00	$914.00	$1,309.00
Cost/SF	0.43	1.02	1.45
POST-TENSIONED CONCRETE			
Concrete Beam 12" x 24"			
Formwork (150 SF)	354.00	153.00	507.00
Concrete (2.22 CY)	61.00	85.00	146.00
Post-Tensioned Cables	244.00	280.00	524.00
Finishing Beam Top (30 FT)	8.00		8.00
	$667.00	$518.00	$1,185.00
Cost/SF	0.74	0.57	1.31

TABLE A-5 (*Cont.*)

SUPERSTRUCTURE

PRIMARY FRAMING ASSEMBLIES

SPAN FACTORS
(COLUMN SPACING)

SPAN	16'	20'	25'	30'	40'	50'	80'
Wood Timber	0.4	0.5	0.7	1.0			
Laminated Wood	0.4	0.5	0.9	1.0	1.7		
Structural Steel	0.6	0.7	0.8	1.0	1.5	2.0	3.5
Reinforced Concrete		0.7	0.8	1.0	1.9	2.5	
Precast Concrete		0.7	0.8	1.0	1.9	2.5	
Post-Tensioned Conc.		0.8	0.9	1.0	1.7	2.3	5.0

LOAD FACTORS

LIVE LOAD	50#	60#	80#	100#	125#	150#	200#
Wood Timber	.50	.60	.80	1.0	1.3	1.6	
Laminated Wood	.50	.60	.80	1.0	1.3	1.6	
Structural Steel	.70	.75	.85	1.0	1.2	1.4	1.7
Reinforced Concrete	.75	.80	.90	1.0	1.2	1.4	1.8
Precast Concrete	.75	.80	.90	1.0	1.2	1.4	1.8
Post-Tensioned Conc.	.80	.85	.90	1.0	1.2	1.4	1.8

TABLE A-5 (*Cont.*)

SUPERSTRUCTURE

COMPARATIVE COST CALCULATIONS

Any framing assembly average cost may be adjusted to meet the requirements of a given building by the formula:

ADJUSTED PRIMARY FRAMING ASSEMBLY COST

EQUALS

AVERAGE FRAMING ASSEMBLY COST X SPAN FACTOR X LOAD FACTOR

If the same framing assembly is used throughout the building, the adjusted framing assembly cost is equivalent to the framing cost per gross square foot for the building.

EXAMPLE

Steel frame building, 30-foot span, 125# live load. Adjusted Primary Framing Cost = 1.29 x 1.0 x 1.2 = 1.55 per sq. ft.

If different framing assemblies are used in the same building, each applicable adjusted framing assembly cost must be converted to reflect its percentage involvement in the building under consideration, by use of the formula given on the next page.

SUPERSTRUCTURE

CONVERTED PRIMARY FRAMING ASSEMBLY COST

EQUALS

ADJUSTED FRAMING ASSEMBLY COST X PERCENTAGE INVOLVEMENT

For a particular building, the framing cost per gross square foot is equal to the sum of the converted assembly costs for both the primary and secondary framing.

TABLE A-5 (*Cont.*)

SUPERSTRUCTURE

SECONDARY FRAMING ASSEMBLIES AVERAGE COSTS

    The cost figures given below are based on a 30-foot span and 100 pounds per square foot live load. Following these are tables that adjust for the relative cost effect of varying spans and floor loads for each of the framing assemblies.

	LABOR	MATERIAL	TOTAL
PLYWOOD JOIST (30 SF OF AREA)			
Double 2 x 4 top and bottom 3/4" ply web 12" oc	$ 21.00	$ 41.00	$ 62.00
Cost/SF	0.70	1.36	2.06
WOOD TIMBER (120 SF OF AREA)			
6" x 18" Fir 48" oc	100.00	154.00	254.00
Cost/SF	0.83	1.28	2.11
LAMINATED WOOD (120 SF OF AREA)			
6" x 18" Laminated 48" oc 270 BF	86.00	297.00	383.00
Cost/SF	0.72	2.47	3.19
TRUSS JOIST (60 SF OF AREA)			
16" Member 24" oc	28.00	89.00	117.00
Cost/SF	0.47	1.48	1.95

TABLE A-5 (*Cont.*)

SUPERSTRUCTURE

	LABOR	MATERIAL	TOTAL
BAR JOIST (60 SF OF AREA)			
16 H 5 approx. 234 LBS 24" oc	$ 30.00	$ 83.00	$113.00
Cost/SF	0.50	1.38	1.88
STRUCTURAL STEEL (225 SF OF AREA)			
16 B 31 930 LBS 7'6" oc	126.00	330.00	456.00
Cost/SF	0.56	1.47	2.03
REINFORCED CONCRETE (180 SF OF AREA)			
8" x 18" Conc. Beam 6' oc			
Formwork 110 SF	180.00	68.00	248.00
Concrete 1.1 CY	37.00	43.00	80.00
Reinf. Steel (268 LBS)	62.00	59.00	121.00
Finish Beam Top (20 SF)	5.00		5.00
	284.00	170.00	454.00
Cost/SF	1.58	0.94	2.52
PRECAST CONCRETE (180 SF OF AREA)			
6" x 18" Conc. Beam 6' oc	108.00	220.00	328.00
Cost/SF	0.60	1.22	1.82

TABLE A-5 (*Cont.*)

SUPERSTRUCTURE

SECONDARY FRAMING ASSEMBLIES

SPAN FACTORS

SPAN	16'	20'	25'	30'	40'	50'	80'
Plywood Joists	0.4	0.5	0.7	1.0			
Wood Timber	0.4	0.5	0.7	1.0			
Truss Joists	0.5	0.6	0.7	1.0	1.5	2.3	
Bar Joists		0.6	0.8	1.0	1.4	1.8	3.0
Structural Steel		0.6	0.8	1.0	1.5	2.0	3.5
Reinforced Concrete		0.7	0.8	1.0	1.8	2.3	
Precast Concrete		0.7	0.8	1.0	1.9	2.5	

LOAD FACTORS

LIVE LOAD	50#	60#	80#	100#	125#	150#	200#
Plywood	0.5	0.6	0.8	1.0			
Wood Timber	0.5	0.6	0.8	1.0			
Truss Joists	0.6	0.7	0.8	1.0	1.3	1.5	
Bar Joists	0.6	0.7	0.8	1.0	1.3	1.5	
Structural Steel	0.7	0.8	0.9	1.0	1.2	1.4	1.7
Reinforced Concrete	0.7	0.8	0.9	1.0	1.2	1.4	1.8
Precast Concrete	0.8	0.8	0.9	1.0	1.2	1.4	1.8

TABLE A-5 (*Cont.*)

SUPERSTRUCTURE

COMPARATIVE COST CALCULATIONS

Any framing assembly average cost may be adjusted to meet the requirements of a given building by the formula:

ADJUSTED SECONDARY FRAMING ASSEMBLY COST

EQUALS

AVERAGE FRAMING ASSEMBLY COST X SPAN FACTOR X LOAD FACTOR

If the same framing assembly is used throughout the building, the adjusted framing assembly cost is equivalent to the framing cost per gross square foot for the building.

EXAMPLE

Building with bar joist secondary framing, 25-foot span, 150# live load.

Adjusted Secondary Framing cost = 1.91 x 0.8 x 1.5 = 2.29 per gross square foot.

If different framing assemblies are used in the same building, each applicable adjusted framing assembly cost must be converted to reflect its percentage involvement in the building under consideration, by use of the formula given on the next page.

TABLE A-5 (*Cont.*)

SUPERSTRUCTURE

CONVERTED SECONDARY FRAMING ASSEMBLY COST

EQUALS

ADJUSTED FRAMING ASSEMBLY COST X PERCENTAGE INVOLVEMENT

For a particular building, the framing cost per gross square foot is equal to the sum of the converted assembly costs for both the primary and secondary framing.

TABLE A-6

EXTERIOR WALLS
MASONRY

112101 6" BLOCK	LABOR	MAT'L	TOTAL
CONCRETE MASONRY UNIT	1.42	0.65	2.07
HORIZONTAL REINFORCING	0.08	0.12	0.20
MORTAR	--	0.14	0.14
TOOL JOINTS & CLEAN	0.08	0.05	0.13
TOTAL PER SQ FT	1.58	0.96	2.54

112102 8" BLOCK	LABOR	MAT'L	TOTAL
CONCRETE MASONRY UNIT	1.64	0.77	2.41
HORIZONTAL REINFORCING	0.08	0.12	0.20
MORTAR	--	0.14	0.14
TOOL JOINTS & CLEAN	0.08	0.05	0.13
TOTAL PER SQ FT	1.80	1.08	2.88

112103 8" BLOCK & STUCCO	LABOR	MAT'L	TOTAL
CONCRETE MASONRY UNIT	1.64	0.77	2.41
HORIZONTAL REINFORCING	0.08	0.12	0.20
MORTAR	--	0.14	0.14
TOOL JOINTS & CLEAN	0.09	0.05	0.14
STEEL LATH	0.27	0.24	0.51
STUCCO	0.71	0.38	1.09
PAINT 3 COATS	0.27	0.14	0.41
TOTAL PER SQ FT	3.06	1.84	4.90

112104 12" BLOCK	LABOR	MAT'L	TOTAL
CONCRETE MASONRY UNIT	2.32	0.99	3.31
HORIZONTAL REINFORCING	0.08	0.15	0.23
MORTAR	--	0.14	0.14
TOOL JOINTS & CLEAN	0.09	0.05	0.14
TOTAL PER SQ FT	2.49	1.33	3.82

Source: Dodge Building Cost Services (McGraw-Hill Information Systems Company) with Wood & Tower Inc., *1979 Dodge Construction Systems Costs,* McGraw-Hill, New York, 1978.

TABLE A-6 (*Cont.*)

EXTERIOR WALLS
MASONRY

```
112109                           LABOR     MAT'L     TOTAL
12" BRICK & BLOCK WALL

   4" FACE BRICK                 2.35      1.02      3.37
   WALL TIES                     0.06      0.07      0.13
   8" CONCRETE MASONRY UNIT      1.60      0.77      2.37
   HORIZONTAL REINFORCING        0.08      0.13      0.21
   MORTAR                         --       0.16      0.16
   TOOL JOINTS & CLEAN           0.20      0.05      0.25
                                -----     -----     -----
   TOTAL PER SQ FT              4.29      2.20      6.49


112110                           LABOR     MAT'L     TOTAL
12" BLOCK (SOLID) LOAD BEARING

   CONCRETE MASONRY UNIT         3.26      1.09      4.35
   WALL TIES                     0.06      0.07      0.13
   HORIZONTAL REINFORCING        0.08      0.16      0.24
   MORTAR                         --       0.14      0.14
   TOOL JOINTS & CLEAN           0.09      0.05      0.14
                                -----     -----     -----
   TOTAL PER SQ FT              3.49      1.51      5.00


112111                           LABOR     MAT'L     TOTAL
8" MODULAR BRICK & TILE

   4" MODULAR BRICK              2.25      1.22      3.47
   4" TILE BACKUP                1.66      0.66      2.32
   WALL TIES                     0.06      0.07      0.13
   MORTAR                         --       0.13      0.13
   TOOL JOINTS & CLEAN           0.20      0.05      0.25
                                -----     -----     -----
   TOTAL PER SQ FT              4.17      2.13      6.30
```

TABLE A-6 *(Cont.)*

EXTERIOR WALLS
MASONRY

```
112116                              LABOR      MAT'L      TOTAL
10" STONE & BLOCK

   2" CUT STONE                     4.55       4.50       9.05
   8" CONCRETE MASONRY UNIT         1.60       0.77       2.37
   STONE TIES                       0.06       0.07       0.13
   HORIZONTAL REINFORCING           0.08       0.12       0.20
   MORTAR                            --        0.17       0.17
   TOOL JOINTS & CLEAN              0.23       0.05       0.28
                                   -----      -----      -----
   TOTAL PER SQ FT                  6.52       5.68      12.20



112117                              LABOR      MAT'L      TOTAL
10" BRICK & TILE CAVITY WALL

   4" MODULAR BRICK                 2.25       1.22       3.47
   4" TILE BACKUP                   1.66       0.66       2.32
   WALL TIES                        0.06       0.07       0.13
   MORTAR                            --        0.14       0.14
   TOOL JOINTS & CLEAN              0.20       0.05       0.25
                                   -----      -----      -----
   TOTAL PER SQ FT                  4.17       2.14       6.31



112118                              LABOR      MAT'L      TOTAL
10" BRICK CAVITY WALL-INSULATED

   4" MODULAR BRICK                 2.25       1.22       3.47
   4" MODULAR BRICK                 2.25       1.22       3.47
   WALL TIES                        0.06       0.07       0.13
   MORTAR                            --        0.14       0.14
   INSULATION                       0.07       0.13       0.20
   TOOL JOINTS & CLEAN              0.20       0.05       0.25
                                   -----      -----      -----
   TOTAL PER SQ FT                  4.83       2.83       7.66
```

TABLE A-6 (*Cont.*)

EXTERIOR WALLS
CONCRETE

113101 4" CONCRETE WALL	LABOR	MAT'L	TOTAL
CONCRETE	0.17	0.55	0.72
FORM & STRIP	2.86	0.64	3.50
REINFORCING	0.25	0.26	0.51
RUB CONCRETE	0.54	0.06	0.60
	-----	-----	-----
TOTAL PER SQ FT	3.82	1.51	5.33

113102 6" CONCRETE WALL	LABOR	MAT'L	TOTAL
CONCRETE	0.23	0.83	1.06
FORM & STRIP	2.86	0.64	3.50
REINFORCING	0.26	0.32	0.58
RUB CONCRETE	0.54	0.06	0.60
	-----	-----	-----
TOTAL PER SQ FT	3.89	1.85	5.74

113103 8" CONCRETE WALL	LABOR	MAT'L	TOTAL
CONCRETE	0.30	1.09	1.39
FORM & STRIP	2.86	0.64	3.50
REINFORCING	0.36	0.46	0.82
RUB CONCRETE	0.54	0.06	0.60
	-----	-----	-----
TOTAL PER SQ FT	4.06	2.25	6.31

113104 10" CONCRETE WALL	LABOR	MAT'L	TOTAL
CONCRETE	0.38	1.34	1.72
FORM & STRIP	2.86	0.64	3.50
REINFORCING	0.48	0.60	1.08
RUB CONCRETE	0.54	0.06	0.60
	-----	-----	-----
TOTAL PER SQ FT	4.26	2.64	6.90

TABLE A-6 (*Cont.*)

EXTERIOR WALLS
PRECAST CONCRETE

```
115101                              LABOR     MAT'L     TOTAL
PRECAST WALL PANEL

   FLAT WITH PLAIN FINISH           1.53      5.72      7.25
   METAL TIES                       0.06      0.09      0.15
   CAULKING                         0.28      0.14      0.42
                                    -----     -----     -----
   TOTAL PER SQ FT                  1.87      5.95      7.82


115102                              LABOR     MAT'L     TOTAL
PRECAST WALL PANEL

   FLAT WITH SANDBLAST FINISH       1.53      6.45      7.98
   METAL TIES                       0.06      0.09      0.15
   CAULKING                         0.28      0.14      0.42
                                    -----     -----     -----
   TOTAL PER SQ FT                  1.87      6.68      8.55


115103                              LABOR     MAT'L     TOTAL
PRECAST WALL PANEL

   FLAT WITH EXPOSED AGGREGATE      1.75      7.50      9.25
   METAL TIES                       0.06      0.09      0.15
   CAULKING                         0.28      0.14      0.42
                                    -----     -----     -----
   TOTAL PER SQ FT                  2.09      7.73      9.82


115104                              LABOR     MAT'L     TOTAL
PRECAST WALL PANEL

   SHAPED WITH PLAIN FINISH         1.75      8.61     10.36
   METAL TIES                       0.06      0.09      0.15
   CAULKING                         0.28      0.14      0.42
                                    -----     -----     -----
   TOTAL PER SQ FT                  2.09      8.84     10.93
```

TABLE A-6 (Cont.)

EXTERIOR WALLS
CURTAIN WALL

```
118104                              LABOR     MAT'L      TOTAL
STAINLESS STEEL FRAME

   FRAME                            1.68      12.63      14.31
   SPANDREL (40%) STAINLESS STEEL   0.77       2.94       3.71
   INSULATION                       0.09       0.15       0.24
   1/4" PLATE GLASS (60%)           1.24       1.16       2.40
                                    -----      -----      -----
   TOTAL PER SQ FT                  3.78      16.88      20.66


118105                              LABOR     MAT'L      TOTAL
BRONZE FRAME

   FRAME                            1.68      13.27      14.95
   SPANDREL (40%) BRONZE            0.77       2.98       3.75
   INSULATION                       0.09       0.15       0.24
   1/4" PLATE GLASS (60%)           1.24       1.16       2.40
                                    -----      -----      -----
   TOTAL PER SQ FT                  3.78      17.56      21.34


118106                              LABOR     MAT'L      TOTAL
COLORED ALUMINUM FRAME

   FRAME                            1.53       5.99       7.52
   SPANDREL (40%) ALUMINUM          0.52       1.84       2.36
   INSULATION                       0.09       0.15       0.24
   1/4" PLATE GLASS (60%)           1.22       1.16       2.38
                                    -----      -----      -----
   TOTAL PER SQ FT                  3.36       9.14      12.50
```

TABLE A-6 (Cont.)

EXTERIOR WALLS
CURTAIN WALL (GLASS)

118107 GLASS	LABOR	MAT'L	TOTAL
3/8" CLEAR PLATE	2.65	3.28	5.93
	-----	-----	-----
TOTAL PER SQ FT	2.65	3.28	5.93

118108 GLASS	LABOR	MAT'L	TOTAL
1/2" CLEAR PLATE	3.45	3.92	7.37
	-----	-----	-----
TOTAL PER SQ FT	3.45	3.92	7.37

118109 GLASS	LABOR	MAT'L	TOTAL
1/2" CLEAR TEMPERED	3.45	6.00	9.45
	-----	-----	-----
TOTAL PER SQ FT	3.45	6.00	9.45

118110 GLASS	LABOR	MAT'L	TOTAL
3/4" CLEAR PLATE	4.60	6.50	11.10
	-----	-----	-----
TOTAL PER SQ FT	4.60	6.50	11.10

118111 GLASS	LABOR	MAT'L	TOTAL
1" CLEAR PLATE	5.20	8.94	14.14
	-----	-----	-----
TOTAL PER SQ FT	5.20	8.94	14.14

TABLE A-6 (*Cont.*)

EXTERIOR WALLS
SPECIAL DOORS

118501 ROLL UP METAL DOOR, CHAIN PULL	LABOR	MAT'L	TOTAL
DOOR 20 GA GALVANIZED	4.30	4.70	9.00
	-----	-----	-----
TOTAL PER SQ FT	4.30	4.70	9.00

118502 ROLL UP METAL DOOR, MOTORIZED	LABOR	MAT'L	TOTAL
DOOR 20 GA GALVANIZED	4.30	4.70	9.00
MOTORS & CONTROLS	1.10	5.50	6.60
	-----	-----	-----
TOTAL PER SQ FT	5.40	10.20	15.60

118503 REVOLVING DOOR 7' DIAMETER	LABOR	MAT'L	TOTAL
(ADD AS APPROPRIATE)			
DOOR - ALUMINUM	1,250	11,500	12,750
	-----	-----	-----
TOTAL PER EACH	1,250	11,500	12,750

118504 REVOLVING DOOR 7' DIAMETER	LABOR	MAT'L	TOTAL
(ADD AS APPROPRIATE)			
DOOR - STAINLESS STEEL	1,250	13,500	14,750
	-----	-----	-----
TOTAL PER EACH	1,250	13,500	14,750

118505 REVOLVING DOOR 7' DIAMETER	LABOR	MAT'L	TOTAL
(ADD AS APPROPRIATE)			
DOOR - BRONZE	1,300	15,500	16,800
	-----	-----	-----
TOTAL PER EACH	1,300	15,500	16,800

TABLE A-6 (*Cont.*)

EXTERIOR WALLS
EXTERIOR DOORS

119508 ARCHITECTURAL METAL	LABOR	MAT'L	TOTAL
1 3/4" ALUMINUM ENTRANCE PLAIN	5.40	6.50	11.90
ALUMINUM FRAME 3'X7'	1.90	4.24	6.14
GLAZING	2.12	1.80	3.92
HARDWARE	2.06	2.90	4.96
	-----	-----	-----
TOTAL PER SQ FT	11.48	15.44	26.92

119509 ARCHITECTURAL METAL	LABOR	MAT'L	TOTAL
1 3/4" ALUM. ENTRANCE PLAIN 3'X7'	5.40	6.50	11.90
ALUMINUM FRAME & SIDELITE	2.08	6.14	8.22
GLAZING	2.80	2.38	5.18
HARDWARE	2.06	2.90	4.96
	-----	-----	-----
TOTAL PER SQ FT	12.34	17.92	30.26

119510 ARCHITECTURAL METAL	LABOR	MAT'L	TOTAL
1 3/4" ALUM. ENTRANCE PLAIN 3'X7'	5.40	6.50	11.90
ALUM. FRAME, SIDELITE & TRANSOM	2.53	7.60	10.13
GLAZING	3.05	3.38	6.43
HARDWARE	2.25	3.18	5.43
	-----	-----	-----
TOTAL PER SQ FT	13.23	20.66	33.89

119511 ARCHITECTURAL METAL ANODIZED	LABOR	MAT'L	TOTAL
1 3/4" ALUMINUM ENTRANCE 3'X7'	5.50	8.30	13.80
ALUM. FRAME, SIDELITE & TRANSOM	2.80	10.02	12.82
GLAZING	3.05	3.38	6.43
HARDWARE	2.31	3.18	5.49
	-----	-----	-----
TOTAL PER SQ FT	13.66	24.88	38.54

TABLE A-6 (*Cont.*)

EXTERIOR WALLS
WINDOWS

118501 ALUMINUM	LABOR	MAT'L	TOTAL
4'X5' AWNING	1.82	5.36	7.18
STANDARD GLAZING	1.20	1.12	2.32
	-----	-----	-----
TOTAL PER SQ FT	3.02	6.48	9.50

118502 ALUMINUM	LABOR	MAT'L	TOTAL
4'X5' CASEMENT	1.82	5.06	6.88
STANDARD GLAZING	1.20	1.12	2.32
	-----	-----	-----
TOTAL PER SQ FT	3.02	6.18	9.20

118503 ALUMINUM	LABOR	MAT'L	TOTAL
4'X5' DOUBLE HUNG	2.44	3.90	6.34
STANDARD GLAZING	1.20	1.12	2.32
	-----	-----	-----
TOTAL PER SQ FT	3.64	5.02	8.66

118504 ALUMINUM	LABOR	MAT'L	TOTAL
4'X5' GLIDING	1.84	4.04	5.88
STANDARD GLAZING	1.20	1.12	2.32
	-----	-----	-----
TOTAL PER SQ FT	3.04	5.16	8.20

118505 ALUMINUM (THERMAL BREAK)	LABOR	MAT'L	TOTAL
4'X2' DBL GLAZED 2 PANEL	1.84	8.90	10.74
	-----	-----	-----
TOTAL PER SQ FT	1.84	8.90	10.74

TABLE A-7

ROOFING
SLATE

163501 PENNA. RIBBON	LABOR	MAT'L	TOTAL
3/4" PLYWOOD SHEATHING	0.28	0.55	0.83
FELT	0.06	0.07	0.13
SLATE SHINGLES	0.92	0.74	1.66
	-----	-----	-----
TOTAL PER SQ FT	1.26	1.36	2.62

163502 PENNA. CLEAR	LABOR	MAT'L	TOTAL
3/4" PLYWOOD SHEATHING	0.28	0.55	0.83
FELT	0.06	0.07	0.13
SLATE SHINGLES	0.92	0.94	1.86
	-----	-----	-----
TOTAL PER SQ FT	1.26	1.56	2.82

163503 VERMONT GRAY	LABOR	MAT'L	TOTAL
3/4" PLYWOOD SHEATHING	0.28	0.55	0.83
FELT	0.06	0.07	0.13
SLATE SHINGLES	0.92	1.36	2.28
	-----	-----	-----
TOTAL PER SQ FT	1.26	1.98	3.24

163504 VERMONT RED NON FADE	LABOR	MAT'L	TOTAL
3/4" PLYWOOD SHEATHING	0.28	0.55	0.83
FELT	0.06	0.07	0.13
SLATE SHINGLES	0.92	2.42	3.34
	-----	-----	-----
TOTAL PER SQ FT	1.26	3.04	4.30

Source: Dodge Building Cost Services (McGraw-Hill Information Systems Company) with Wood & Tower Inc., *1979 Dodge Construction Systems Costs,* McGraw-Hill, New York, 1978.

TABLE A-7 (*Cont.*)

ROOFING
METAL PITCHED

```
164101                          LABOR     MAT'L     TOTAL
COPPER FLAT SEAM

   INSULATION                   0.15      0.18      0.33
   3/4" PLYWOOD SHEATHING       0.28      0.55      0.83
   ROSIN PAPER                  0.05      0.06      0.11
   16 OZ COPPER                 1.64      2.45      4.09
                                -----     -----     -----
   TOTAL PER SQ FT              2.12      3.24      5.36


164102                          LABOR     MAT'L     TOTAL
COPPER BATTEN SEAM

   INSULATION                   0.15      0.18      0.33
   3/4" PLYWOOD SHEATHING       0.28      0.55      0.83
   ROSIN PAPER                  0.05      0.06      0.11
   2"X2" WOOD BATTENS           0.51      0.50      1.01
   16 OZ COPPER                 1.53      2.35      3.88
                                -----     -----     -----
   TOTAL PER SQ FT              2.52      3.64      6.16


164103                          LABOR     MAT'L     TOTAL
COPPER STANDING SEAM

   INSULATION                   0.15      0.15      0.30
   3/4" PLYWOOD SHEATHING       0.28      0.55      0.83
   ROSIN PAPER                  0.05      0.06      0.11
   16 OZ COPPER                 1.73      2.50      4.23
                                -----     -----     -----
   TOTAL PER SQ FT              2.21      3.26      5.47


164104                          LABOR     MAT'L     TOTAL
LEAD COATED TIN FLAT SEAM

   INSULATION                   0.15      0.18      0.33
   3/4" PLYWOOD SHEATHING       0.28      0.55      0.83
   ROSIN PAPER                  0.05      0.06      0.11
   11 OZ LEAD COATED TIN        0.94      1.55      2.49
                                -----     -----     -----
   TOTAL PER SQ FT              1.42      2.34      3.76
```

TABLE A-7 (*Cont.*)

ROOFING
BUILT-UP ON METAL DECK

```
168101                           LABOR     MAT'L     TOTAL
20 GA STEEL DECK

   1 1/2" RECTANGULAR RIBS 6" OC  0.35      0.78      1.13
   2" RIGID INSULATION            0.25      0.37      0.62
   4 PLY BUILT UP (20 YEAR)       0.31      0.31      0.62
                                  -----     -----     -----
   TOTAL PER SQ FT                0.91      1.46      2.37


168102                           LABOR     MAT'L     TOTAL
20 GA STEEL DECK

   3" RECTANGULAR RIBS 8" OC       0.37      0.96      1.33
   2" RIGID INSULATION            0.25      0.37      0.62
   4 PLY BUILT UP (20 YEAR)       0.31      0.31      0.62
                                  -----     -----     -----
   TOTAL PER SQ FT                0.93      1.64      2.57


168103                           LABOR     MAT'L     TOTAL
20 GA STEEL DECK

   4 1/2" DEEP RIBS               0.50      1.14      1.64
   2" RIGID INSULATION            0.25      0.37      0.62
   4 PLY BUILT UP (20 YEAR)       0.31      0.31      0.62
                                  -----     -----     -----
   TOTAL PER SQ FT                1.06      1.82      2.88


168104                           LABOR     MAT'L     TOTAL
16/16 GA CELLULAR STEEL DECK

   1 1/2" DEEP RIBS               0.81      1.66      2.47
   2" RIGID INSULATION            0.25      0.37      0.62
   4 PLY BUILT UP (20 YEAR)       0.31      0.31      0.62
                                  -----     -----     -----
   TOTAL PER SQ FT                1.37      2.34      3.71
```

TABLE A-7 (*Cont.*)

ROOFING
BUILT-UP ON POURED TOPPING

166501 3" INSULATING CONCRETE	LABOR	MAT'L	TOTAL
CONCRETE	0.33	0.52	0.85
VAPOR BARRIER	0.17	0.14	0.31
5 PLY BUILT UP (20 YEAR)	0.36	0.34	0.70
	-----	-----	-----
TOTAL PER SQ FT	0.86	1.00	1.86

166502 3" LIGHTWEIGHT CONCRETE TOPPING	LABOR	MAT'L	TOTAL
CONCRETE	0.33	0.54	0.87
2 1/2" RIGID INSULATION	0.23	0.42	0.65
5 PLY BUILT UP (20 YEAR)	0.36	0.34	0.70
	-----	-----	-----
TOTAL PER SQ FT	0.92	1.30	2.22

166503 2" VERMICULITE	LABOR	MAT'L	TOTAL
VERMICULITE	0.30	0.47	0.77
2 1/2" RIGID INSULATION	0.23	0.42	0.65
5 PLY BUILT UP (20 YEAR)	0.36	0.34	0.70
	-----	-----	-----
TOTAL PER SQ FT	0.89	1.23	2.12

166504 3" VERMICULITE	LABOR	MAT'L	TOTAL
VERMICULITE	0.33	0.65	0.98
2 1/2" RIGID INSULATION	0.23	0.42	0.65
5 PLY BUILT UP (20 YEAR)	0.36	0.34	0.70
	-----	-----	-----
TOTAL PER SQ FT	0.92	1.41	2.33

TABLE A-8

PARTITIONS
DRYWALL

```
121101                               LABOR    MAT'L    TOTAL
WOOD STUD & 1/2" GYPSUM BOARD

    1/2" GYPSUM BOARD                0.19     0.15     0.34
    2"X4" WOOD STUDS 16" OC          0.21     0.32     0.53
    1/2" GYPSUM BOARD                0.19     0.15     0.34
    TAPING & SPACKLING               0.21     0.06     0.27
                                     -----    -----    -----
    TOTAL PER SQ FT                  0.80     0.68     1.48


121102                               LABOR    MAT'L    TOTAL
STEEL STUD & 1/2" GYPSUM BOARD

    1/2" GYPSUM BOARD                0.19     0.15     0.34
    3" STEEL STUDS 16" OC            0.40     0.32     0.72
    1/2" GYPSUM BOARD                0.19     0.15     0.34
    TAPING & SPACKLING               0.21     0.06     0.27
                                     -----    -----    -----
    TOTAL PER SQ FT                  0.99     0.68     1.67


121103                               LABOR    MAT'L    TOTAL
STEEL STUD & 1/2" GYPSUM BOARD INSUL.

    1/2" GYPSUM BOARD                0.19     0.15     0.34
    3" STEEL STUDS 16" OC            0.40     0.32     0.72
    3 1/2" BATT INSULATION           0.12     0.16     0.28
    1/2" GYPSUM BOARD                0.19     0.15     0.34
    TAPING & SPACKLING               0.21     0.06     0.27
                                     -----    -----    -----
    TOTAL PER SQ FT                  1.11     0.84     1.95


121104                               LABOR    MAT'L    TOTAL
STEEL STUD & 1/2" LAM. GYPSUM BOARD

    TWO-1/2" GYPSUM BOARD            0.38     0.30     0.68
    3" STEEL STUDS 16" OC            0.40     0.32     0.72
    TWO-1/2" GYPSUM BOARD            0.38     0.30     0.68
    ADHESIVE                         0.18     0.10     0.28
    TAPING & SPACKLING               0.21     0.06     0.27
                                     -----    -----    -----
    TOTAL PER SQ FT                  1.55     1.08     2.63
```

Source: Dodge Building Cost Services (McGraw-Hill Information Systems Company) with Wood & Tower Inc., *1979 Dodge Construction Systems Costs,* McGraw-Hill, New York, 1978.

TABLE A-8 (Cont.)

PARTITIONS
LATH AND PLASTER

```
122101                          LABOR    MAT'L    TOTAL
WOOD STUD, GYPSUM LATH & PLASTER

   PLASTER 2-COATS              0.60     0.10     0.70
   GYPSUM LATH 3/8"             0.30     0.19     0.49
   2"X4" WOOD STUDS 16" OC      0.21     0.32     0.53
   GYPSUM LATH 3/8"             0.30     0.19     0.49
   PLASTER 2-COATS              0.60     0.10     0.70
                                -----    -----    -----
   TOTAL PER SQ FT              2.01     0.90     2.91


122102                          LABOR    MAT'L    TOTAL
WOOD STUD, STEEL LATH & PLASTER

   PLASTER 3-COATS              0.82     0.16     0.98
   STEEL LATH                   0.27     0.28     0.55
   2"X4" WOOD STUDS 16" OC      0.21     0.32     0.53
   STEEL LATH                   0.27     0.28     0.55
   PLASTER 3-COATS              0.82     0.16     0.98
                                -----    -----    -----
   TOTAL PER SQ FT              2.39     1.20     3.59


122103                          LABOR    MAT'L    TOTAL
STEEL STUD, STEEL LATH & PLASTER

   PLASTER 3-COATS              0.82     0.16     0.98
   STEEL LATH                   0.27     0.28     0.55
   3" STEEL STUDS 16" OC        0.40     0.32     0.72
   STEEL LATH                   0.27     0.28     0.55
   PLASTER 3-COATS              0.82     0.16     0.98
                                -----    -----    -----
   TOTAL PER SQ FT              2.58     1.20     3.78


122104                          LABOR    MAT'L    TOTAL
2" SOLID PLASTER

   PLASTER 3-COATS              0.82     0.16     0.98
   STEEL LATH                   0.27     0.28     0.55
   STEEL CHANNELS               0.32     0.27     0.59
   PLASTER 2-COATS              0.60     0.10     0.70
                                -----    -----    -----
   TOTAL PER SQ FT              2.01     0.81     2.82
```

TABLE A-8 (*Cont.*)

PARTITIONS
MASONRY

```
123101                              LABOR     MAT'L     TOTAL
4" MASONRY BLOCK

   CONCRETE MASONRY UNIT            1.38      0.46      1.84
   HORIZONTAL REINFORCING           0.08      0.11      0.19
   MORTAR                            --       0.13      0.13
   TOOL JOINTS & CLEAN              0.07      0.05      0.12
                                   -----     -----     -----
   TOTAL PER SQ FT                  1.53      0.75      2.28


123102                              LABOR     MAT'L     TOTAL
6" MASONRY BLOCK

   CONCRETE MASONRY UNIT            1.42      0.57      1.99
   HORIZONTAL REINFORCING           0.08      0.11      0.19
   MORTAR                            --       0.13      0.13
   TOOL JOINTS & CLEAN              0.07      0.05      0.12
                                   -----     -----     -----
   TOTAL PER SQ FT                  1.57      0.86      2.43


123103                              LABOR     MAT'L     TOTAL
8" MASONRY BLOCK

   CONCRETE MASONRY UNIT            1.62      0.66      2.28
   HORIZONTAL REINFORCING           0.08      0.11      0.19
   MORTAR                            --       0.14      0.14
   TOOL JOINTS & CLEAN              0.07      0.05      0.12
                                   -----     -----     -----
   TOTAL PER SQ FT                  1.77      0.96      2.73


123104                              LABOR     MAT'L     TOTAL
8" SOLID MASONRY BLOCK

   CONCRETE MASONRY UNIT            1.88      0.74      2.62
   HORIZONTAL REINFORCING           0.08      0.11      0.19
   MORTAR                            --       0.14      0.14
   TOOL JOINTS & CLEAN              0.07      0.05      0.12
                                   -----     -----     -----
   TOTAL PER SQ FT                  2.03      1.04      3.07
```

TABLE A-8 (*Cont.*)

PARTITIONS
STRUCTURAL GLAZED TILE

```
126101                               LABOR     MAT'L      TOTAL
4" STRUCTURAL GLAZED TILE 1-FACE

    STRUCTURAL GLAZED TILE           2.90      2.24       5.14
    MORTAR                            --       0.14       0.14
    TOOL JOINTS & CLEAN              0.07      0.07       0.14
                                    -----     -----      -----
    TOTAL PER SQ FT                  2.97      2.45       5.42


126102                               LABOR     MAT'L      TOTAL
4" STRUCTURAL GLAZED TILE 2-FACE

    STRUCTURAL GLAZED TILE           3.10      4.10       7.20
    MORTAR                            --       0.14       0.14
    TOOL JOINTS & CLEAN              0.08      0.10       0.18
                                    -----     -----      -----
    TOTAL PER SQ FT                  3.18      4.34       7.52


126103                               LABOR     MAT'L      TOTAL
6" STRUCTURAL GLAZED TILE 1-FACE

    STRUCTURAL GLAZED TILE           3.30      3.10       6.40
    MORTAR                            --       0.14       0.14
    TOOL JOINTS & CLEAN              0.07      0.07       0.14
                                    -----     -----      -----
    TOTAL PER SQ FT                  3.37      3.31       6.68


126104                               LABOR     MAT'L      TOTAL
6" STRUCTURAL GLAZED TILE 2-FACE

    STRUCTURAL GLAZED TILE           3.50      3.90       7.40
    MORTAR                            --       0.14       0.14
    TOOL JOINTS & CLEAN              0.08      0.10       0.18
                                    -----     -----      -----
    TOTAL PER SQ FT                  3.58      4.14       7.72
```

TABLE A-8 (Cont.)

PARTITIONS
DOORS

```
129505                          LABOR    MAT'L    TOTAL
KALAMEIN

   1 3/4" 2 HR FIRE RATED DOOR   3.20    5.32     8.52
   METAL FRAME                   2.08    2.45     4.53
   HARDWARE                      1.04    1.42     2.46
   PAINT                         0.26    0.12     0.38
                                -----   -----    -----
   TOTAL PER SQ FT               6.58    9.31    15.89


129506                          LABOR    MAT'L    TOTAL
HOLLOW CORE BIRCH

   1 3/8" DOOR 3'X7'             2.77    1.34     4.11
   WOOD FRAME & TRIM             0.50    0.77     1.27
   HARDWARE                      1.04    1.42     2.46
   PAINT OR STAIN               0.26    0.12     0.38
                                -----   -----    -----
   TOTAL PER SQ FT               4.57    3.65     8.22


129507                          LABOR    MAT'L    TOTAL
HOLLOW CORE BIRCH

   1 3/4" DOOR 3'X7'             2.77    2.00     4.77
   WOOD FRAME & TRIM             0.50    0.80     1.30
   HARDWARE                      1.04    1.42     2.46
   PAINT OR STAIN               0.26    0.12     0.38
                                -----   -----    -----
   TOTAL PER SQ FT               4.57    4.34     8.91


129508                          LABOR    MAT'L    TOTAL
SOLID CORE BIRCH

   1 3/4" DOOR 3'X7'             2.77    4.20     6.97
   WOOD FRAME & TRIM             0.75    1.77     2.52
   HARDWARE                      1.04    1.42     2.46
   PAINT OR STAIN               0.26    0.12     0.38
                                -----   -----    -----
   TOTAL PER SQ FT               4.82    7.51    12.33
```

TABLE A-9

INTERIOR WALL FINISHES
THIN COVERING

135106 FINISH ON WOOD	LABOR	MAT'L	TOTAL
FILL, STAIN & 3 COAT VARNISH	0.38	0.15	0.53
	-----	-----	-----
TOTAL PER SQ FT	0.38	0.15	0.53

135107 PAINT ON MASONRY	LABOR	MAT'L	TOTAL
2 COAT LATEX	0.30	0.10	0.40
	-----	-----	-----
TOTAL PER SQ FT	0.30	0.10	0.40

135108 PAINT ON MASONRY	LABOR	MAT'L	TOTAL
3 COAT LATEX	0.33	0.12	0.45
	-----	-----	-----
TOTAL PER SQ FT	0.33	0.12	0.45

135109 VINYL WALL COVERING	LABOR	MAT'L	TOTAL
15 OZ VINYL SHEET	0.42	0.36	0.78
ADHESIVE	0.09	0.05	0.14
	-----	-----	-----
TOTAL PER SQ FT	0.51	0.41	0.92

135110 CORK WALL COVERING	LABOR	MAT'L	TOTAL
1/8" CORK SHEET	0.62	2.20	2.82
ADHESIVE	0.09	0.05	0.14
	-----	-----	-----
TOTAL PER SQ FT	0.71	2.25	2.96

Source: Dodge Building Cost Services (McGraw-Hill Information Systems Company) with Wood & Tower Inc., *1979 Dodge Construction Systems Costs,* McGraw-Hill, New York, 1978.

TABLE A-9 (*Cont.*)

INTERIOR WALL FINISHES
THIN COVERING

```
135116                              LABOR     MAT'L     TOTAL
WALL PAPER

   36 SF ROLL ALLOWANCE 3.00        0.32      0.20      0.52
   ADHESIVE                         0.08      0.02      0.10
                                   -----     -----     -----
   TOTAL PER SQ FT                  0.40      0.22      0.62


135117                              LABOR     MAT'L     TOTAL
WALL PAPER

   36 SF ROLL ALLOWANCE 6.50        0.36      0.34      0.70
   ADHESIVE                         0.08      0.02      0.10
                                   -----     -----     -----
   TOTAL PER SQ FT                  0.44      0.36      0.80


135118                              LABOR     MAT'L     TOTAL
WALL PAPER

   MURAL DESIGN                     1.16      0.50      1.66
   ADHESIVE                         0.08      0.02      0.10
                                   -----     -----     -----
   TOTAL PER SQ FT                  1.24      0.52      1.76


135119                              LABOR     MAT'L     TOTAL
GRASS CLOTH COVERING

   CLOTH WITH LINER                 1.26      0.84      2.10
   ADHESIVE                         0.10      0.02      0.12
                                   -----     -----     -----
   TOTAL PER SQ FT                  1.36      0.86      2.22
```

TABLE A-9 (*Cont.*)

INTERIOR WALL FINISHES
TILE

137101 CERAMIC-MUDSET	LABOR	MAT'L	TOTAL
2"X2" TILE MULTI-COLOR	0.98	1.22	2.20
MUD BED	0.28	0.29	0.57
GROUT JOINTS & CLEAN	0.13	0.05	0.18
	-----	-----	-----
TOTAL PER SQ FT	1.39	1.56	2.95

137102 CERAMIC TILE ADHESIVE BOND	LABOR	MAT'L	TOTAL
1/2" GYPSUM BOARD WATER RESISTANT	0.19	0.22	0.41
PRIMER COAT	0.07	0.05	0.12
ADHESIVE	0.14	0.08	0.22
2"X2" TILE MULTI-COLOR	0.98	1.22	2.20
GROUT JOINTS & CLEAN	0.13	0.05	0.18
	-----	-----	-----
TOTAL PER SQ FT	1.51	1.62	3.13

137103 CERAMIC TILE THINSET	LABOR	MAT'L	TOTAL
2"X2" TILE MULTI-COLOR	0.98	1.22	2.20
THINSET BASE	0.08	0.12	0.20
GROUT JOINTS & CLEAN	0.13	0.05	0.18
	-----	-----	-----
TOTAL PER SQ FT	1.19	1.39	2.58

137104 CERAMIC TILE THINSET	LABOR	MAT'L	TOTAL
2"X2" CUSTOM DESIGN	0.98	2.00	2.98
THINSET BASE	0.08	0.12	0.20
GROUT JOINTS & CLEAN	0.13	0.05	0.18
	-----	-----	-----
TOTAL PER SQ FT	1.19	2.17	3.36

TABLE A-10

FLOOR FINISHES
RESILIENT

141106 1/8" VINYL ASBESTOS	LABOR	MAT'L	TOTAL
12"X12" TILE	0.28	0.57	0.85
MASTIC	0.13	0.05	0.18
	-----	-----	-----
TOTAL PER SQ FT	0.41	0.62	1.03

141107 .08 VINYL	LABOR	MAT'L	TOTAL
12"X12" TILE	0.28	1.04	1.32
MASTIC	0.13	0.05	0.18
	-----	-----	-----
TOTAL PER SQ FT	0.41	1.09	1.50

141108 3/16" CONDUCTIVE VINYL	LABOR	MAT'L	TOTAL
12"X12" TILE	0.28	2.28	2.56
MASTIC	0.13	0.05	0.18
	-----	-----	-----
TOTAL PER SQ FT	0.41	2.33	2.74

141109 3/16" RUBBER	LABOR	MAT'L	TOTAL
9"X9" TILE	0.28	1.28	1.56
MASTIC	0.13	0.05	0.18
	-----	-----	-----
TOTAL PER SQ FT	0.41	1.33	1.74

141110 1/8" CORK	LABOR	MAT'L	TOTAL
9"X9" TILE	0.28	0.82	1.10
MASTIC	0.13	0.05	0.18
	-----	-----	-----
TOTAL PER SQ FT	0.41	0.87	1.28

Source: Dodge Building Cost Services (McGraw-Hill Information Systems Company) with Wood & Tower Inc., *1979 Dodge Construction Systems Costs,* McGraw-Hill, New York, 1978.

TABLE A-10 (*Cont.*)

FLOOR FINISHES
WOOD

143116 25/32" YELLOW PINE	LABOR	MAT'L	TOTAL
2 1/4" FIRST GRADE	0.99	0.96	1.95
SAND & FINISH	0.50	0.10	0.60
	-----	-----	-----
TOTAL PER SQ FT	1.49	1.06	2.55

143117 5/16" OAK PARQUET	LABOR	MAT'L	TOTAL
6"X6" OAK PARQUETRY	1.00	1.24	2.24
MASTIC BASE	0.28	0.09	0.37
SAND & FINISH	0.50	0.10	0.60
	-----	-----	-----
TOTAL PER SQ FT	1.78	1.43	3.21

143118 5/16" WALNUT PARQUET	LABOR	MAT'L	TOTAL
6"X6" WALNUT PARQUETRY	1.00	1.70	2.70
MASTIC BASE	0.28	0.09	0.37
SAND & FINISH	0.50	0.10	0.60
	-----	-----	-----
TOTAL PER SQ FT	1.78	1.89	3.67

143119 5/16" TEAK PARQUET	LABOR	MAT'L	TOTAL
6"X6" TEAK PARQUETRY	1.00	1.52	2.52
MASTIC BASE	0.28	0.09	0.37
	-----	-----	-----
TOTAL PER SQ FT	1.28	1.61	2.89

TABLE A-10 (*Cont.*)

FLOOR FINISHES
MASONRY

144101 7/8" SLATE MUDSET	LABOR	MAT'L	TOTAL
SLATE	3.16	4.08	7.24
3/4" SETTING BED	0.29	0.12	0.41
MORTAR JOINTS	0.16	0.04	0.20
CLEAN	0.20	0.01	0.21
	-----	-----	-----
TOTAL PER SQ FT	3.81	4.25	8.06

144102 7/8" SLATE THINSET	LABOR	MAT'L	TOTAL
SLATE	2.90	3.46	6.36
CEMENT BED	0.16	0.05	0.21
MORTAR JOINTS	0.16	0.04	0.20
CLEAN	0.20	0.01	0.21
	-----	-----	-----
TOTAL PER SQ FT	3.42	3.56	6.98

144103 1" MARBLE MUDSET	LABOR	MAT'L	TOTAL
MARBLE	3.24	4.84	8.08
3/4" SETTING BED	0.29	0.12	0.41
MORTAR JOINTS	0.16	0.04	0.20
CLEAN	0.20	0.01	0.21
	-----	-----	-----
TOTAL PER SQ FT	3.89	5.01	8.90

144104 7/8" MARBLE THINSET	LABOR	MAT'L	TOTAL
MARBLE	2.94	4.32	7.26
CEMENT BED	0.16	0.05	0.21
MORTAR JOINTS	0.16	0.04	0.20
CLEAN	0.20	0.01	0.21
	-----	-----	-----
TOTAL PER SQ FT	3.46	4.42	7.88

TABLE A-10 (*Cont.*)

FLOOR FINISHES
TERRAZZO

144301 1 3/4" BONDED TERRAZZO	LABOR	MAT'L	TOTAL
4'X4' PANELS, TERRAZZO TOPPING	1.72	0.71	2.43
MORTAR BED	0.36	0.14	0.50
METAL DIVIDER	0.15	0.36	0.51
	-----	-----	-----
TOTAL PER SQ FT	2.23	1.21	3.44

144302 2 1/2" BONDED TERRAZZO	LABOR	MAT'L	TOTAL
4'X4' PANELS, TERRAZZO TOPPING	1.82	0.92	2.74
MORTAR BED	0.42	0.23	0.65
METAL DIVIDER	0.15	0.36	0.51
	-----	-----	-----
TOTAL PER SQ FT	2.39	1.51	3.90

144303 3" TERRAZZO (NOT BONDED)	LABOR	MAT'L	TOTAL
4'X4' PANELS, TERRAZZO TOPPING	1.94	1.14	3.08
MORTAR BED	0.46	0.23	0.69
1/4" SAND CUSHION	0.07	0.02	0.09
METAL DIVIDER	0.15	0.36	0.51
	-----	-----	-----
TOTAL PER SQ FT	2.62	1.75	4.37

144304 2 1/4" PRECAST TERRAZZO	LABOR	MAT'L	TOTAL
1 1/2" TERRAZZO PANELS	1.96	2.56	4.52
3/4" SETTING BED	0.36	0.14	0.50
	-----	-----	-----
TOTAL PER SQ FT	2.32	2.70	5.02

TABLE A-10 (*Cont.*)

FLOOR FINISHES
CARPETING

145106 CARPETING	LABOR	MAT'L	TOTAL
ACRYLIC SCULPTURED	0.32	1.04	1.36
	-----	-----	-----
TOTAL PER SQ FT	0.32	1.04	1.36

145107 CARPETING	LABOR	MAT'L	TOTAL
ACRYLIC PLUSH	0.32	1.24	1.56
	-----	-----	-----
TOTAL PER SQ FT	0.32	1.24	1.56

145108 CARPETING	LABOR	MAT'L	TOTAL
COMMERCIAL ACRYLIC PILE	0.32	1.46	1.78
	-----	-----	-----
TOTAL PER SQ FT	0.32	1.46	1.78

145109 CARPETING	LABOR	MAT'L	TOTAL
COMMERCIAL NYLON	0.32	1.11	1.43
	-----	-----	-----
TOTAL PER SQ FT	0.32	1.11	1.43

145110 CARPETING	LABOR	MAT'L	TOTAL
INDOOR-OUTDOOR FOAM BACK	0.25	0.80	1.05
	-----	-----	-----
TOTAL PER SQ FT	0.25	0.80	1.05

TABLE A-11

CEILINGS
GYPSUM BOARD

151101 1/2" GYPSUM BOARD ON WOOD JOISTS	LABOR	MAT'L	TOTAL
GYPSUM BOARD	0.20	0.15	0.35
TAPING & SPACKLING	0.11	0.04	0.15
3 COATS PAINT	0.24	0.08	0.32
	-----	-----	-----
TOTAL PER SQ FT	0.55	0.27	0.82

151102 1/2" GYPSUM BOARD ON WOOD HANGERS	LABOR	MAT'L	TOTAL
2"X4" WOOD HANGERS & FURRING	0.46	0.44	0.90
GYPSUM BOARD	0.20	0.15	0.35
TAPING & SPACKLING	0.24	0.08	0.32
	-----	-----	-----
TOTAL PER SQ FT	0.90	0.67	1.57

151103 5/8" GYPSUM BOARD ON WOOD JOISTS	LABOR	MAT'L	TOTAL
GYPSUM BOARD	0.21	0.16	0.37
TAPING & SPACKLING	0.11	0.04	0.15
3 COATS PAINT	0.25	0.08	0.33
	-----	-----	-----
TOTAL PER SQ FT	0.57	0.28	0.85

151104 5/8" GYPSUM BOARD ON WOOD HANGERS	LABOR	MAT'L	TOTAL
2"X4" WOOD HANGERS & FURRING	0.49	0.44	0.93
GYPSUM BOARD	0.19	0.16	0.35
TAPING & SPACKLING	0.11	0.04	0.15
3 COATS PAINT	0.25	0.08	0.33
	-----	-----	-----
TOTAL PER SQ FT	1.04	0.72	1.76

Source: Dodge Building Cost Services (McGraw-Hill Information Systems Company) with Wood & Tower Inc., *1979 Dodge Construction Systems Costs,* McGraw-Hill, New York, 1978.

TABLE A-11 (*Cont.*)

CEILINGS
LATH AND PLASTER

153101	LABOR	MAT'L	TOTAL
PLASTER ON GYPSUM LATH			
GYPSUM LATH	0.23	0.19	0.42
PLASTER 3 COATS	0.95	0.16	1.11
	-----	-----	-----
TOTAL PER SQ FT	1.18	0.35	1.53

153102	LABOR	MAT'L	TOTAL
PLASTER ON STEEL LATH			
STEEL LATH	0.21	0.26	0.47
PLASTER 3 COATS	1.00	0.16	1.16
	-----	-----	-----
TOTAL PER SQ FT	1.21	0.42	1.63

153103	LABOR	MAT'L	TOTAL
PLASTER ON SUSPENDED LATH			
STEEL SUSPENSION SYSTEM	0.47	0.26	0.73
STEEL LATH	0.21	0.26	0.47
PLASTER 3 COATS	1.00	0.16	1.16
	-----	-----	-----
TOTAL PER SQ FT	1.68	0.68	2.36

153104	LABOR	MAT'L	TOTAL
KEENES PLASTER ON SUSPENDED LATH			
STEEL SUSPENSION SYSTEM	0.47	0.26	0.73
STEEL LATH	0.21	0.26	0.47
PLASTER 3 COATS	0.84	0.16	1.00
	-----	-----	-----
TOTAL PER SQ FT	1.52	0.68	2.20

TABLE A-11 (*Cont.*)

CEILINGS
ACOUSTICAL

155111 LAY IN 24"X24" GRID	LABOR	MAT'L	TOTAL
STEEL SUSPENSION SPLINED SYSTEM	0.40	0.38	0.78
5/8" FIBERGLASS	0.31	0.39	0.70
	-----	-----	-----
TOTAL PER SQ FT	0.71	0.77	1.48

155112 LAY IN 24"X48" GRID	LABOR	MAT'L	TOTAL
STEEL SUSPENSION SPLINED SYSTEM	0.40	0.38	0.78
5/8" FIBERGLASS TILE	0.31	0.34	0.65
	-----	-----	-----
TOTAL PER SQ FT	0.71	0.72	1.43

155113 LAY IN 24"X48" GRID	LABOR	MAT'L	TOTAL
STEEL SUSPENSION SPLINED SYSTEM	0.40	0.38	0.78
3/4" FIBERGLASS TILE	0.31	0.34	0.65
	-----	-----	-----
TOTAL PER SQ FT	0.71	0.72	1.43

155114 LAY IN 24"X24" GRID	LABOR	MAT'L	TOTAL
STEEL SUSPENSION SYSTEM	0.40	0.38	0.78
3/16" ASBESTOS BEVELED PERFORATED	0.17	0.29	0.46
	-----	-----	-----
TOTAL PER SQ FT	0.57	0.67	1.24

155115 LAY IN 24"X48" GRID	LABOR	MAT'L	TOTAL
STEEL SUSPENSION SYSTEM	0.24	0.23	0.47
3/16" ASBESTOS BEVELED PERFORATED	0.17	0.29	0.46
	-----	-----	-----
TOTAL PER SQ FT	0.41	0.52	0.93

TABLE A-11 (*Cont.*)

CEILINGS
METAL

157101 METAL LAY IN 12"X12" GRID	LABOR	MAT'L	TOTAL
STEEL SUSPENSION SYSTEM	0.40	0.36	0.76
STEEL PANELS	0.38	0.98	1.36
TOTAL PER SQ FT	0.78	1.34	2.12

157102 METAL LAY IN 12"X12" GRID	LABOR	MAT'L	TOTAL
ALUMINUM SUSPENSION SYSTEM	0.63	0.62	1.25
ALUMINUM PANELS	0.40	0.90	1.30
TOTAL PER SQ FT	1.03	1.52	2.55

157103 METAL LAY IN 12"X12" GRID	LABOR	MAT'L	TOTAL
ALUMINUM SUSPENSION SYSTEM	0.63	0.62	1.25
STAINLESS STEEL PANELS	0.40	2.98	3.38
TOTAL PER SQ FT	1.03	3.60	4.63

157104 METAL LAY IN 12"X12" GRID	LABOR	MAT'L	TOTAL
STAINLESS STEEL SUSPENSION SYSTEM	0.64	3.10	3.74
STAINLESS STEEL PANELS	0.40	2.98	3.38
TOTAL PER SQ FT	1.04	6.08	7.12

157105 METAL LAY IN 12"X12" GRID	LABOR	MAT'L	TOTAL
STEEL SUSPENSION SYSTEM	0.40	0.38	0.78
STEEL PANELS	0.38	1.24	1.62
SOUND ABSORBING PADS	0.08	0.18	0.26
TOTAL PER SQ FT	0.86	1.80	2.66

APPENDIX B
PROJECT PROCEDURES

FIGURE B-1

EXTRACTS FROM AN ARCHITECT–ENGINEER AGREEMENT

NOLEN–SWINBURNE AND ASSOCIATES

Gentlemen:

This letter constitutes an agreement between us, NOLEN–SWINBURNE and ASSOCIATES, and _____

_____ .

It sets forth the service which you shall render and the professional and legal obligations which you shall assume in preparing plans, details, specifications and cost estimates; in reviewing, approving and accepting shop drawings or fixture and equipment information; and in field observation and accepting the construction of all the mechanical/electrical portions of the work of project _____

_____ .

You SHALL PROVIDE THE FOLLOWING SERVICES:

DESIGN AND PRELIMINARY INFORMATION

1. Receive required production time schedule from us and agree to provide manpower and time to meet this schedule.

2. Prepare comparative design studies required by nature of project, dovetailing with our studies in SCHEMATIC DESIGN and DESIGN DEVELOPMENT PHASES. These shall involve systems design, complete with cost analysis of each system. Submit written report analyzing each system and make recommendation of final selections.

3. Prepare preliminary specifications covering general systems design and the kind of materials and equipment necessary for its operation.

4. We will retain the services of a Cost Consultant to prepare the Project Estimate, the Consulting Engineer shall cooperate by providing all information necessary to complete the estimate or integrate his cost estimate with that of the Cost Consultant within the established time schedule required in Paragraph 1 above.

5. Submit written statement to us that the work as recommended can be completed in accordance with all applicable codes and laws affecting the construction and use of the project.

6. Mechanical spaces, riser shafts, and required horizontal clearances shall be sized and located in early stages of schematic design.

FINAL DOCUMENTS

1. Prepare plans, sections, details, diagrams, and schedules necessary to completely cover the work. Two-line piping drawings and isometrics must be used where necessary for clarity or showing detailed arrangements and clearances. All drawings shall be made with pencil on pencil cloth which will be supplied by us.

2. Supply us all necessary blueprints during design and production stages. We will issue and pay for all prints required for bidding and construction.

3. At completion of work all Engineering tracings are your property; you are to reproduce one set for your purposes, upon completion of as-built drawings.

4. Provide sufficient time to coordinate and cross-check each part of the Engineering drawings and specifications within your firm with the work of other Consultants and with our drawings and specifications.

5. Supply us with typewritten draft of final specifications. Copy shall be

double-spaced and follow format in use by us. After review and approval by us, type final specifications, single-spaced, on master sheets for offset printing. We will print and pay for all required specifications.

6. Prepare written final cost estimates of the work. These estimates shall be reasonably accurate and reflect a high professional concern for this responsibility. If, during the course of design and production, estimates are too high for project budget, work shall be re-studied and adjusted to fall within budget allowances. If after bidding the costs are beyond budget allowances, the work shall be re-executed to fall within such allowances in the manner you recommend, at no additional cost to us. Should we retain the services of a Cost Consultant to prepare the Project Estimate, the Consulting Engineer shall cooperate by providing all information necessary to complete the estimate or integrate his cost estimate with that of the Cost Consultant within the established time schedule required in Paragraph 1 above.

7. Submit written statement to us that the work as completed and cross-checked is in complete accordance with all applicable codes and laws affecting the construction and use of the project.

CONSTRUCTION OF THE WORK

1. Provide field observation services on a routine basis of at least once a week and as emergencies may require, to insure that the portion of the work for which you are responsible is being constructed in accordance with your drawings and specifications. Examine sub-surface conditions as they are exposed to view and be fully responsible for re-design and safety of this part of the work caused by actual conditions.

2. During these field observation services on the portion of the work for which you are responsible you shall observe that the contractor and sub-contractors are taking proper precautions concerning the safety of workmen and other people at the site of the work. Your only obligation here is to notify responsible parties when an unsafe condition exists and needs correction.

3. Examine, process and approve shop drawings and other fixture and equipment information and data sheets, or catalog cuts relating to your part of the work. In doing so you assume responsibility for their being in accordance with your plans and specifications. It will be your responsibility to coordinate the work of other trades when a substitution of a material or item of equipment is approved by you. Maintain one set to be delivered to the Owner upon completion of the work.

4. Prepare drawings, details and specifications for required Bulletins, Addenda and Change Orders.

5. Observe all special field tests and the testing and adjustment of systems as well as the balancing of the air supply, return and chill water systems. You shall be required to submit field reports approved by you attesting that the field tests, system adjustments and balancing have been accomplished in accordance with contract documents. It shall be your responsibility to see that the Mechanical and Electrical Contractors instruct the Owner on operation of their systems and that the specified operating manuals are prepared in a manner satisfactory to you. If Owner's representative is changed and requires additional instruction, then you will be reimbursed for this work.

6. Continue consulting engineering services for a period of one year after accepting the work. One month prior to termination of year's guarantee, a thorough inspection of the work shall be made and a punch list prepared of all items requiring adjustments or correction. This inspection will include only that required for warranty of equipment and will not include inspection to determine whether equipment or systems are being operated or properly maintained. Should your field observation indicate that improper operation or maintenance will seriously affect system life or performance, a separate report shall be submitted to us for review with the Owner. You will submit a report of all items requiring adjustments or corrections of warranty.

RESPONSIBILITIES

1. We acknowledge that we are directly responsible to the Owner in connection with all architectural services, and we assume all the proper professional and legal obligations that our contract with the Owner provides. However, in choosing to use you to perform certain portions of the work instead of executing it under our own name, we require you to accept full responsibility for your portion of the work.

2. We have in effect, in the amounts stated, the following insurance:

Professional liability	$_____	Workmens' comp. and empl. liability	$_____
Comp. gen. auto liability bodily injury and property damage	$_____	Valuable papers	$_____
General liability	$_____	Insurance (fire and burglary) on office contents	$_____

3. You herewith accept all professional and legal responsibilities for all that part of the work covered by your designs, your drawings, your specifications, your shop drawing approval procedures, and the coordination with other trades for changes or substitutions approved by you as well as your observation in the field of work exposed to view during routine inspection. You acknowledge these are not our responsibility, and we acknowledge you are not responsibile for any other part of the project.

4. You agree to carry insurance in at least the following amounts:

        Professional liability $_____

        General liability $_____

        Bodily injury $_____

        Valuable documents $_____

5. Errors and omissions under our Contract with the Owner are our direct responsibility with the Owner. If any such errors are your responsibility under this agreement, you shall bear the cost thereof. We will deduct the amount from the engineering fee. In no event will the Owner be billed said cost as an extra.

6. On Public Work Projects, where we are required to sign mandatory contracts, you agree to accept the same responsibilities and obligations for yourself on your portion of the work.

FEE

1. We agree to pay you $_____ (_____).

2. You shall also be paid for re-design caused by sub-surface conditions being at variance with reasonable original assumptions at a rate of two (2) times technical payroll.

3. It is to be expected that routine changes of ideas and solutions by us will occur during the normal process of design and working drawings. No additional compensation will be given for this work. If substantial changes initiated and/or approved by the Owner occur after Owner's approval of the preliminary drawings, additional work thus caused will be compensated at a rate of two (2) times technical payroll.

4. Routine revisions to the work as construction advances will be done without additional charge. Substantial changes, if not the result of your errors in the original contract documents, will be compensated at a rate of two (2) times technical payroll. Prior to any revisions, you will review them with us, and together we shall mutually determine whether they are routine or substantial.

5. Payment of Fee will be made when we have been paid our fee by the Owner. Payment shall be prorated in the same percentage as the payment to us for that stage of the work.

(Other sections omitted)

FIGURE B-2

FORM LETTER APPROVING SUBCONTRACTORS

NOLEN–SWINBURNE AND ASSOCIATES

Gentlemen:

We have your request dated _____ to approve _____ as subcontractor for _____. They are approved with the understanding they assume all their responsibilities to you as set forth in the Contract Documents, with particular emphasis on the following:

They have had ample time to thoroughly examine the drawings and specifications and are acquainted with all reasonable conditions which can be expected to prevail at the location and time when the work is to be done. The stated time for completion is adequate and they shall expedite their work to meet this date.

They have carefully considered all areas where other trades adjoin or affect the performance of their work and find there are no conditions that prevent its proper completion. They agree that the act of performing work on any surface constitutes acceptance of that surface as a proper base for their work. If the surface is not a proper one, they shall perform no work on it until conditions are made satisfactory by the trade that constructed such surface.

They acknowledge that the Architects have specified materials by trade name, which when properly installed, can produce the results specified. If they elect to substitute "or equal" materials, they agree they do so at their own risk. If the Architects approve the substitution when requested, the subcontractor accepts complete responsibility for proper results and performance. If they do not measure up to the specified standards, they shall be improved or replaced until they do meet such standards without additional expense to the Architects or Owner.

They agree the drawings and specifications are reasonably complete and proper for their portion of the work. If not, they shall state in writing where any deficiencies occur, and these shall be adjusted by corrective drawings and specifications. This shall continue until agreement is reached on scope, performance and materials required for the work prior to approval of this subcontractor. The purpose of this procedure is to firmly establish a full understanding of the requirements necessary to perform the work and properly estimate its cost.

This approval does not displace your position as prime contractor. Although you have selected this subcontractor to execute certain parts of the work, you are still responsible for the quality of material and workmanship supplied by him and for his scheduling of materials and labor to precisely meet the completion date established in your agreement with the Owner.

Yours very truly,

cc: Owner

FIGURE B-3

FORM LETTER ESTABLISHING JOB SAFETY PROCEDURES

NOLEN–SWINBURNE AND ASSOCIATES

Gentlemen:

We have experienced a rising concern over the methods of insuring the safety of all people working on our several projects now under construction, and in the methods used to protect the work and Owner's property during construction. We are sure you share this concern with us and understand why we emphasize its importance at this time on your particular project.

Contained within the General Conditions and sections of the project Contract Specifications are various applicable articles and paragraphs that establish your responsibility for the safety of the work, property, and all individuals and employees on the contract site; and provide the methods for assuring safe working conditions.

Will you please supply us with the name of the person who will be charged with carrying out these requirements?

We also wish to point out that our assigned Field Representative has been instructed to report to our office and to the person you will designate to be in charge of safety, any areas of the work or conditions he considers to be unsafe. However, he is also being instructed that in no way whatsoever is he to give any instructions to your people on the methods or procedure required to rectify an unsafe condition or produce a safe one, as this lies within your responsibility where we are sure you would insist that it be.

We are not aware of any unsafe conditions on the job at the present time. However, with the delivery and erection of the various structural or architectural components, the many hazards inherent in this building(s) are apparent.

We wanted to emphasize by this letter, how important we consider safety on this project.

Yours very truly,

cc: Owner

FIGURE B-4

PROJECT COMPENSATION WORKSHEET*

Project: **Franklin Elementary**
Project #: **7701** Date: **1-10-77**
Owner: **Alton School Board**
Architect: **Apple & Bartlett Assoc.**

ITEM	LINE	TOTAL HOURS	TOTAL DOLLARS	Schematic Design Hrs.	Schematic Design $	Design Development Hrs.	Design Development $	Construction Documents Hrs.	Construction Documents $	Bidding or Negotiations Hrs.	Bidding or Negotiations $	Construction Contract Administration Hrs.	Construction Contract Administration $
@ $	1							360	5,040				
@ $	2							466	4,660				
@ $	3							310	2,480				
@ $	4							296	1,776				
@ $	5							158	632				
Direct In-house Salary Expense	6	3519	32,417	370	3,890	647	5,835	1,590	14,588	142	1,297	770	6,807
Direct @ 125% of 6 Personnel Expense	7		40,521		4,862		7,294		18,235		1,621		8,509
Indirect Expense @ 84% of 7	8		34,038		4,084		6,127		15,317		1,362		7,148
Other Nonreimbursable Direct Expense	9		2,237		268		403		1,007		89		470
Total In-house Expense	10		76,796		9,214		13,824		34,559		3,072		16,127
Outside Services Expense	11		25,200		1,500		6,000		11,200		750		5,750
Estimated Total Expense	12		101,996		10,714		19,824		45,759		3,822		21,877
Contingency	13		6,854										
Profit	14		16,150										
Proposed Compensation	15		125,000										
Estimated Reimbursable Expense	16		5,900										

FIGURE B-5

THE ARCHITECTURAL AREA AND VOLUME OF BUILDINGS*

THE AMERICAN INSTITUTE OF ARCHITECTS

AIA Document D101

THE ARCHITECTURAL AREA
AND VOLUME OF BUILDINGS

*Establishing Definitions for the Architectural
Area and Architectural Volume of Buildings*

ARCHITECTURAL AREA OF BUILDINGS

The ARCHITECTURAL AREA of a building is the sum of the areas of the several floors of the building, including basements, mezzanine and intermediate floored tiers and penthouses of headroom height, measured from the exterior faces of exterior walls or from the centerline of walls separating buildings.

- Covered walkways, open roofed-over areas that are paved, porches and similar spaces shall have the architectural area multiplied by an area factor of 0.50.

- The architectural area does not include such features as pipe trenches, exterior terraces or steps, chimneys, roof overhangs, etc.

ARCHITECTURAL VOLUME OF BUILDINGS

The ARCHITECTURAL VOLUME (cube or cubage) of a building is the sum of the products of the areas defined above (using the area of a single story for multistory portions having the same area on each floor) and the height from the underside of the lowest floor construction system to the average height of the surface of the finished roof above for the various parts of the building.

*AIA Document D101 has been reproduced with permission of the American Institue of Architects, under application number 78065. Further reproduction, in part or in whole, is not authorized. Because AIA documents are revised from time to time, users should ascertain from AIA the current edition of the document that has been reproduced above.

FIGURE B-5 (*Cont.*)

THE ARCHITECTURAL AREA AND VOLUME OF BUILDINGS

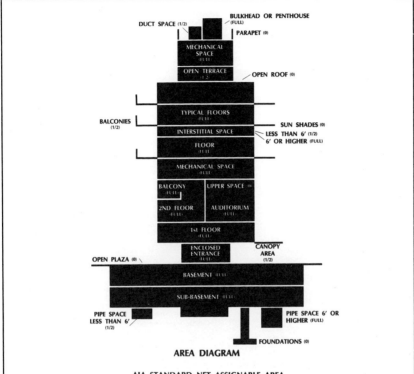

AREA DIAGRAM

AIA STANDARD NET ASSIGNABLE AREA

The STANDARD NET ASSIGNABLE AREA is that portion of the area which is available for assignment or rental to an occupant, including every type of space usable by the occupant.

The Standard Net Assignable Area should be measured from the predominant inside finish of permanent outer walls to the office side of corridors or permanent partitions and from center line of adjacent assigned spaces. Where there are interior spaces surrounded by corridors, measurement shall be from the inside face of enclosing walls. Included should be space subdivisions for occupant use; i.e., offices, file rooms, office storage rooms, etc. Deductions should not be made for columns and projections necessary to the building or for partitions subdividing space.

NOTE: There are two variations of the Net Area which may be useful:
(1) Single Occupant Net Assignable Area includes the space from the inside finish of exterior walls to the office side of permanent partitions and including toilets. The Single Occupant Net Assignable Area is different from the Standard Net Assignable Area by the addition of corridors and toilets, but excludes elevator shafts, elevator lobbies, stair enclosures, mechanical equipment rooms and electrical closets.

(2) Store Net Assignable Areas are from the exterior front face of the building or store front line through to the exterior rear face of the building and from center line to center line of walls between adjacent spaces.

FIGURE B-6

QUALITY ASSURANCE CHECKLIST*

The following list of recommendations for avoiding professional liability losses has been developed from an examination of more than 22,000 claims filed against architects and engineers. It is hoped that design professionals will compare this checklist against current practices within their firms. We urge you to circulate this list in your firm. If you wish, you may make copies for distribution to each firm member.

I CLIENT SELECTION

(a) Do assure yourself that your client has a financial capacity to undertake the proposed project.

(b) Do avoid undertaking projects for clients whose past record indicates they are prone to litigation.

(c) Do avoid undertaking projects of a purely speculative nature unless the client has a proven record of completing such projects.

II SELECTION OF CONSULTANTS

(a) Do select your consulting professionals on the basis of their competence, and ability to perform the specific project at hand.

(b) Do be certain that work performed by consultants is under written contract.

(c) Do be certain that the contract with the consultant clearly outlines his scope of responsibility.

(d) Do be sure that your consultants have an adequate number of staff personnel.

(e) Do be sure that your consultants have evidence of sufficient financial responsibility, such as professional liability insurance, for the project.

III PERFORMANCE BY STAFF MEMBERS

(a) Do appoint a qualified and experienced member of your firm to coordinate in-house quality control efforts.

(b) Do establish checking procedures to detect simple errors and omissions in plans and specifications.

(c) Do have the work of less experienced staff members carefully checked by a principal of the firm or by a responsible, experienced employee.

(d) Do establish an office manual setting forth the duties and responsibilities of all positions in the firm.

IV CONTRACT DOCUMENTS

(a) Do be thoroughly familiar with the terms of your agreement with your client.

(b) Do be certain to have a written contract, preferably one of the NSPE or AIA standard forms, for every project, regardless of size.

(c) Do be thoroughly familiar with the rights, duties and responsibilities assigned to you in the general conditions of the contract between the owner and the contractor.

(d) Do use extreme care in modifying or supplementing standard forms of professional services contracts.

(e) Do consult your lawyer concerning the effects of such modifications.

(f) Do check with your insurance counsellor about the effect that contract changes may have on your insurance coverage.

(g) Do be certain that any changes in services to be performed are reduced to writing and made on the basis of an amendment or supplement to the original agreement with the client.

(h) Do not use non-standard contract forms without consulting your legal counsel to determine whether such non-standard contract forms impose responsibilities which you cannot or are not willing to assume.

(i) Do be certain that the client understands that estimates of probable construction costs cannot be guaranteed.

(j) Do be certain that the owner understands that an estimate of probable construction costs is not a promise to design the structure within a cost limitation.

(k) Do make certain that all changes, directions or orders affecting fees, cost of the project or design or scope of the project are confirmed in writing.

V SPECIFICATIONS

(a) Do inform all project personnel concerning the proposed content of the specifications while the drawings are being prepared.

(b) Do coordinate the preparation of the drawings and specifications throughout the Con-

Checklist
I

*This document has been reproduced with permission of the Office for Professional Liability Research of Victor O. Schinnerer & Company, Inc.

FIGURE B-6 (*Cont.*)

QUALITY ASSURANCE CHECKLIST

struction Documents Phase.

(c) Do begin preparing the specifications when work on the drawings is begun; do not wait until the drawings are virtually complete.

(d) Do not "over" specify or "under" specify— use just the right amount of text to communicate project requirements to the contractor.

(e) Do use standard specification language so that all parties will be able to understand what is intended by the written word.

(f) Do review the text of all specifications carefully to ascertain whether (1) it really reflects the intent of the design, and (2) the items specified can meet the performance requirements.

(g) Do beware of typographic errors in the final version of the specifications.

(h) Do consider subscribing to a master specification system such as MASTERSPEC.

VI USE OF MATERIALS AND EQUIPMENT

(a) Do not use new materials or equipment without determining their suitability for the exact purpose for which you are specifying them.

(b) Do not rely on producer's sales literature regarding the suitability of new material or equipment.

(c) Do not rely on test reports furnished by the manufacturer unless the scope of the test and reputation of the tester are known.

(d) Do make certain that the producer of new material or equipment knows how his product is to be used in your particular application.

VII CONSTRUCTION PHASE SERVICES

(a) Do be certain that the owner understands that you are not and cannot be a guarantor of the contractor's performance.

(b) Do be certain that the owner understands that his greatest protection against faulty workmanship lies in the competence and integrity of the contractor he selects.

(c) Do avoid contractual language that might have the effect of making you responsible for the safety of personnel at the job site.

(d) Do be careful that all of your dealings and those of your field representatives are through the general contractor and not directly with subcontractors.

(e) Do not disapprove of subcontractors except in an objective and factual way, so as to avoid any possible claim for defaming a subcontractor.

(f) Do be certain that the contractor and subcontractors fully understand the agreed on procedure for handling shop drawings.

(g) Do not approve shop drawings in a manner that indicates approval for other than conformance to the design concept of the project and compliance with the specifications and drawings prepared by you.

(h) Do make certain that all instructions to the contractor are confirmed in writing.

VIII BUILDING CODES AND ZONING RESTRICTIONS

(a) Do be familiar with all zoning laws, building codes and restrictions applicable to the project.

(b) Do be aware of the fact that in most cases building codes requirements are minimums.

IX OCCUPATIONAL SAFETY AND HEALTH ACT

(a) In the Office—Know Your Responsibilities as an Employer

1. Contact the Occupational Safety and Health Administration for copies of pertinent documents published in connection with the Act.

2. Examine safety and health facilities in your office for compliance with the Act.

3. Post required notices furnished by the OSHA Administration.

4. Hold periodic meetings with your office staff to review safety and health requirements.

5. If an inspector calls, be aware of the extent of his authority.

6. Keep records of "recordable" injuries.

(b) At the Construction Site—Know Your Responsibilities as an Architect or Engineer

1. Instruct your own employees to not intentionally expose themselves to hazardous conditions during periodic visits to the site.

2. Do *not* include a safety program in the Project Manual or the technical specifications.

3. Do not interfere with the contractors' responsibilities to provide a safe and healthful work environment for their employees.

(c) In the Design—Know Your Responsibilities as a Design Professional

1. Be aware of OSHA standards which affect design conditions.

2. Review applicable building codes in conjunction with a review of OSHA standards to determine when the Act takes precedence.

3. Advise the owner of budgetary adjustments necessitated by the Act's requirements.

FIGURE B-7

PRESERVING THE RECORD*

Defending any professional liability claim against an architect or engineer can be expensive and time consuming, even when the professional's responsibility appears to be minimal or non-existent. A proper response to a claim requires detailed preparation, often developed from documentation contained in project files. This Guideline will outline some suggestions for preparing those files and laying the foundation for a successful defense in the event of a professional liability claim.

Background

An earlier article on documentation in the *Guidelines for Improving Practice* series, "To Write or Not to Write" by Margaret Bates Ellison, Esquire, (Volume I, Number 6; General Information - 4), contains a number of recommendations for developing and preserving records which could prove useful in defending against allegations of professional negligence. While listing specific items requiring attention during the planning, construction and post-construction phases of a project, that *Guideline* notes that the real value of "putting it in writing" lies in the necessity of having to stop and think in order to do so. The preparation of a written record will enable the architect or engineer to better discharge his duty to clients and the public and will provide tangible evidence of the professional's thought process in weighing those factors which affected the project. Thus, it should facilitate establishing that the professional did, in fact, exercise his best judgment in meeting the ordinary standard of care imposed by the law.

For many people, and this applies to others as well as to design professionals, preparing written records and documenting their activities is a burdensome task. Although this often may be true, the potential benefits of documentation must be weighed against the contemporary expenditure of effort, particularly when that effort may be the best defense for avoiding professional liability.

Documentation Before and During Design

Every project has limitations imposed upon it which primarily affect one or more of the following parameters: scope, quality, cost or time. These limiting features are always (or should be) subjects of discussion with the client as soon as professional services commence. While decisions flowing from these discussions can be changed many times prior to completion of the project, written documentation of those discussions and decisions is the first step in producing a project file that is loss prevention oriented.

A classic and recurring genesis of disputes between client and design professional is often found in misunderstandings arising out of the client's failure to temper his expectations with the project limitations he himself has imposed. To effectively protect against the consequences of such misunderstandings, an architect or engineer should prepare memoranda immediately after all discussions involving what the client anticipates will result from the project. Each memorandum should be very candid in matching the client's wishes with the project limitations, pointing out in clear language any inconsistencies, potential problems, solutions, recommendations and decisions. One copy of each memorandum should be placed in the project file and one copy forwarded to the client. It is not necessary that the client sign or otherwise acknowledge receipt of his copy. While the client's written acceptance of the memorandum would be ideal, an inability to secure his acknowledgement should in no way discourage this practice. As noted above, a very important benefit resulting from this procedure is that it not only reduces to writing the design professional's understanding of the matters which were discussed but also enhances his ability to serve the client's needs by particularizing the problems and solutions.

When the client is disappointed by one or more elements of the resulting project, all too frequently the courtroom dialogue, reduced to its simplest, sounds something like this:

Documentation - II

FIGURE B-7 (*Cont.*)

PRESERVING THE RECORD

Client: "I told him what I wanted and he didn't give it to me."

A/E: "Yes; he said he wanted that but I told him it would not be possible within the project budget."

From this, both parties' testimony often then deteriorates, and the outcome must be determined by some arbitrary selection of whichever seems more believable. It would be far better, easier and less expensive if the architect or engineer could simply refer to his project file and produce a copy of a memorandum documenting the discussion alluded to in the courtroom. The existence of such a memorandum might even dissuade the client from bringing suit in the first place. Even if it does not, the professional's testimony will be much more persuasive when compared to the other side testifying from memory. Lawsuits frequently take years to get to trial and memories are convenient, especially when substantial dollars are at stake. Recollections, recorded contemporaneously with the event, will have significant impact on a judge and jury trying to decide who is telling the truth. Properly and consistently prepared, the project memorandum can provide a solid basis for not holding the design professional liable for the client's alleged disappointment with the project.

Making Documentation a Regular Practice

While many architects and engineers are quick to prepare memoranda and other records whenever anything goes wrong, they often fail to appreciate the significance of having an established practice of documenting the normal course of a project. The credibility of a design professional's records is enhanced immeasurably when it can be shown that such records are prepared as a usual practice, irrespective of the circumstances, and are not formulated only under emergency conditions. In order to facilitate the preparation of regular reports on conditions at the construction site, the AIA publishes Document G711, "Architect's Field Report." Likewise, to assist in maintaining an orderly record of the receipt, processing and disposition of shop drawings and samples, AIA publishes Document G712, "Shop Drawing and Sample Record." The regular use of these forms should enable an architect or engineer to both serve his client better and to establish effective project records in these two important areas.

An unappreciated aspect of regularly preparing records is that this will document the dates on which various events occur during the life of a project. Under numerous state laws, the happening of such events can trigger the commencement of the statute of limitations period applicable to claims which might arise therefrom. The earlier the design professional's records show when something actually occurred, the sooner the statute of limitations period can run its course. Without knowing from which events a claim could sub-

sequently develop, a regular practice of documentation is the only way to achieve this protection.

Making Use of Equipment

Written memoranda in the project files are not the only way to document the development of, and decisions attendant to, the progress of a project. A large variety of mechanical recording devices and photographic equipment is available to assist in the effort to preserve the record. Many architects and engineers regularly utilize portable tape recorders to describe their visits to the construction site. The information on the tapes is then transcribed for insertion into the project files.

Photographs also can provide an effective record of the project. In addition to using a camera to show regular progress during the construction phase, the ready availability of photographic equipment can be invaluable in the event of bodily injury, material failure, collapse or any other occurrence which could give rise to a professional liability claim. A few years ago, a radio news bulletin reported a structural collapse which had occurred during a concrete pour. On the basis of this, a photographer and defense attorney, on behalf of the design professionals for the project, were sent to the job site. Photographs taken immediately after the collapse showed vividly the haphazard and inadequate nature of the concrete formwork shoring and bracing in areas which remained standing. After being ordered to leave by the contractor's personnel, they returned a few days later to take additional pictures. By then, however, all the shoring and bracing had been replaced properly, indicating that much remedial effort had taken place in the interim. By letting it be known that the two series of pictures existed, no claim was filed against the architect or his consultants because of this serious structural failure.

This vignette points up the importance of documenting as quickly as possible all circumstances surrounding any event or situation from which a professional liability claim could develop. In an emergency, the effective use of a camera often can do more than any number of written reports to limit the possibility of a professional liability claim.

How Long Should Records Be Retained

The Office for Professional Liability Research occasionally receives an inquiry about how long should an architectural or engineering firm retain record documents in its files. For many firms, project records become quite voluminous, and the cost of internal or external storage or microfilming represents a significant expenditure.

Unfortunately, there is no easy answer to this question. Often, factors other than potential professional liability concerns bear on the decision to retain or

FIGURE B-7 (Cont.)

PRESERVING THE RECORD

dispose of records. If a firm has a continuing relationship with a client, the client may expect the design professional to retain records of its (the client's) projects, particularly if the client itself has no centralized capability for this function. The design professional's files may be the only source of information providing an historical record of the project or the basis for alteration and maintenance work.

From a professional liability standpoint, it is suggested that records be retained for at least the period of the applicable statute of limitations. However, even this does not provide a definitive answer. In many states, the special statute of limitations applicable to architectural and engineering services has not been tested successfully and upheld by the jurisdiction's highest appellate court. The problem is compounded further when the design professional's firm is located in one state, and the client or project is located in another. Thus, it could be risky to rely on the special statute of limitations to establish the time frame for retaining documents, but at least it does give some guidance.

If a project had an unusual number of problems (in the architect's or engineer's judgment) because of attitudes exhibited by the client, contractors or others, the design professional should be prepared to preserve indefinitely extensive project records. The same would be true if new building products or systems had been utilized (or if established products or systems had been used in a new way.)

No definitive chronological limit exists for retaining records which would be generally applicable to all firms and all projects, and there is a constant urge to cull unneeded material from past project files. However, it should be recognized that such material should not be disposed of indiscriminately simply because of storage or other problems. Even if a firm were going out of business or dissolving, strong consideration should be given to retaining the files and records for a reasonable period.

Selected Checklist for Project Records

Most firms recognize the need to retain record sets of drawings and specifications and other data directly related to the construction process. It is equally important to keep on file pertinent documents showing that all services, judgments and decisions were in accordance with the applicable legal standard of care, and they conformed to the provisions of the professional service contract. The following checklist contains some items which are frequently overlooked when preparing project files.

- Memoranda of informal conferences and telephone conversations.
- Documentation of the owner's authorization to enter into the contract with the design profession-

al (if the owner is other than a sole proprietor or partnership.)

- Copies of owner-furnished data, such as the program, survey, soil reports, legal material, and so forth.
- Documentation of key design decisions, and the owner's response thereto.
- Documentation of the owner's written approval to proceed from one phase of professional service to the next. This specific requirement is a condition of the standard AIA Owner-Architect and NSPE Owner-Engineer agreement forms and is very often not adhered to. (There have been cases in which the design professional has been denied his fees because he failed to secure written approval before proceeding.)
- Copies of all contracts entered into by the design professional *and* his client—whether the client is the owner or another design professional. (Even though it may be difficult to secure copies of contracts to which the design professional is not a party, effort should be made to do so if those contracts affect him in any way.)

When Not To Write

When preparing project documentation, there are certain cautions which should be observed because in the event of a lawsuit project records and files are subject to discovery (review by other parties and opponents in the legal action.) Therefore, it is just as important to avoid recording some things as it is to preserve others. The following lists some of the circumstances in which the written record can be detrimental. It is given for the purpose of emphasis and to provide examples so that design professionals will have some idea of when "To Write Or Not To Write".

1. Avoid all references to personalities. Document the performance of others by stating objective facts; measure that performance by comparing it to the requirements of the contract documents. Do not use statements which tend to debase another person. For example, use: "The contractor failed to install .... as required by Section .... of the specifications", rather than: "The contractor is doing a lousy job".

2. When investigating an injury to persons or damage to property, record only what has been actually observed, and the names and addresses of witnesses to the event. *Do not* record opinions or conclusions as to the cause of the incident or how it could have been avoided.

3. Communications with third parties (i.e., parties other than the client) should be limited to and in accordance with the requirements of the professional

FIGURE B-7 (*Cont.*)

PRESERVING THE RECORD

service contract with the client. Do not volunteer or perform gratuitous services.

4. When recording the minutes of construction site meetings (if required by the professional service contract), state clearly which party is responsible for each of the matters discussed. For instance, if job site safety is the subject of discussion, be sure the minutes reflect the fact that it is the contractor's responsibility to take whatever actions are necessary.

Whether or not the architect's or engineer's records and files will form the first line of defense in the event a professional liability claim arises depends almost entirely on his willingness to prepare those records and files in an effective and comprehensive manner. The time, money and effort to achieve a successful defense in the absence of good records will far outweigh what they would have been to prepare those records properly in the first place.

FIGURE B-8

SHOP DRAWINGS*

SHOP DRAWINGS

Architects and engineers review and approve shop drawings as part of their normal professional services. Questions raised by numerous design professionals about the potential for a professional liability claim to arise out of shop drawings have prompted the Office for Professional Liability Research to review its files on this subject and prepare this Guideline to report on its findings.

Background

Architectural and engineering practice frequently involves the processing, review and approval of shop drawings. The use of shop drawings plays an important role in the design professional's ability to render appropriate professional services on behalf of his client. Whether or not a professional liability claim will result from the processing and approval of shop drawings often is determined by a number of factors. These include how well the architect or engineer understands the function and purpose of shop drawings, as well as their relationship to the design and the contract documents. Another factor involves the willingness of the design professional to insist that all parties adhere to the procedures for handling shop drawings set forth in the General Conditions. Rarely has a professional liability claim arisen from the design professional's approval of shop drawings when he has exercised reasonable care in processing and approving them and has insisted that others meet their contract obligations, as well, in connection with submitting shop drawings.[1]

Shop Drawings Defined

A commonly accepted definition of shop drawings is found in the *Glossary of Construction Industry Terms* published by the American Institute of Architects (Document M101). This definition reads as follows:

> **Shop Drawings:** Drawings, diagrams, illustrations, schedules, performance charts, brochures and other data prepared by the Contractor or any Subcontractor, manufacturer, supplier or distributor, which illustrate how specific portions of the Work shall be fabricated and/or installed.

As will be shown below, the concepts contained in this definition are reflected in the provisions of the standard AIA and NSPE General Conditions. Thus, it is quite important to understand exactly what the shop drawings are. Equally important, it is necessary to perceive what the shop drawings are not: Shop drawings are not part of the "contract documents". The standard General Conditions define which documents constitute the "contract documents" for the project, and neither the AIA nor the NSPE General Conditions includes shop drawings within that definition. A quick review of the definitions for the "contract documents" contained in the standard General Conditions will indicate that the component parts of the contract documents are prepared by or with the assistance of the design professional.[2] However, as can be seen by the definition for shop drawings set forth above, the shop drawings are prepared by the contractor (or someone directly responsible to the contractor). As a result, it would be inappropriate to include shop drawings within the definition of those documents which are the responsibility of the design professional.

The concept of requiring shop drawings to be prepared by the contractor to show how he will implement the requirements of the design and working drawings prepared by the architect or engineer has been part of the construction industry for a long time. Its origin has been lost in time, but one writer on the subject in the early part of the Twentieth Century had this to say:

> No matter how carefully the Architect's drawings may be made, they do not completely cover the constructive details of all the trades employed upon the work, nor would the masters of those trades wish the Architect to enter more fully than he does into such details. The drawings made by the several trades, the so-called shop drawings, are a necessary step between the Archi-

Shop Drawings

*This document has been reproduced with permission of the Office for Professional Liability Research of Victor O. Schinnerer & Company, Inc.

FIGURE B-8 (*Cont.*)

SHOP DRAWINGS

tect's drawings and actual construction. Even if it were proper for him to do it, the Architect could not make the shop drawings acceptable to the mechanics because in most cases, such drawings speak not merely the language of the trade but the language of the very shop in which the work is to be made.[3]

This same source goes on to discuss the role of the architect in reviewing shop drawings after they have been prepared by the respective trades. In reviewing and approving shop drawings, the design professional will be determining whether or not the specific details reflected in the shop drawings conform to the overall design intent and are compatible with other aspects of the project which are beyond the responsibility of the preparer of the specific shop drawings.

Therefore, keep in mind certain points about shop drawings:

- Shop drawings are not contract documents.
- Shop drawings are prepared by the contractor or by someone directly or indirectly responsible to the contractor.
- Shop drawings illustrate how specific portions of the work are to be fabricated and/or installed, but are not a substitute for proper design and working drawings and specifications.

With regard to this third point, there often is no clear line of demarcation between what information should be shown in the shop drawings and what information belongs in the contract documents. If the information relates to fundamental design criteria for the project or will affect the public health, safety or welfare, it normally should be covered in the contract documents. On the other hand, elements of the work which are subject to specific fabrication, manufacturing, assembly or installation requirements are often left to be shown in detail in the shop drawings.

If the architect or engineer prepared (or could prepare) drawings and specifications which were complete and perfect in the literal sense of those words, there would be no need for shop drawings; the contract documents would show everything exactly as it is to be constructed. But, neither does the law demand nor does human fallibility permit architects and engineers to prepare perfect contract documents. And even if perfect contract documents could be prepared, it would not be in the best interest of the work to do so (as was seen above by the need to allow the respective trades to perform the work according to each one's specific approach to the details). In addition, the owner's economic interest would suffer because inflexibility in details while arriving at the desired end result would prevent the contractor from seeking the lowest bid from a number of sources of supply, none of whom might utilize the exact approach set forth in the contract documents to meet the design requirements.

Contract Requirements Related to Shop Drawings

The standard General Conditions published by AIA and NSPE contain detailed requirements for processing

shop drawings.[4] These provisions are found in Subparagraphs 4.13.1 through 4.13.8 in AIA Document A201 (1970 Edition) and in Paragraphs 6.23 through 6.28 in NSPE Document 1910-8 (1974 Edition). For all intents and purposes, the terms in the AIA and NSPE General Conditions parallel each other.

As mentioned above, the contractor is obligated to prepare the shop drawings, or have them prepared by a subcontractor, manufacturer, supplier or distributor. He also is obligated by contract to check and approve shop drawings before submitting them to the architect or engineer. The contractor's check and approval involves far more than simply seeing that the shop drawings called for by the contract documents are prepared. He clearly is required to carefully verify field dimensions and construction criteria.

An important, and often overlooked, provision in the General Conditions requires the contractor to notify the architect or engineer in writing about any information in the shop drawings which deviates from the requirements of the contract documents. An approval of the shop drawings by the design professional does not relieve the contractor from responsibility for a deviation unless the contractor has given specific notice in writing, and the design professional has consented in writing to the specific deviation. The architect's or engineer's approval does not, in and of itself and pursuant to the contract provisions, relieve the contractor from responsibility for errors or omissions in the shop drawings.[5] However, to retain this important contractual protection, it is important for the design professional to follow the contract requirements carefully; failure to do so could result in a waiver of the contractor's obligations. This will be covered in more detail below.

Inherent in an adequate shop drawing approval process is the need to establish procedures for the receipt, review, approval and return of shop drawings to the contractor. The General Conditions make it incumbent on the contractor to submit shop drawings to the architect or engineer with reasonable promptness and in an orderly sequence so as to avoid causing delay in the work. It is also the responsibility of the contractor to properly identify the shop drawings he submits, as required by the contract documents.

The architect or engineer should document the date he receives shop drawings and the date on which they are returned to the contractor. The provisions in the General Conditions require the design professional to review and approve shop drawings with reasonable promptness. Obviously, the amount of time required to review shop drawings will vary with the complexity of the project and the specific shop drawings submitted by the contractor, so it is important to establish a schedule for processing the shop drawings within the office.

If the contractor submits shop drawings which have not been checked and approved by him, the architect or engineer should return the shop drawings unapproved. This should be done promptly so that there

FIGURE B-8 (*Cont.*)

SHOP DRAWINGS

will be no opportunity for the contractor to claim that he was unduly delayed by the design professional's failure to inform him of the non-approval. If an architect or engineer accepts shop drawings without the contractor's approval and proceeds to check and approve them, there is a serious risk of being held solely liable for any errors in the shop drawings which may be detected subsequently. Even though the provisions in the General Conditions are quite explicit in regard to the contractor's duty to check and approve shop drawings, these provisions can be waived and rendered ineffective by the design professional's actions. When the architect or engineer does the contractor's job for him, in effect, he creates for himself a serious risk of a professional liability claim. Not only will he have to spend a great deal of time to corroborate the information in the shop drawings, he also may be assuming unilaterally a responsibility for the adequacy and accuracy of the shop drawings.

The Shop Drawing Stamp

Both the AIA and the NSPE General Conditions require the contractor to stamp his approval on the shop drawings before submitting them to the architect or engineer for review and approval. In this regard, it would be helpful to read Subparagraph 4.13.4 in AIA Document A201 and Paragraph 6.26 in NSPE Document 1910-8. These provisions state that the contractor, by approving and submitting shop drawings, represents that he has determined and verified all field measurements and quantities, field construction criteria, materials, catalog numbers and similar data, and that he has reviewed and coordinated the information in the shop drawings with the requirements of the work and the contract documents. If the design professional would require the contractor's shop drawing approval stamp to contain language which reflects these terms in the General Conditions, it might reduce the propensity of some contractors to submit shop drawings which have been given inadequate attention in their offices or in the field. If the architect or engineer accepts shop drawings which have not been checked properly, and proceeds to review and approve them, it will be difficult to establish a defense on the basis of the contract requirements should a professional liability claim ensue at some later date.

The architect's or engineer's shop drawings stamp also should be in conformance with the provisions of the contract documents. In both the AIA and the NSPE General Conditions, the pertinent provisions state that the design professional's review and approval of shop drawings is only for conformance with the design concept of the project and with the information given in the contract documents. Recommended language for the architect's shop drawing stamp is found in the AIA *Handbook of Professional Practice*, Chapter 18 at page 8. Likewise, recommended language for the engineer's shop drawing stamp is found at page 30 in the *Commentary on the Contract Documents* (NSPE Document 1910-9) prepared for NSPE by John R. Clark, Esq. In order to avoid potential conflicts between design professionals on a given project, the architects and engineers should agree to utilize shop drawing stamps which are compatible and consistent with each other's.

There has been a significant amount of discussion among design professionals about the potential exposure to professional liability claims which might result if the architect's or engineer's shop drawing stamp states that he "approves" shop drawings. The following paragraph contained in NSPE Document 1910-9 assesses this concern, and reaches a conclusion which is shared by the Office for Professional Liability Research.

> Recently some writers on the subject have advised against the use of the word "approve" to describe the extent of the Engineer's responsibility when reviewing Shop Drawings and other similar submissions. Words such as "check," "examine," "accepted" and "not rejected" have been suggested instead of "approve"—on the assumption that thereby the Engineer will have reduced the extent of his exposure for letting an incorrect submission pass through. The PEPP Contract Documents Committee and this author are persuaded that use of these other words will be more likely to deceive the Engineer than to reduce his liability. Once the submission is given to him, the Engineer approves or disapproves of it to the extent that it is or is not responsive to the data given in the Contract Documents. The Owner and the Contractor are entitled to rely upon the Engineer's approving or disapproving these submissions. The newly suggested language is considered to be without legal merit. It would involve reliance on "weasel words" which the Committee has studiously tried to avoid. It would be more likely to lull the Engineer into a sense of false security than have any material effect on a judge or jury.

If a design professional allows a contractor to proceed with the fabrication or installation of an item covered by a shop drawing, it is unlikely that the design professional will not be deemed to have approved the shop drawing—regardless of what word might have been used on the shop drawing stamp. It is far better to recognize the professional obligation which relates to the approval of shop drawings than to believe that liability can be avoided by the simplistic substitution of one word for another.

Conclusion and Recommendations

In order to avoid potential professional liability claims arising out of the processing of shop drawings, architects and engineers should fully comprehend their role and the roles of others in preparing, checking, submitting and approving shop drawings throughout the course of a project. Adherence to the procedures related to shop drawings set forth in the standard AIA and NSPE General Conditions will do much to minimize the possibility of liability problems. To achieve this, the following recommendations should be considered in establishing administrative procedures within the firm:

▶ Insist that office and field personnel read and follow the provisions related to shop drawings contained in the General Conditions.

FIGURE B-8 (*Cont.*)

SHOP DRAWINGS

Hold a pre-bid or pre-award meeting with the contractor(s) to specifically point out the contract requirements in regard to the processing of shop drawings. Insist throughout the project that the contractor adhere to his contractual obligations to check and approve shop drawings before submitting them to the design professional.

Confine the architect's and engineer's review and approval of shop drawings to a determination of whether or not they conform to the design concept and the requirements of the contract documents. It should be made clear that any approval does not extend to information not called for in the contract documents.

Do not do the contractor's job for him—if shop drawings have been submitted without having been checked and approved by the contractor, do not accept them.

Do not accept shop drawings from anyone but the contractor. Shop drawings should not be submitted directly to the design professional from subcontractors or suppliers.

Establish and maintain a log in the office to record the dates on which shop drawings are received and returned.

If shop drawings cannot be approved, document carefully and in writing the reasons why shop drawings have been rejected or returned without approvals.

Ask the contractor to utilize a shop drawing approval stamp which reflects the provisions of Subparagraph 4.13.4 in AIA Document A201 or Paragraph 6.26 in NSPE Document 1910-8.

Utilize a shop drawing stamp for the design professional's approval which reflects the language recommended by AIA or NSPE; i.e. approval is only for conformance with the design concept and with the information given in the contract documents.

In conclusion, the potential for professional liability problems arising out of processing and approving shop drawings is directly related to the care and diligence with which the design professional adheres to contract requirements and adequate administrative procedures. Neither vaguely worded shop drawing stamps nor total avoidance of shop drawings will provide the architect or engineer with protection from liability claims—and in fact, the failure to meet professional standards of care will increase the possibility of claims.

[1] Many aspects of this *Guideline* on shop drawings are also applicable to the review and approval of samples submitted by the contractor.

[2] See AIA Document A201, Paragraph 1.1 (1970 Edition); and NSPE Document 1910-8, Article 1 (1974 Edition).

[3] American Institute of Architects, *The Handbook of Architectural Practice*, p. 65, The AIA Press, New York, New York, 1920.

[4] For another discussion on procedures for processing shop drawings, see *Guidelines for Improving Practice*, Vol. IV, Number 11 (General Information—21), "Protecting Yourself Against Claims for Delays or Extras" by Richard M. Bryan, Esq., p. 2, Washington, D. C., 1974.

[5] A case illustrating this principle is *Appeal of Dawson Construction Co.*, GSBCA No. 3685, 72/2 BCA 9758 (Oct. 31, 1972) in which a government contractor was denied a claim for extra compensation after it had to replace work installed pursuant to owner-approved shop drawings. The claim was rejected because the contractor was responsible for creating the deficiencies in the shop drawings, and the owner's approval was considered conditional on the shop drawings meeting contract requirements. Approval of an incorrect shop drawing did not change contract requirements.

METRIC CONVERSION FACTORS

(approximate conversions from customary to metric and vice versa)

	When you know:	You can find:	If you multiply by:
Length	inches	millimeters	25.0
	feet	centimeters	30.0
	yards	meters	0.9
	miles	kilometers	1.6
	millimeters	inches	0.04
	centimeters	inches	0.4
	meters	yards	1.1
	kilometers	miles	0.6
Area	square inches	square centimeters	6.5
	square feet	square meters	0.09
	square yards	square meters	0.8
	square miles	square kilometers	2.6
	acres	square hectometers	0.4
	square centimeters	square inches	0.16
	square meters	square yards	1.2
	square kilometers	square miles	0.4
	square hectometers	acres	2.5
Mass	ounces	grams	28.0
	pounds	kilograms	0.45
	short tons	megagrams (met. tons)	0.9
	grams	ounces	0.035
	kilograms	pounds	2.2
	megagrams	short tons	1.1
Liquid volume	Ounces	milliliters	30.0
	pints	liters	0.47
	quarts	liters	0.95
	gallons	liters	3.8
	cubic feet	cubic meters	0.03
	cubic yards	cubic meters	0.76
	milliliters	ounces	0.034
	liters	points	2.1
	liters	quarts	1.06
	liters	gallons	0.26
Temperature	degrees Fahrenheit	degrees Celsius	5/9 (after subtracting 32)
	degrees Celsius	degrees Fahrenheit	9/5 (then add 32)

INDEX

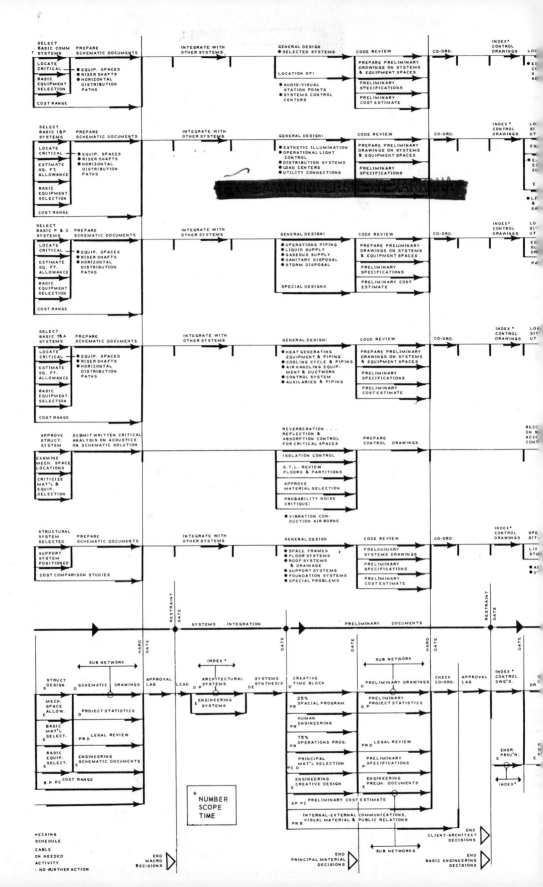